Historians and Africanist History: A Critique

Arnold Temu and
Bonaventure Swai

Historians and Africanist History: A Critique

Post-Colonial Historiography Examined

Arnold Temu and Bonaventure Swai

Zed Press, 57 Caledonian Road, London N1 9DN

Historians and Africanist History: A Critique was first
published by Zed Press, 57 Caledonian Road,
London N1 9DN in November 1981.

Copyright © Arnold Temu and Bonaventure Swai, 1981

Copyedited by Mandy MacDonald
Proofread by Penelope Fryxell
Designed by Mayblin/Shaw
Cover design by Jan Brown
Typeset by Jenny Donald
Printed by Krips Repro, Holland.

ISBN Hb 0 905762 78 9
     Pb 0 905762 79 7

All rights reserved

British Library Cataloguing in Publication Data
Temu, Arnold
Historians and Africanist History
1. Historiography — Africa
I. Title II. Swai, Bonaventure
907'.206   DT19
ISBN 0 905762 78 9

U.S. Distributor
Lawrence Hill and Co., 520 Riverside Avenue, Westport,
Conn. 06880, U.S.A.

Dedicated to Walter Rodney

'African peasants and workers will undoubtedly achieve the goal of unity, but it will be a unity in struggle and unity through struggle — ideological, economic and military. On the ideological front, our task as revolutionary African youth is to interpret the present realities of Africa from the viewpoint of the majority of its peoples who are toilers. We must interpret it in order to understand the direction of change and to see to it that progressive and revolutionary trends are brought to the forefront. The degree to which we serve that function is the degree to which we may be judged revolutionary.'

'Scientific socialist analysis is by its very nature historical analysis, since it must lay bare the process by which social relations and institutions come to being.'

The Nationalist (Dar es Salaam) 17 December 1969.

Dedicated to Walter Rodney

Contents

Dedication v
Preface ix
1. Crisis in Africanist History 1
   The Contemporary Study of History 2
     Limitations of Social History (2)
     The Call for Militancy (3)
     Obstacles to Radicalism (4)
   People's History: What Is The Problem? 6
     The 'African Factor' (6)
   Paralysis of Professional Africanism 7
     Limitations of Development Ideology (9)
     Empiricists versus Radicals (11)
   The Way Ahead 12
2. The African Factor 18
   The Postcolonial School of Africanist Historiography 21
     On Social Change (22)
     On African Achievements (22)
     On Resistance to Colonialism (23)
   The Concept of Local Initiative: A Critique 25
     Its Analysis of the European Response to African Resistance (26)
     Its Analysis of African Rebellions: Form, Not Content (28)
   The Material Basis of Colonial Violence and Resistance 32
     Capitalist Penetration and the Colonial State (34)
   From the Age of Resistance to the Age of Improvement? 39
     Laziness and the Work Ethic (43)
     The Colonial Reign of Terror (45)
   Transcending Africanist Historiography 49

3. **Local Initiative: The Crisis from Within**   61
    From the Golden Age of African Historiography to
        Pessimism   63
    The Nihilist School as an Alternative   66
        The New Breed of Imperial Historians (71)
    From Africanist Economic History to the Notion of
        Development of Underdevelopment   74
        An Evaluation of This New Approach (76)
    The Cul-de-Sac of Postcolonial Africanist Historiography   77
    Towards Materialist History: An Example   82
        The State in African History (82)
        The Trade Thesis (84)
        The Case of Madagascar (87)
        The Case of Zanzibar (93)
        The Case of Ukimbu, Western Tanzania (95)
        Merchant Capital and Violence (97)
    The Failure Summed Up   98

4. **The Cult of Facts and Fetishism in Africanist History**   111
    The Enigma of Appearances   112
        The Fallacy of Objectivism (115)
    The Material Basis of Academia   120
        Universities and Professionalism (123)
        Truth as Usefulness (129)
    The Failures of the Empirical Method: An Example   131
        Critical Theory: The Only Historiographic Alternative (135)
        The Case of Joseph Merinyo and the KNPA in Tanganyika (138)
    Conclusion   143

5. **Towards An International Problematic for Africanist Studies**   153
    A Summing Up   153
    The Essential Context for Understanding — The Era of
        Imperialism   154
    An Application of the Theoretical Problematic Being
        Proposed   160
        The Political Economy of Tanzanian Educational History (160)
        Attitudes versus Conditions as an Explanation of Primary School
          Leavers' Behaviour (162)
        The Basis of Education in Colonial and Post Colonial Societies (164)
    Conclusion   169

Select Bibliography   177

Index   185

Preface

This study has been undertaken with the awareness that it is 'sometimes much more difficult to state a problem correctly than to find a solution for it', but that this endeavour is 'necessary if the Promethean task of storming the heavens and so take control of the process of development and deliberate planning of the future is to be accomplished'.[1] It has also, on the one hand, been designed to offer an analysis of postcolonial Africanist historiography now that Africanist history has come of age, a fact which has made a 'study of the history of Africanist history' the more necessary;[2] and, on the other, to suggest a scientific alternative relevant to this field of inquiry.[3]

The discipline of history, like other professions, has a strong tradition. Its practitioners have a firm sense of identity. Thus it has been underlined: 'As a professional man [history is very much a profession, and very much a man's profession at that: there is only one woman lecturer in a faculty of thirty at Cambridge] [4] he shares a similar class position to the nineteenth century administrator, in the middle or lower echelons of the bourgeoisie.' His vocation as an historian places him above the *hoi polloi* whom he 'surveys . . . retrospectively as the agents – or subjects – of change. He may feel sympathy for the mass, but hardly solidarity.'[5] For this reason, perhaps, the English professional historian A.J.P. Taylor has urged his fellows that 'a good historian should ride the waves and not swim in them'.[6] Such seems to be the attitude which professional Africanist historians 'have taken along with mother's milk'. If there were any debates about the 'historian's craft'[7] and even more so the method and concepts utilized by the professional historian to produce historical knowledge, they came to an end with Leopold von Ranke's assertion of 'objectivism'[8] and the seminar method. Since then the historical method has been considered as natural as the Talmud: its historical perspectives have been thrown overboard.[9]

Yet a generation or so of African historians has passed through a system of this kind following the founding and institutionalization of the study of Africanist history since the Second World War.[10] Many such historians, inheritors of the professional method, are involved in universities, colleges and schools, peddling what has been bequeathed to them. Historical associations of various strengths and sizes are also engaged in a similar enterprise, publishing pamphlets and holding seminars on Africanist history. Around such activities have crystallized various schools of Africanist historiography geared to creating intellectual autarky in support of 'nationalist' obscurantism.[11] Thus emerged the Dar es Salaam, Nairobi, Ibadan and Makerere schools of nationalist historiography and so forth. Each of these schools claims that truth is on its side.[12] Rather than starting their study of the past 'with criticism of politics, with taking sides in politics, hence with *actual* struggles' and identifying themselves with such struggles, spokesmen of the various schools have faced 'the world in doctrinaire fashion with a new principle, declaring, here is truth, kneel here!' But principles of the world should be developed 'out of principles of the world. We do not tell the world, Cease your struggles, they are stupid. We merely show the world why it actually struggles; and the awareness of this is something which the world *must* acquire even if it does not want to.'[13] Short of this, studying the past becomes an ideological enterprise.[14] Indeed such has been the case with postcolonial Africanist historiography.

Africanist historiography was constituted as an ideological response to colonial historiography.[15] In this encounter it also remained trapped, thereby making it a 'negative mirror image of liberal historiography'.[16] The rival schools of Africanist historiography in Africa, in conformity with Ranke's dictum, claim that theirs is a task 'simply to show how it really was' or to 'ascertain the facts'. Facts or events of the past, they claim, are the sole basis of the generalizations they make.[17] But such positivist methodology or empiricism is itself ideological. 'The choice of a particular field of investigation, the choice of a given range of concepts with which to investigate that field, all express assumptions about the nature of society and about what is theoretically significant and what is not.' Knowledge is produced within specific problematics which are either idealist or materialist. 'Science proceeds by challenging the deceptive obviousness of everyday observation and common sense.' Dominant in observations of everyday life are world views or ideologies which are class-based.[18]

> Ideology, however, is not apology, although it may and often does entail it. Ideologies are world-views which, despite their partial and possibly critical insights, prevent us from understanding the society in which we live and the possibility of changing it. They are world-views which correspond to standpoints of classes and social groups whose interests in the existing social system and incapacity to change it make it impossible for them to see it as a whole. A large number of different ideologies have been developed by thinkers tied to bourgeois society, and there is constant development and change. But they are all part of *bourgeois ideology*, not because they express immediate interests of the ruling class or are developed by it, but because they are limited, in theory, by the limits of bourgeois society in reality; because their development, including even their criticism of bourgeois society, is governed by the development of bourgeois society and unable to go beyond it.[19]

Such too has been the case with the endeavour to assert the 'African factor' in Africanist history.

Critics who have attempted to dislodge this perspective with the use of a radical perspective have been termed 'pessimists'. For professional Africanist historians, however, the term 'pessimist' has been used loosely as a word of contempt embracing all those radical critics considered at loggerheads with the conventional wisdom dominant in Africanist historiography. Such are what have been dubbed 'radical pessimists associated with Dar es Salaam' and, we would imagine, Zaria.[20] On the opposite pole of the 'radical school' of Africanist history, which is also called the 'new school', are a number of conservative and bourgeois historians largely based at Africanist departments, schools, and institutes in metropolitan universities: a collection of nihilist and imperial historians who have from time to time posed as the 'conscience' of professional Africanist history.[21] The groups of voices thus claiming to be the core of Africanist historiography appear many and contradictory. Each group contends that truth is on its side: the nationalist school, which is parcellized into various national loyalties; the school which subscribes to the notion of the development of underdevelopment; the 'new school' of Africanist historiography, which claims to be Marxist in its approach;[22] the nihilist school which 'springs from an emphasis upon the variety and complexity of historical events, so great as to reject any of those general categories which form the texture of most theories of historical interpretation and to deny any validity to frontier-lines between historical epochs';[23] and the group of imperial historians which gets its inspiration from Cambridge University and which is but a crude refurbishment of the now defunct colonial historiography.

However, the different schools aside, save for the new school of Marxist historiography which, as far as African history is concerned, is still in its infancy,[24] the rest of the factions share the same idealist problematic. For them, the idea takes precedence over matter, thought over being.[25] Nevertheless, as E.H. Carr has observed with regard to the endeavour by bourgeois historians to write 'ultimate history', where the leading pundits among Africanist historians contradict one another so flagrantly, the field is open for inquiry.[26] For this reason, therefore, this study has been designed as an introductory work for students and general readers who are interested in the study of African history. It is hoped that it will be useful not only to undergraduate students of history but also to postgraduates who have not had much previous grounding in the development of postcolonial Africanist historiography. Moreover, while articles and papers of one kind or another have been written about postcolonial Africanist historiography, to our knowledge this is the first time that an attempt has been made to synthesize the efforts and to put them in book form.[27]

In the course of preparing this study we gained immensely from the criticism and encouragement of many of our colleagues at Zaria and Dar es Salaam. We also learned a great deal from the postgraduate seminars in history at Ahmadu Bello University and the staff seminar programme of the Department of History at the University of Dar es Salaam. We are indebted to all those colleagues who were kind enough to give us their comments. While we cannot name them all owing to the lack of space, to mention a few would be an injustice to the rest.

The criticism which we received led us to revise this study in many places. The work sometimes made very slow progress, perhaps because we took suggestions too seriously. But revision is important. In 1858 when Marx was working on the *Contribution to the Critique of Political Economy* he wrote to Lassalle: 'The job is making very slow progress because things which one has for many years made the chief object of one's investigation constantly exhibit new aspects and call forth new doubts whenever they are to be put in final shape. Besides, I am not the master of my time but rather its servant.'[28] We often found ourselves repeating statements of a similar nature. But there also comes a time 'when collective criticism is important'. This step, however, presupposes publication.[29] In preparing this work for publication, we received a great deal of help from the Zed Press staff. We wish to mention in particular Roger van Zwanenberg, who is himself an Africanist, and who gave us a number of suggestions on matters of substance with regard to how to improve this work. To him, and to Robert Molteno, also of Zed Press, we are most grateful.

Many of the examples used in this book are drawn from East and Central Africa. This is by no means indicative of any nationalist chauvinism on our part. Nor is it intended to suggest that the study of history in East and Central Africa is more advanced than elsewhere in Africa. Rather it arises from the fact that both of us are East Africans by an accident of birth. It might also be of interest to observe that many of the themes stressed by the 'Dar school of nationalist historiography', for example, were also given similar, if not equal, emphasis by other schools like that of Ibadan, the subjective differences between them notwithstanding.[30]

Lastly, it needs to be underlined that this book is designed as a critical appraisal of Africanist history as it is currently taught and written throughout the West and in English-speaking Africa. It seeks to lock horns with the conventional wisdom dominant in Africanist historiography with a view to destroying its very fundamentals. For this reason, this study is intended as a contribution to the still young but rapidly growing 'new school of Africanist historiography'. The book is divided into five chapters. The first chapter, Crisis in Africanist Historiography, is given by way of a prolegomenon. It is intended to delineate the crisis which is documented more appropriately in Chapter 3. The second chapter seeks to analyse the rise and institutionalization of Africanist history, the so-called African historiographical revolution.[31] The crisis in Africanist history has forced more and more scholars to go back to the classics, to adopt the tools of political economy, and eventually to turn to the Marxist method;[32] this phenomenon is examined in Chapter 4. The fifth chapter is intended as a conclusion and a pointer to the future of African history. We hope that this book will be of use to students of African history, and that orthodox Africanist historians will not be unduly alarmed.

Preface

References

1. R. Garaudy, *Marxism in the Twentieth Century*, London 1970.
2. L. Kapteijns, *African Historiography written by Africans 1955-1973: The Nigerian Case*, Leiden 1977. Bonaventure Swai, 'The latest Cinderella of professional African history', *Tanzania Zamani*, 20, 1978. T.L. Eriksen, *Modern African History: Some Historical Observations*, Uppsala 1979.
3. Bonaventure Swai, 'Local initiative in African history: a critique', *Tanzania Zamani*, 19, 1977; 'Opportunism, pragmatism, and African history', *Utafiti*, 4, 1979. H. Bernstein and J. Depelchin, 'The object of African history: a materialist perspective', *History in Africa*, 5, 1978.
4. As late as in the 1960s Dr Pamela Nightingale, who is a specialist on South Asian history, found it very difficult to convince some of her supervisors at Cambridge that it was worthwhile for a woman to pursue postgraduate work in such a field of specialization. However she eventually pulled through and wrote a thesis which has been published under the title *Trade and Empire in Western India 1786-1804*, Cambridge 1970.
5. R. Samuel (ed.), *Village Life and Labour*, London 1975, p. xvi.
6. Quoted by Bonaventure Swai, *Antinomies of Local Initiative in African History*, Dar es Salaam, 1979, p. 1.
7. G. Kitson Clark, *The Critical Historian*, London 1965.
8. This term has been used in this way by V. Kelle and M. Kovalson to underline the difference between bourgeois and scientific objectivity. See their book, *Historical Materialism*, Moscow 1973.
9. A.J. Temu and Bonaventure Swai, 'Old and new themes in African history', *Proceedings of the Workshop for the Teaching of African History in African Universities*, Lagos 1977; 'Poverty of African history: the case of Tanzanian historiography', *Cahiers d'études africaines*, Vol. 77-78, 1981. Bonaventure Swai, 'Recovery of local initiative in African history or the realization of the nation state', Dar es Salaam 1977, mimeo.
10. C. Fyfe (ed.), *African Studies Since 1945*, London 1976.
11. The term 'nationalist' has been used deliberately to underline its difference from the appellation 'nation'. J. Blaut, 'Are the Puerto Ricans a national minority?' *Monthly Review*, 29, 1977. H.B. Davis, *Nationalism and Socialism: Marxist and Labour Theories of Nationalism to 1917*, New York 1967.
12. T.O. Ranger, *Recovery of African Initiative in Tanzanian History*, Dar es Salaam 1969. D. Denoon and A. Kuper, 'The nationalist historians in search of a nation: the "new historiography" in Dar es Salaam', *African Affairs*, 69, 1970. M.L. Chanock, 'Development and change in the history of Malawi', and R.H. Palmer, 'Johnson and Jameson: a comparative study in the imposition of colonial rule', in B. Pachai (ed.), *Early History of Malawi*, London 1972. T.O. Ranger, 'Towards a usable past', in Fyfe (ed.), *African Studies Since 1945*.
13. K. Marx to A. Ruge, September 1843, H. Selsam, D. Goldway and H. Martel (eds.), *Dynamics of Social Change: A Reader in Marxist*

Social Science, New York 1970.
14. J. Depelchin, 'Towards a problematic history of Africa', *Tanzania Zamani*, 18, 1976; 'African history and the ideological reproduction of exploitative relations of production', *Africa Development*, II, 1977.
15. Bonaventure Swai, 'Trade and politics in eighteenth century Malabar', Dar es Salaam 1979, mimeo.
16. N.N. Luanda, 'The negative mirror images of African initiative: colonial resistance and collaboration', Dar es Salaam 1979, mimeo. Bonaventure Swai, 'Collaboration versus resistance and beyond', Dar es Salaam 1978, mimeo. J.R. Mbwiliza, 'Resistance and collaboration or the struggle of the unity of opposites: the dilemma of the comprador class at Sancul, Mozambique 1750-1850', *Utafiti*, 4, 1979.
17. G.S. Jones, 'History: the poverty of empiricism', in R. Blackburn (ed.), *Ideology in the Social Sciences*, London 1978.
18. See the introduction by Blackburn, in Blackburn (ed.), *op. cit.*
19. M. Shaw, 'The coming crisis of radical sociology', Blackburn (ed.), *op. cit.*, pp. 33-4.
20. See the introduction by T.O. Ranger (ed.), *Emerging Themes of African History*, Nairobi 1968. A.D. Roberts, review of D.A. Low and A. Smith (eds.), *History of East Africa*, Vol. III (Oxford 1976), in *Journal of African History*, XIX, 1978, p. 149.
21. See the introduction in Fyfe (ed.), *African Studies Since 1945*. S. Marks, 'South African Studies since World War Two', in Fyfe (ed.), *op. cit.*; D. O'Meara, review of T.R.H. Davenport, *South Africa: A Modern History* (Toronto 1979), in *Utafiti*, 4, 1979.
22. J. Depelchin, 'The coming of age of political economy in African studies', *International Journal of African Historical Studies*, XI, 1978.
23. M. Dobb, *Studies in the Development of Capitalism*, London 1975, p. 1. Bonaventure Swai, 'Nihilists and African history', Dar es Salaam 1977, mimeo.
24. Bernstein and Depelchin, 'The object of African history: a materialist perspective'.
25. J. Depelchin, 'Notes towards the production of a materialist precolonial Central African history', Dar es Salaam 1977, mimeo.
26. E.H. Carr, *What is History?*, London 1962.
27. Bernstein and Depelchin, 'The object of African history: a materialist perspective'. Swai, *Antinomies of Local Initiative in African History*.
28. Quoted by L. Seve, *Man in Marxist Theory*, Hassocks, Sussex, 1978.
29. *Ibid.*
30. J.F.A. Ajayi, *Christian Missions in Nigeria 1841-1891*, London 1965; 'West African states at the beginning of the nineteenth century', in J.F.A. Ajayi and I. Espie (eds.), *A Thousand years of West African History*, Ibadan 1965; 'The continuity of African institutions under colonialism', in Ranger (ed.), *Emerging Themes of African History*. Kapteijns, *African Historiography Written by Africans 1955-1973: The Nigerian Case.*
31. T. Hodgkin, 'Where the paths began', and S. Marks, 'South African studies since World War Two', both in C. Fyfe (ed.), *African Studies Since 1945*.
32. Depelchin, 'The coming of age of political economy in Africa'.

1. Crisis in Africanist History

Courage, it has been said, is necessary if orthodoxy is to be dislodged. Thus a leading English politician of the nineteenth century, Disraeli, remarked: 'If the history of England be ever written by one who has the knowledge and the courage, because both qualities are equally necessary for the understanding, the world would be more astounded than when reading the annals of Niebuhr. Generally speaking, all the great events have been distorted, most of the important causes concealed, some of the principal characters never appear and all who figure are so misunderstood and misrepresented that the result is a complete mystification.'[1] Mystification is the word; but perhaps it is also salutary to emphasize that sheer courage alone is not enough to remedy this kind of parody. Neither is information on its own sufficient. As C. Wright Mills has remarked in the context of the discipline of sociology:

> It is not only information that they [scholars] need – in this Age of Fact, information often dominates their attention and overwhelms their capacities to assimilate. It is not only the skills of reason that they need – although their struggles to acquire these often exhaust their limited moral energy.
> What they need, and what they feel they need, is a quality of mind that will help them to use information and to develop reason in order to achieve lucid summations of what is going on in the world and of what may be happening within themselves. It is this quality . . . that journalists and scholars, artists and publics, scientists and editors are coming to expect of what may be called the sociological imagination.[2]

Here sociology seems to be at variance with professional history: 'History rarely ventures beyond a timid empiricism while sociology soars into empty abstraction.'[3] For most professional historians, discussion of method, other than the 'instinctively followed procedures' and the 'explicitly formulated rules of thumb', is anathema. The hard facts, it is alleged, are at variance with the cloudy theories; there is a marked distinction between theory and facts unless the former is distilled from the latter.[4] This attitude, however, has led the writing of history to acquire the image of sorcery.[5] In line with an ambition cherished by Macaulay, the nineteenth-century English statesman and man of letters, it has been assumed that the historian's pen, like the alchemist's stone, can turn the most obscure 'historical sources', especially written documents, into a celebrated study that may 'replace the latest novel on the lady's dressing table'[6] – without wasting too much energy on theoretical formulations.

The Contemporary Study of History

The study of history has undergone radical change, and even an 'inversion'.[7] Initially history meant the story of kings, wars and empires. Thus in his inaugural lecture as Professor of History at Cambridge University in 1861 Charles Kingsley averred:

> The new science of little men can be no science at all; because the average man is not the normal man; and never yet has been; because the great man is rather the normal man, as approaching more nearly than his fellows to the true 'norma' and the standard of a complete human character . . . to turn to the mob for your theory of humanity is (I think) about as wise as to ignore the Apollo and the Theseus, and to determine the proportions of the human figure from a crowd of dwarfs and cripples. The object of history therefore is to find out what great men did with the various aspects of public life in which they were involved.[8]

History, according to Professor Kingsley, was the story of great men and great deeds, rather than a tale of the horrors of the *menu peuple* who laboured on the lord's estate or built tombs for megalomaniac rulers and their concubines.

The 'social realities and forces of our epoch' have compelled the recognition of the history of the oppressed. Such history has 'even penetrated the hermetically sealed citadel of the university'. 'A whole cluster of researchers, for the most part young, have set themselves the task of forging new working instruments, inventorying sources, compiling bibliographies, publishing documents, and writing monographs. Specialized institutes arise and colloquia multiply. The field of investigation expands.' New and wider theoretical fields have been opened. 'The accent has shifted' and the 'problematic itself has changed'.[9] Such is what Georges Haupt, a militant intellectual who 'devoted his life to the study of the workers' movement, and was perhaps the foremost contemporary analyst of it as a world force', had to say about European social history.[10]

Limitations of Social History

As a discipline, European social history is a fairly new field of study.[11] Nevertheless, 'it is no longer necessary to apologize too profusely for taking the common people of the past on their own terms and trying to understand them'.[12] To study history from the 'bottom up' is now a very popular enterprise.[13] To many professional Africanist historians, the enterprise has also proved very popular because they too claim to be concerned with the history of the inarticulate.[14] They have, therefore, always wanted to compare the results of their enterprise to the spectacular discoveries of European social history, especially one of its leading variants – labour history.[15] But if labour history has been a source of inspiration to those who have subscribed and continue to subscribe to postcolonial Africanist historiography, it has to be noted that this discipline is also engulfed in a crisis. It has, for example, been lamented that the discipline is not as popular in schools and colleges as it used to be. African governments are putting pressure on professional historians to justify their place in universities, and the students who still register for history courses are demanding a relevant kind of history. Yet the crisis in Africanist history is not merely a crisis of demand and supply but one of method. African universities started 'with a mission that gave them little time to evaluate the type of social science teaching and research that could concern itself with the production of knowledge'.[16] The methodological intervention continues to be not only empiricist, but also superficial. Such has been termed 'the esoteric version of history': a history which, although purportedly written from below, remains history written from above. For this reason, this kind of history continues to be dedicated to the study of ideological and organizational forms of institutions and movements rather than their social content, and has been 'miniaturized in this way into pedantic detailed studies lacking any general perspective'. Thus it is 'capable of rousing only a very limited interest'.[17]

The Call for Militancy
Perhaps this occurrence should be attributed to the professionalization of this specific segment of history, for it has been observed that, whenever professionals penetrate a new area of study, there is a tendency for the knowledge which is produced to lose the audience for which it is intended.[18] Thus Fonvieille-Alquier has rejected professional historians *en bloc*. Instead he has called for a revival of the saga of militants. It is for this reason that he has quipped:

> History? But what history? Certainly not a history that is sterilized, carefully balanced, patiently dissected, measured to the millimetre, devitalized as a result of its confrontation with itself and its sources, the history with which we are left when the historians are done with it. No! We want a history rich with colours of life, vast frescoes burning with passion, with republican spirit – an album of vivid images that cry out, where blood, sweat, tears, and powder are mixed together. This is no longer doubtless history with a capital letter, but rather the politics of the past as it was lived and made by generations of men whose hopes were only illusions and who have found up to now only deception at the end of their dreams. In this guise, history remains the daily companion of the militant.[19]

What history has lost in the course of being professionalized by 'scribblers in the pay of the ruling class', therefore, is its militancy. Professionalization of history denotes its miniaturization with the intent to render it harmless. This kind of history is not written with the view to 'recapturing a forgotten, inspiring, memorable past', an enterprise which Hobsbawm categorizes as 'a fit task for historians', but only a segment of it.[20] History becomes 'a big cake from which each could cut off a piece according to one's taste or one's appetite'.[21] Such is the ritualization of the past; a 'reactionary cult of the past'.[22]

Indeed there has been an attempt to write history along the lines recomended by Fonvieille-Alquier. But here too problems have been encountered. More efforts have been given to 'conjuring away the embarrassing realities' of the past rather than capturing it with all its vividness. The history of the inarticulate, as Johann Jacoby, a militant worker of the nineteenth century, observed, still remains to be written. What has been done so far is very much like 'a resounding church-bell, a tinkling sleigh-bell, or a step in the course of a career'.[23] Such is the situation which has produced intellectual freaks; a kind of lumpen-intelligentsia more engrossed in its own psycho-dramas than the concrete: best known for its verbal ferocity which is intended to foreclose further argument rather than to promote discussion. Thus Stalin had no respect for documents; Popper sees a place for the history of various aspects of human life but none for the history of mankind; and it has been asserted of late that little is to be gained from historical writing and historical research.[24]

Obstacles to Radicalism

The crisis is neither restricted to social history nor the discipline of history alone.[25] Rather, it involves the social sciences in general and even the natural sciences.[26] The 'collapse of consensus politics; the decomposition of the affluent society and the failure of the Americans to win a decisive victory in Vietnam', coupled with the general crisis of late capitalism, are some of the elements which have forced the conventional orthodoxy in the social sciences into disarray. In its place are emerging a number of 'anti-texts' which are pushing received wisdom into further obscurantism.[27] The crisis in which the social sciences as practised in the metropolitan countries are engulfed has been summarized admirably by Bernal:

> In the age in which we live we can observe both tendencies of conservatism and those of change. In the orbit of so-called Western civilization, that is capitalist countries on both sides of the Atlantic, we can see the last stages of the general suppression and mystification of the knowledge of society. There is great insistance that the study of society is a pure and objective science, divorced from direct concern with changes in society. This, though it ostensibly puts the social sciences in the category of the respectable physical and natural sciences, removes from them the possibilities of experimental test, the only

means of solid advance. Social science becomes an accumulation of harmless platitudes with disconnected empirical additions. Where the social sciences are involved it is to justify the existing order, either directly by pointing out the essential harmonies of the system, or indirectly by pointing both to the impossibility and the wickedness of any suggestion of changing it.[28]

Such then is the situation to which the social sciences have been relegated. The endeavour to use the methods of quantification with a view to introducing an element of precision to the study of humanity has not been of much help. Frustrations continue in abundance. The time when the millennium will dawn and so wipe out the anguish in which social scientists are enmeshed has yet to come. Meanwhile the gulf between obscurantist scholarship and radical practice continues to widen.

A similar crisis exists in Africanist history. For one thing, Africanist history is but a branch of bourgeois history as it is practised in metropolitan countries; for another, much of the social malaise bedevilling the metropolitan countries, given the global nature of capital, continues to have extremely adverse effects in backward capitalist countries. Africanist history was conceived as a kind of people's history.[29] However, the efforts to write a 'people's history' have yet to show encouraging results. This is so because the framework of problematic within which this type of history is to be produced has not been examined seriously. The meaning of the term 'people's history' has also not been located. In both cases the colonizer-colonized problematic has been turned on its head by Africanist historians, but rarely the right way up. Thus, while in colonial historiography it was normally the history of the colonizer which was taken seriously, with the emergence of Africanist history the story of the colonized has come in to the limelight. Moreover, this is what has also been called people's history, the history of the oppressed. But colonial oppression was mediated by various layers of local classes. Africanist historians, however, have been content with viewing the colonized as an amorphous mass, and people as simply aggregates of individuals. Without showing the determinants of people's interactions and thus the classes which they constitute, the history of the colonized as a history of the oppressed continues to be a strange hotchpotch. It ranges from so-called drum and trumpet history to the story of the strife of African peasantries. Notwithstanding the intervention of radical historians, which is now on the increase, frustrations, as has already been said, abound.[30] Thought is still arrested at the level which the founding fathers of Africanist history achieved in the latter part of the nineteenth century. Africanist history still labours under the same aims as it did then: to vindicate the African past.[31] The notions employed in postcolonial Africanist historiography remain reductionist. The problem has been reduced to that of the need to search for more evidence. But this cannot be undertaken at the expense of 'scrupulous inquiry into historical practice'.[32]

For most professional Africanist historians, the criterion for writing history of the people is still elusive.³³ What goes for history of the people continues to look more like 'a telephone directory – an enumeration of names unconnected with one another' than serious and rigorous historical work.³⁴ Professional Africanist history which purportedly is a history written from 'bottom up' remains 'drum and trumpet history'. While in Europe social history denotes the activities of workers amongst other social categories, in Africa the study remains a description of the lives of chiefs and their headmen, nationalist fighters and trade union leaders.³⁵ It has already been pointed out that European social history also has a number of shortcomings; the crisis of postcolonial Africanist historiography appears to be more serious. The notions employed in the study of Africanist history are still very crude, the assertions rampant. Postcolonial Africanist historiography has yet to acquire the scholarly rigour found in European social history, notwithstanding claims that this is being realized.³⁶

People's History: What Is the Problem?

Failure to produce authentic history of the people, as has already been indicated, has been misinterpreted as a crisis of information. But it has also been realized of late that 'the manner in which an historical problem is posed will also determine the answer';³⁷ that the problematic within which specific history is constituted is just as important as the information necessary for the reconstruction of that history.³⁸ Like the bourgeois history practised in metropolitan countries, professional Africanist history, an appendage of the former, is based on the problematic of the subject. Pioneers of the 'African historiographical revolution' sought to transform the 'colonized peoples of Africa' who constituted the object of this historical enterprise from objects to subjects of history. In so doing, the 'objective structural features' of the African colonial social formations articulated within an imperialist hegemony were reduced 'to the intentions, motives and interpersonal relations of individual agents'.³⁹ This idealist problematic was considered as a given, and thus natural. So, too, were the rules of the game which are supposed to have determined the conditions under which the interpersonal relations of the individual agents were conducted.⁴⁰

The African Factor
The pioneers of postcolonial Africanist historiography, in their endeavour to destroy the primacy of colonial historiography, asserted the 'African factor' in the making of history. Thus in the case of Tanzanian history it has been observed: while 'it *is* true, as the Arusha Declaration says, that Tanzanians have been pushed around and acted upon a great deal', and while it is obviously true that 'the achievement of a really effective Tanzanian initiative is the task of the statesman even more than of the historian', there has all the same been 'more initiative at all periods of Tanzanian history than has been generally allowed'.⁴¹ Thus the African past has been glorified in the

endeavour to assert the African factor in history.[42] As another result, what amounts to a crude 'Whig interpretation' of African history has been produced whose *telos* has been assumed to be the creation of the postcolonial state.[43] Assessing in 1930 the achievements of the historiography of the French Revolution Karl Korsch remarked:

> The schema applied by this political historiography consisted simply of making the Revolution coincide with the political result it attained at a given point in its revolutionary development. This point was fixed at different stages in the development of a new revolutionary state by the various factions of bourgeois historiography, and all the parties, individuals, events, concepts, trajectories, and tendencies were ranked as progressive or backward according to whether they contributed to the advent and strengthening of this revolutionary result or whether they struggled against it. Beginning from this point, parties, persons, events, etc. are judged positive or negative, revolutionary or counter-revolutionary, according to the words of the Scripture: 'But let your communication be, Yea, yea; Nay, nay: for whatsoever is more than these cometh of evil.'[44]

Korsch pinpointed the teleological approach dominant in the study of the French Revolution. The same observation should be made about postcolonial Africanist historiography.[45] Segments of African history have been selected for analysis and continuities with other periods of history drawn without due consideration being given to the concrete conditions within which the historical events were precipitated.

Paralysis of Professional Africanism

While the African past has been praised as the golden age of African genius and continuities with the recent past established, contemporary events in Africa have not been so bright. Events in the Congo in 1960 during which the world witnessed the murder of Patrice Lumumba; the so-called African political instabilities which have seen Africa engulfed in all kinds of military dictatorship, the worst of which were those established by Nguema, Bokassa and Idi Amin; the political assassinations in the so-called models of African political development, like the murder of Josiah Mwangi Kariuki; the detention of leading African intellectuals like Ngugi-wa-Thiong'o; the brutal coercion of peasants and workers in the so-called African socialist republics with a view to forcing them to produce more in the name of 'foreign exchange'; the Sahel famine, which to say the least was only the tip of the iceberg of the economic crisis dominant in Africa, and so forth: all these events and more have forced some Africanist scholars to re-examine their profession. Further, in professional Africanist history, in place of the golden age of consensus when most professional Africanist historians thought alike, the iron age of nihilism has emerged. The idea of progress in professional Africanist history has been superseded by the notion of history without a pattern.[46] The optimism once dominant in Africanist history has come to an end.[47]

Obscurantist professional Africanist historians have sought to resolve the crisis with which they are confronted by sinking more deeply into the past. Their task, they say, is to describe the past meticulously and nothing more.[48] As in Vidia Naipaul's novel, *The Mimic Men*, professional Africanist historians have proved unable to cope with the crisis confronting them. These historians have recommended all sorts of remedies to contain the crisis – for example, the call to collect more information and so be better able to make sound historical judgements – but such suggestions have only proved cosmetic.[49] Meanwhile the crisis rages on.

This sense of helplessness is not restricted to professional historians of Africa. Rather it is typical of the dominant social groups which these historians objectively defend.[50] Thus on the question of economic development within the imperialist camp and the possibilities of an alternative, it has been said:

> You all know very well that, if we want to go very quickly in our economic changes, we cannot easily do it without creating a certain amount of trouble in this country [Nigeria].... The imperialists have got various means of defending their monopoly. They have got their newspapers and televisions and they go to any extent to tell lies. If we want to really set about improving the economy of our country in a particular way, they may say we are Communists. They can make our countrymen suspect our every move. If they do not succeed by false propaganda, by calling us all sorts of names, if they fail to make us unpopular in order to win their case, they can arrange assassination. They can go to any extent without discrimination.[51]

For such a 'mimic man' the forces against Africa seem gargantuan. They appear overwhelming, and in such a situation there is little that can be done. People of this sort find themselves happier defending than re-examining the system which they have inherited. Obscurantist Africanist historians find themselves in a similar boat. At best they preach contentment, speak of the wonderful past, and reiterate how difficult it is to write a work of history.

In his poem 'A Worker Reads History', Bertolt Brecht has something similar to say about ruling classes and their intellectual coolies:

> Those who take the meat from the table
> Preach contentment ...
> Those who eat their fill speak to the hungry
> Of wonderful times to come ...
> Those who lead the country into abyss
> Call ruling too difficult
> For the ordinary.[52]

But just as conventional historians preach contentment with the past, some of the leading Africanist historians have begun to stress that the relevance of the past is to be found in the way in which it is used to explain the present. Thus in the preface to his book *How Europe Underdeveloped Africa* Walter Rodney says: 'This book derives from a concern with the contemporary African situation. It delves into the past only because otherwise it would be impossible to understand how the present came into being and what the trends are for the near future. In the search for an understanding of what is now called "underdevelopment" in Africa, the limits of inquiry have had to be fixed as far apart as the fifteenth century, on the one hand, and the end of the colonial period, on the other hand.'[53]

The African crisis, therefore, has called for a re-examination of the manner in which the past has been studied with a view to illuminating the present. It has been realized that the social sciences can no longer explain social phenomena adequately, and hence the need to question the present mode of conceptualization with intent to transcend it.[54] There is a general disillusionment with 'the traditions of liberal scholarship'. Bourgeois scholarship, it has been discovered, is too fragmented, unsatisfactory and inadequate for explaining social phenomena. In place of the empiricist mode of investigation, therefore, has been posed the critical approach. The acceptability of the latter approach, moreover, is on the increase because 'it does not take the commonsense definitions of social groups and institutions as given, but seeks to specify and analyse them in its own terms.' It is also acceptable because it promises to apprehend social phenomena more comprehensively.[55]

Limitations of Development Ideology

In Africanist studies, the 'ideology of development' replaced the world view of the 'mission to civilize' in the aftermath of the Second World War. The ideology of development was reflected in Africanist history by such ideas as social change, continuity of African institutions and African struggles. But 'the unexpected gap between conventional social science theories and the objective reality of the African countries' is now with us.[56] Moreover, the realization that such a gap exists is not restricted to the leading radical scholars of Africanist studies, but also shared by their students. In a dossier which was intended to analyse their teachers, some student leaders at the University of Nairobi noted:

> Apparently convinced that the best concepts are foreign ones (from USA, UK, etc.) and only occasionally paying lip service to the initiative and needs of the fifteen million 'other' Kenyans, these gentlemen of learning perverted the truth about Kenya's past, present and future potential. Many even announced to us in various classrooms that Kenya's salvation lay in becoming more and more dependent on the imperialist masters 'because we have no skills, no capital, no wealth'. They called this higher education. We do not agree with what we saw every day with our own eyes in Kenyan society.[57]

A number of running battles have been fought in classrooms and in the streets by university students not only in Kenya, but also elsewhere in Africa. The ruling classes have responded with a sledgehammer. The classroom, observed Mao Tse-tung, has been the stage of intense class struggle.[58] Education reforms which have been undertaken at the instigation of capital have been accompanied by the intensification of authoritarianism. The latter has been justified by the allegation that coercion has to be increased because people are unable to exercise 'responsibly' their own rights of freedom.[59]

The difference between what is alleged and the reality is also becoming clear to ordinary people. Who eats the fruits of independence, and who waters the tree on which the fruits grow is becoming as clear as the difference between day and night. So too is the idea of nation building:

> So the PS had ulcers too
> My ulcers I think are equally painful
> Only they are caused by hunger
> Not by sumptuous lunches!
>
> So two nation builders
> Arrived home this evening
> With terrible stomach pains
> The result of building the nation
> Different ways.[60]

The ulcers of one of the nation builders arise from delicious dishes eaten at state banquets and other important occasions, and those of the other from hunger, notwithstanding his having sold his labour time the whole day. Such are the two ways of nation building, by eating and by sheer donkeywork.[61]

It has so far been emphasized that postcolonial Africanist historiography is engulfed in a crisis, that this crisis is neither restricted to Africanist history nor to the social sciences as they apply to Africa only, and that this crisis has ultimately to be related to the crisis of society. The nationalist euphoria which dominated postcolonial African social formations has been evaporated by all kinds of malaise: economic, social, political and so on. However, these are mere symptoms of the crisis of capital, which is now in its moribund stage.[62] The crisis of postcolonial Africanist historiography has thrown many a scholar off balance. Many have been given to lamenting about the 'golden age' which has already passed rather than seek new avenues for resolving the crisis.[63]

It has been noted about crises in general that they are not natural; rather they are social occurrences: they are not acts of God. For Marx, 'the importance of crisis [in society] lies, on the one hand, in its ability to lay bare the inner workings and dynamics of a specific social formation, and on the other, in exposing the contradictions inherent in that social formation.' Crises are 'not an aberration, but rather an integral and necessary part of a given formation'.[64] But if this can be said about society, it can also be argued about the discipline of history in general and postcolonial Africanist historiography in particular. This is so because 'there is no necessary disjunction between the particular and the general: on the contrary [there is] – or ought to be – a dialectical interplay between the two.'[65] If crises reveal the major contradictions dominant in a specific social formation, they do likewise in the discipline of history. The main concern of Africanist historians, then, should be to reveal those contradictions with a view to providing an alternative. 'The philosophers', it was observed by the leading materialist of the nineteenth century, 'have only interpreted the world in various ways; the point, however, is to *change* it.'[66]

Empiricists versus Radicals
To understand the crisis in which postcolonial Africanist historiography is engulfed, it is necessary to examine the contradictions inherent in the empiricist problematic which has been so influential in the writing of Africanist history. This will be analysed in Chapter 4. It is also necessary to observe that there have been attempts to offer an alternative problematic to the empirical method. This has been done with a view to writing African history which is concrete.[67] To do this it has been necessary to try to restore 'critical theory' in the study of African history. Critical theory was developed with a view to seeing better the 'invisible in the visible, or of the essential in the appearing'. The Socratic method which was constituted as part of critical theory was presented as a procedure to discover 'the essential by ruling out what it is not'. With the Socratic method, 'Plato shows the basic concept of reason as a critique of conventional mystification which releases a changed praxis [action] in the individual's life.' With Hegel 'it became the critique of one-sided social-cultural forms that distort human spontaneity and, in Marx, the critique of political-economic forms that separate and block the essential productive processes of society'.[68] But the 'critical theory' is eschewed by professional historians because it is considered too rarefied.[69] The concern of the historian, it is said, is not with theory – much of which is ideological – but with the 'hard facts'.[70] Nevertheless the call for relevance is greater today than it has ever been before.[71]

This demand has been interpreted as a call for commitment, a violation of professional ethics since partisanship is treated as a mark of delinquency in rigour. Thus it has been asserted: 'Africanist scholars in the West have been criticized for doing research that is irrelevant to Africa, and for being mainly interested in the building of academic careers. Research on Africa should be both useful to Africa and committed ... or revolutionary. It would lead me too far to go into the complicated question of what this "new" anthropology, or history for that matter, should be, and how it should be done.'[72] Such an academic venture might sound complicated; but it is into this kind of arena that the debate is veering. The complexity or simplicity of the subject at such a juncture is irrelevant.[73]

The call for relevant history has been misinterpreted and confused with a view to avoiding the issue of scholarly rigour. It has also been regarded as an invitation to respond pragmatically to the issue in question. However, the call for relevance is an issue which is intended to shift the debate to its proper terrain: the production of social knowledge.[74] This is the arena in which obscurantists and radicals are at loggerheads. It has already been observed that professional historians claim they use no theory in the production of historical knowledge. Rather it is discovered, together with the facts, in the course of conducting research. Too much theorization, therefore, is to them unprofessional; it is not conducive to the writing of proper history. But it has also been observed: 'the positivist attitude of scientists who pretend to have no need of philosophy . . . amounts in practice to thinking according to the principles of a philosophy which remains implicit and unconscious, and therefore which is uncriticized. As Engels said, they are "no less in bondage to philosophy, but unfortunately in most cases to the worst philosophy". Those who abuse philosophy most are slaves to precisely the worst vulgarized relics of the worst philosophies.'[75] Professional historians' claim that their enterprise is concerned with the story of man. But is it not right that a subject which claims to be dealing with man should have some form of philosophy of what man is? Such is the 'original simplicity' of philosophy. The skeleton in the cupboard of many professional historians is the abstract individual. However, why such professionals should place a premium on the abstract rather than the concrete individual is in question. Historians should concern themselves with not only data but also their own assumptions or unarticulated premises.[76]

The Way Ahead

Historians should be aware of the logic they use in the course of producing historical knowledge. The formalism dominant in postcolonial Africanist historiography should be challenged and destroyed. The 'relations between thought and reality, more specifically, between logic and the external world' should be emphasized. Logic, it must be stressed, is not 'sealed in the mind' and thus has no 'necessary and unbreakable connections with society and nature' or the object of study; on the contrary, the two are organic.[77] The issue of historical practice is long overdue in professional Africanist historiography. Indeed, while the 'question of method is just as important as the object of investigation',[78] theory and practice or empirical matter are dialectical. Without theory it is hard to comprehend empirical matter, and without the latter it is impossible to sharpen the former.[79] 'The historical actors tell their own story but, as every historian knows, that story has had to be discovered by a complex process of reading and "decoding" the sources; and this process involves a "dialogue" between the evidence and the conceptual framework' of the historian.[80] The empiricist tradition has unduly devalued rigorous conceptualization; but it is also important to note that 'undue theorization may produce a kind of creeping epistemological paralysis – the nightmare fear that our knowledge may not be fully "rigorous"

— inhibits any engagement with empirical material.' Hence the need for a constant movement back and forth between theory and empirical matter 'in which theoretical insights are woven into the texture of historical and political arguments'.[81]

This historical practice is what E.P. Thompson has described as the dialogue between theory and fact, in which the latter is determinant.[82] Perhaps this procedure may help rescue the discipline of history from its impasse of being denied by the very people for whom it was intended. Thus, as Georges Haupt has observed with regard to European working-class history, to rescue the discipline from this predicament entails a 'critical analysis which is neither rhetorical nor a discourse subordinated to the passions, but which instead seeks to grasp the origins of the phenomena'. This implies a 'double articulation'. 'It must place both historical writing and collective memory into relation with the way in which [the oppressed] refer to their own history, with the use they make of it, and with the political and ideological function that they assign to it.'[83] In both cases, though, theory is just as important as the historical events being analysed.[84] To pretend that the two are not dialectical is a travesty of historical practice.[85]

This chapter, as was indicated in the preface, is given by way of an introduction. Many of the issues which are raised here will be tackled more thoroughly in what follows, especially in Chapter 3. This is particularly so with the issue of the crisis in Africanist history and the debate on people's history. Likewise, many of the terminologies used in this chapter will also be clarified in due course. Similarly, the ideological content of the Africanist history will be shown. Critique of ideology is not a pointless enterprise. However, 'an ideological critique is only useful when it remains conscious of its own limitations: it is in no position to handle the object of its research by itself.' Thus it has been emphasized that a 'critique of ideology which is tempted to go beyond its effective limits' and, therefore, which 'remains fixed on the mask instead of what is revealed beneath it', 'itself becomes an ideology'.[86] To avoid relying too greatly on the 'gesture of "unmasking" [which] can turn into a smug ritual', a number of analyses of concrete events have been incorporated into each of the following chapters with a view to demonstrating how an African history which is materialist could be written.

References

1. Quoted by R.P. Dutt, *India Today*, Calcutta 1970, p. 80.
2. C. Wright Mills, *The Sociological Imagination*, Harmondsworth 1970, p. 11.
3. See the introduction in R. Blackburn (ed.), *Ideology in Social Science*, Harmondsworth 1978, p. 10.
4. G.S. Jones, 'History: the poverty of empiricism', *loc. cit.*, G. Novack.

        An Introduction to the Logic of Marxism, New York 1975, p. 5. S. Korner, *Fundamental Questions of Philosophy*, Harmondsworth 1969, p. 3. H. Bernstein and J. Depelchin, 'The object of African history: a materialist perspective', *History in Africa*, 5, 1978.
5.   D.H. Fischer, *Historians' Fallacies*, London 1971.
6.   Quoted by G. Connell-Smith and H.A. Lloyd, *The Relevance of History*, London 1972, pp. 48–9.
7.   G. Haupt, 'Why the history of the working-class movement?' *Review*, II, 1978, p. 6.
8.   Quoted by Jones, 'History: the poverty of empiricism', p. 98.
9.   Haupt, pp. 5–6.
10. *Ibid.*
11. Jones, 'History: the poverty of empiricism'.
12. C. Hill, *The World Turned Upside Down*, Harmondsworth 1975, p. 17.
13. B.J. Bernstein (ed.), *Towards a New Past*, New York 1969. T. Nairn, 'The English working class', in Blackburn (ed.), *Ideology in Social Science.*
14. T.O. Ranger, *Recovery of African Initiative in Tanzanian History*, Dar es Salaam 1969; T.O. Ranger (ed.), *Emerging Themes of African History*, Nairobi 1968; *Dance and Society in Eastern Africa 1890-1970*, London 1975. Bonaventure Swai, 'The contradictory past: historians and African history', Southern African Universities Social Science Conference 1979. W. Freund, 'Theft and social protest among the tin miners of Northern Nigeria', Dar es Salaam 1979, mimeo.
15. Haupt, 'Why the history of the working class movement?'
16. *Ibid*. See also P.A. Nyong'o, 'The teaching of social sciences in East Africa', *Africa Development*, III, 1978. *Tarikh*, 6, 1978. A.E. Afigbo, 'Some thoughts in the teaching of History in Nigeria', Historical Association of Nigeria, n.d. O. Ikime, 'History and the historian in the developing countries', *Proceedings of the Workshop on the Teaching of African History in African Universities*, Lagos 1977.
17. *Ibid*. E. Hobsbawm, 'Labour history and ideology', *Journal of Social History*, VII, 1974. E.P. Thompson, *The Making of the English Working Class*, Harmondsworth 1969. E. Hobsbawm, *Labouring Men*, London 1964.
18. Haupt, 'Why the history of the working class movement?'
19. *Ibid*.
20. *Ibid*.
21. *Ibid*.
22. F. Mehring, *Vita di Marx*, Rome 1966; quoted by Haupt, p. 13.
23. *Ibid*.
24. E.P. Thompson, *The Poverty of Theory and Other Essays*, London 1978. R. Gray, 'E.P. Thompson, history and communist politics', *Marxism Today*, 23, 1979. B. Hindess and P.Q. Hirst, *Precapitalist Modes of Production*, London 1975. L. Althusser, *Essays in Self-Criticism*, London 1977.
25. J.H. Plumb (ed.), *Crisis in the Humanities*, Harmondsworth 1964.
26. F. Green and P. Nore (eds.), *Economics: An Anti-Text*, London 1978. D. Seddon (ed.), *Relations of Production*, London 1978. M. Shaw, *Marxism and Social Science*, London 1977. J.M. Legay, 'Some elements

of the defense of science', *Scientific World*, XVII, 1973.
27. G. Kay, *Development and Underdevelopment*, London 1975. H. Bernstein, 'Capitalism and Underdevelopment: radical critics and Marxist analysis', *Utafiti*, 2, 1977. Green and Nore (eds.), *Economics: An Anti-Text*.
28. J.D. Bernal, *Science and History*, Vol. IV, Harmondsworth 1969, p. 1017.
29. Bonaventure Swai, *Antinomies of Local Initiative in African History*, Dar es Salaam 1979.
30. C.C. Wrigley, 'Historicism in Africa', *African Affairs*, 70, 1971.
   A.J. Temu and Bonaventure Swai, 'Poverty of African history: the case of Tanzanian historiography', *Cahier d'études africaines*, forthcoming.
   J. Depelchin, 'Towards the production of a materialist epistemology', *Utafiti*, 2, 1977.
31. L. Kapteijns, *African Historiography Written by Africans 1955-1973: The Nigerian Case*, Leiden 1977.
32. Thompson, *The Poverty of Theory and Other Essays*, p. 212.
33. H. Kjekshus, *Ecology Control and Economic Development in East Africa*, London 1977.
34. K.M. Panikkar, *A Survey of Indian History*, Bombay 1964, p. ix.
35. M. Chanock, 'Development and change in the history of Malawi', in B. Pachai (ed.), *The Early History of Malawi*, London 1972.
36. Swai, 'The contradictory past: historians and African history'.
37. J. Depelchin, 'Zaire 1960–1977: from colonialism to Mobutism', Dar es Salaam 1977, mimeo.
38. Bernstein and Depelchin, 'The object of African history: a materialist perspective'.
39. N. Abercrombie, B. Turner and J. Urry, 'Class, state and fascism: the work of Nicos Poulantzas', *Political Studies*, XXIV, 1979, p. 512.
40. R. Albritton, 'The game analogy and bourgeois ideology', *Social Praxis*, 3, 1975.
41. Ranger, *The Recovery of African Initiative in Tanzanian History*.
42. J. Depelchin, 'African history and the ideological reproduction of exploitative relations of production', *Africa Development*, II, 1977.
43. J.M. Londsdale, 'The emergence of African nations', in Ranger (ed.), *Emerging Themes in African History*.
44. Haupt, 'Why the history of the working-class movement?' pp. 14–15.
45. Swai, 'The contradictory past: historians and African history'.
   N. Bukharin, *Historical Materialism*, Ann Arbor 1976. B. Hindess, 'Humanism and teleology in sociological theory', in Hindess (ed.), *Sociological Theories of the Economy*, London 1977.
46. C.C. Wrigley, 'Historicism in Africa'.
47. T.O. Ranger, 'Towards a usable past', in C. Fyfe (ed.), *African Studies Since 1945*, London 1976.
48. Wrigley, 'Historicism in Africa'.
49. Ranger, 'Towards a usable past'.
50. I. Oxaal, 'The dependency economist as grassroots politician in the Caribbean', in I. Oxaal, T. Barnett and D. Booth (eds.), *Beyond the Sociology of Development*, London 1975.
51. S. Osoba, 'The deepening crisis of the Nigerian national bourgeoisie',

public lecture at Ahmadu Bello University, Zaria, Nigeria, 4 February 1978, p. 2.
52. Quoted by S. Bowles and H. Gintis, *Schooling in Capitalist America*, New York 1976, p. 3.
53. W. Rodney, *How Europe Underdeveloped Africa*, London 1972, p. 7.
54. J. Copans and D. Seddon, 'Marxism and anthropology: a preliminary survey', in D. Seddon (ed.), *Relations of Production*.
55. *Ibid*. S. Amin, C. Atta-Mills, A. Bujra, G. Hamid and T. Mkandawire, 'Social science and the development crisis in Africa: problems and prospects', *Africa Development*, III, 1978. C.A.O. van Nieuwenhuijze, *The Study of Development and the Need for an Interdisciplinary Approach*, The Hague 1978.
56. Amin *et al.*, *loc. cit*. P.A. Nyongo, 'The teaching of the social sciences in East Africa', *Africa Development, loc. cit*.
57. University of Nairobi Students, 'Education and university must serve the majority of Kenyans: a preliminary critique of the university education, culture and writers in Kenya', *Utafiti*, II, 1977.
58. 'Put Mao Tse-tung through in command of cultural courses', *Peking Review*, 39, 1971. See also Q. Hoare and G.N. Smith (eds.), *Selections from the Prison Notebooks of Antonio Gramsci*, London 1971; Bonaventure Swai, 'The political economy of Tanzanian school leavers: a theoretical consideration', *Taamuli*, 9, 1979.
59. L. Seve, *Man in Marxist Theory*, Hassocks, Sussex, 1978. See also Bowles and Gintis, *Schooling in Capitalist America*.
60. D. Cook and D. Rubadiri (eds.), *Poems from East Africa*, London 1971.
61. *Ibid*.
62. Kay, *Development and Underdevelopment*. E. Mandel, 'The industrial cycle in late capitalism', *New Left Review*, 90, 1975. B. Berberoglu and M. Landsberg, 'Transnational production and the worldwide contradictions of advanced capitalism', *Social Praxis*, 5, 1978. D. O'Meara, review of T.R.H. Davenport, *South Africa: A Modern History* (Toronto 1979), in *Utafiti*, 4, 1979.
63. Ranger, 'Towards a usable past'.
64. M. Watts and R. Shenton, 'Capitalism and hunger in Northern Nigeria', Zaria 1978, mimeo. P. Richards, 'Drought in the Sahel', *African Environment*, I, 1975. P. Sweezy, *The Theory of Capitalist Development*, New York 1942. E. Mandel, *Marxist Economic Theory*, London 1971. A.K. Sen, 'Starvation and exchange entitlements: a general approach and its application to the great Bengal famine', *Cambridge Journal of Economics*, I, 1977. P. Gibbon, 'Colonialism and starvation in Ireland 1845–49', *Race and Class*, 17, 1975. C. Meillassoux, 'Development or exploitation: is the Sahel famine good business?', *Review of African Political Economy*, I, 1974. Bonaventure Swai, 'Are ecological disasters acts of God?', *Kale*, 4, 1979.
65. R. Samuel (ed.), *Village Life and Labour*, London 1975, p. XIX.
66. K. Marx, 'Theses on Feuerbach', R.C. Tucker (ed.), *Marx and Engels Reader*, New York 1963.
67. In their article, 'The object of African history: a materialist perspective', Bernstein and Depelchin have attempted to summarize such efforts.

See also articles in *Utafiti*, 3, 1978. K. Botchwey, 'Marxism, and the analysis of the African reality, *Africa Development*, II, 1977. J.S. Saul, 'Nationalism, socialism and Tanzanian history', L. Cliffe and J.S. Saul (eds.), *Socialism in Tanzania*, Vol. I, Nairobi 1972. J. Depelchin, 'Towards a problematic history of Africa', *Tanzania Zamani*, 18, 1975. G.T. Mishambi, 'The mystification of history: a critique of Rodney's *How Europe Underdeveloped Africa*', *Utafiti*, II, 1977. H. Bernstein, 'Sociology of development versus sociology of underdevelopment', in Bernstein *et al*, *Development Theory: Three Critical Essays*, London 1978.
68. T. Schroyer, *The Critique of Domination: The Origins and Development of Critical Theory*, Boston 1975, pp. 15-16, 18. See also H. Marcuse, *One-Dimensional Man*, London 1973.
69. J. Iliffe, review of H. Kjekshus, *Ecology Control and Economic Development in East African History: The Case of Tanganyika 1850-1950*, London 1977 in *Journal of African History*, XIX, 1978.
70. G.R. Elton, *The Practice of History*, London 1969.
71. G. Connell-Smith and H.A. Lloyd, *The Relevance of History*, London 1972. Atieno Odhiambo, 'A critical analysis of the content of history education in the sub-region of East, Central and Southern Africa including Zaire and Ethiopia', Workshop on the Teaching of History in African Universities, Lagos 1977.
72. L. Kapteijns, *African Historiography written by Africans 1955-1973: The Nigerian Case*.
73. Bonaventure Swai, 'The latest Cinderella of professional African history', *Tanzania Zamani*, 20, 1978.
74. Bernstein and Depelchin, 'The object of African history: a materialist perspective'.
75. F. Engels, *Dialectics of Nature*, Moscow 1974; quoted by L. Seve, *Marxism and the Theory of Human Personality*, London 1975, p. 9.
76. *Ibid*.
77. Novack, *An introduction to the Logic of Marxism*, p. 5.
78. Seve, *Marxism and the Theory of Human Personality*.
79. V.I. Lenin, *Collected Works*, Vol. 38: *Philosophical Notebooks*, Moscow 1961. See especially the section on the question of dialectics, pp. 359-63.
80. Gray, 'E.P. Thompson, history and communist politics', p. 182.
81. *Ibid*.
82. Thompson, *The Poverty of Theory and Other Essays*. See also Mao Tse-tung, *Four Essays on Philosophy*, Peking 1966, A. Mafeje, 'What is historical explanation?' Dar es Salaam 1971, mimeo. J. O'Brien and P. Newcomer, 'Where do good ideas come from?' North Eastern Anthropological Association Meetings 1974, mimeo.
83. Haupt, 'Why the history of the working-class movement?' p. 8.
84. Thompson, *The Poverty of Theory and Other Essays*.
85. Jones, 'History: the poverty of empiricism'.
86. H.M. Enzensburger, 'A critique of political ecology', H. Rose and S. Rose (eds.), *The Political Economy of Science: Ideology in the Natural Sciences*, London 1976, pp. 179-80, 197.

2. The African Factor

For most imperial historians the 'colonial encounter' precipitated in the latter half of the nineteenth century comprised a complex of irrationalities amenable to analysis only in the context of the 'White Man's Burden'. The colonial venture, in their view, was dominated by motives of imperial statesmen to deliver precolonial social formations from the Hobbesian state of nature. Informed by principles of Social Darwinism, the policies formulated by imperial proconsuls were empirical rather than imperial, more preservationist than developmentalist. The endeavour of these imperial proconsuls was to integrate precolonial societies into the mainstream of modern history. Imperial history was intended to describe the motives of such statesmen.[1]

As objects of colonial policy, precolonial and colonial societies existed only in the consciousness of imperial proconsuls: this is the gist of an assertion now vehemently disputed by initiators of the 'African historiographical revolution'.[2] This new historiography was born in the aftermath of the Second World War. Its *forte* lies in the discovery of new methods of data collection; but its main intent is as an *ideological* alternative to colonial historiography. Its initiators have revealed the contradictions dominant in colonial historiography by way of counter-propositions with a view to exposing the inadequacies of imperial presuppositions. Against African inactivity in the making of history has been asserted African agency.[3]

Imperial historians had emphasized the inability of Africans to make their own history because they believed that African institutions were too oppressive and tradition-bound to allow that individual enterprise without which the making of history was well nigh impossible.[4] Besides, African metaphysics stressed unity of the living, the dead and the unborn – an idea thought to be against the notion of social change. The founders of the postcolonial Africanist historiography, however, argued that, although Africa might not have possessed as many historical personalities as Europe, individuals imbued with entrepreneurial sense were a reality of the African past.[5] Indeed, emphasis on unity of the living, dead and unborn was evidence of the African sense of continuity and historical consciousness.[6] The African past, therefore, had personalities around whom the making of history revolved, and this past was as dynamic as European history, the model which Africanist historians have assiduously tried to emulate.

prolific in other things than learning.[10]

Amoo attacked the theoretical justification of slavery and argued that the problem was one of false consciousness. He invoked Roman Law to prove that the imprisonment of one race by another was unjustified. All in all, however, metaphysics proved more captivating to Amoo; the plight of Africans at home and in the diaspora was left unsolved.[11]

Nevertheless, many were subsequently to resurrect Amoo's argument. Believing that racism resulted from misinformation, Blacks in the United States of America, following the collapse of the efforts of reconstruction after the Civil War, sought to educate Americans about Africa's previous achievements. This campaign continued well into the First World War. Egypt was reclaimed from the Mediterranean civilizations and declared a region of African history – an argument renewed by Diop in the 1950s. Songay, Ghana and Mali were also resurrected from oblivion and given wide publicity as African achievements in empire building. The American racist monster, persisted, however.[12] Besides, with the rise of European colonial enlightenment, African institutions were robbed of their historical sense and allowed to exist only in space rather than in time as well. Despite the achievements to recover the African past by professional Black American historians, one of the leading founders of the discipline of Applied Anthropology, Malinowski, declared the African past 'history dead and buried', 'irrelevant mythology';[13] despite also the successful efforts by African 'amateur' historians like Blyden, Sarbah and Johnson to recover the African past for 'purely patriotic reasons' or in 'vindication of the African race' during the second half of the nineteenth century.[14]

The persistence of the notion of African inactivity in the making of history cannot be blamed on misinformation. More value lies in searching out the material basis which allowed the stubborn survival of such 'intellectual monstrosities'. Academics have taken refuge in the dogma of lack of information, whenever they are under siege. To accept such a claim at its face value is to be uncritical, especially when it is advocated so loudly and persistently. On the other hand, to transcend such a claim by showing its ideological content seems an inadequate if necessary step, because the self-assumed superiority of the academic is taken for granted. The observation that an academic is himself produced by the totality of the social process is disregarded.[15]

Contributors to postcolonial Africanist historiography have taken this necessary but inadequate step, showing the ideological content of colonial historiography. This action has been considered radical. This, however, is doubtful if the term *radical* still means to tackle things at the root: to be preoccupied with the fundamental.[16] Nevertheless, the present discussion is not primarily concerned with colonial historiography. Rather it seeks to analyse the mode of conceptualization employed in precipitating the postcolonial Africanist historiography or so-called African historiographical revolution. It is also an attempt to show the possibility of an alternative to the assumed order of arranging facts, with the intent to go beyond the present state of postcolonial Africanist historiography.

The Postcolonial School of Africanist Historiography

Professional historians who subscribed to colonial historiography asserted that the African past was not historical. Africans only existed in the ethnographic present, they argued. Thus, as Dame Perham came to admit:

> In default of true knowledge we, too, often make do with assumptions: the primary one, that Africans are backward; next, that they are all almost equally backward; even that they are inherently, and so permanently, backward. Cut off, as most of us are, from any contact with Africans as individuals, we think of them or deal with them in the mass, according to our various standpoints, as 'natives', or the 'native problem'; as 'the heathen'; as 'hut and poll taxpayers', or as 'native labour'. We see the strange, stupid or cruel things they do and, ignorant of their motives, forgetting what we ourselves did yesterday, what, alas! Christian nations are doing today, think them relatively more stupid and cruel than they are. We allow black skin and negro features to shut Africans off from those perceptions which we turn upon members of our own race.[17]

Such are the assertions which postcolonial Africanist historians have declared mythical and aberrant, a travesty of the empirical method which in the nineteenth century had helped usher in the dawn of scientific, that is critical, historiography.[18] Postcolonial Africanist historians asserted that Africa had a past worth studying. This past constituted an integrated whole and possessed its own motif of development. Postcolonial Africanist historiography was born at a time when the study of history 'from above' was being challenged by studies 'from below'. Africanist history, therefore, was regarded as a contribution to the study of the inarticulate masses who had been denied their 'peoplehood' for too long. In the case of Africa, the history of the inarticulate became synonymous with studies of the colonized, a notion more helpful for its ideological than its theoretical content.[19]

Postcolonial Africanist historiography was intended as an ideological answer to imperial mythology.[20] Departments of History and Institutes of African Studies were established, conferences held, and the results of scholarly enterprise published in learned journals. The various disciplines of anthropology, linguistics, biology and archaeology were brought to bear on the recovery of the African past. Where there were few professional African historians, some were invented.[21] If this seemed too crude an enterprise, professionals of this kind were imported wholesale. Such was the case in East and Central Africa, where the roots of an emerging petty bourgeoisie were still very shallow.[22]

On Social Change
These historians wanted to demonstrate the efficacy of the notions of social change in studying the African past. They wanted to show the ability of precolonial African societies to respond 'rationally' to external and internal stimuli for change and in that way to reveal their evolution from simple to complex entities, a process which was marked by amplified bureaucratic efficiency and universalization of organization.[23] On the problem of response of African societies to colonialism, postcolonial Africanist historians aimed to show that these communities were neither instinctual nor xenophobic in their actions, since they took due consideration of the implications and consequences of the approaches adopted. In view of this dynamism and rationality, it has been concluded by such historians that, left alone, African societies could have modernized very rapidly,[24] and that colonial rule was a mere episode in the evolution of African history, if not a step backwards.[25] Most notions employed in this postcolonial Africanist historiography, however, were entities of unknown quantity. What made African actions rational and therefore real, as was asserted by some professional Africanist historians, remained enigmatic. The encounter between colonial and postcolonial historiography was thoroughly ideological.[26]

On African Achievements
Precolonial as well as colonial history was an object of study. In the precolonial past they showed 'the wonder that was Africa'.[27] The 'hot, smoky, and filthy hut' in which 'men and beasts herded together' 'with a door . . . made only for goats and calves', the habitation which forced human beings to 'crawl in literally on their hands and knees', was not representative of African culture.[28] Africans achieved architectural feats comparable to the best in the world; they built empires and towns bigger than those of contemporary Europe.[29] In reply to those imperialist historians who had pushed further with the question of European cultural superiority, one historian quipped: 'Who in this world is competent to judge whether an Austrian waltz is better than a Makonde ngoma?'[30]

With the exception of emphatic assertions of this kind, which were a pointer to the idea of cultural relativism, it was agreed by most postcolonial historians that Africans contributed to the making of their own history as well as international history. As for the 'Egyptian experiment', Cheikh Anta Diop observed: 'It remains true that . . . [it] was essentially Negro, and that all Africans can draw the same moral advantage that Westerners draw from Graeco-Latin civilization . . . If Plato, Eudore and Pythagoras remained in Egypt for thirteen to twenty years,' he went on to say, 'it was not only to learn recipes.' European scholars could continue to quote Plato as long as they remembered that he was inspired by Africa. Egypt was the 'great initiator of the Mediterranean world' in the fields of philosophy, science and aesthetics.[31]

Concern with precolonial Africanist history was intended to show 'the intellectual capacity of the African people to make their own history'.[32]

It was also intended to show that the endeavour itself was not undertaken for fun but to solve problems of societies which were growing more complex.[33] In so doing, the 'incredible primitiveness of terms and attitudes' with which the problems of African societies were discussed was corrected, and the viability of postcolonial Africanist historiography established.[34] The subtlety of African initiative in the colonial era was also revealed. This kind of initiative was shown not only in the movement of ideas, but also in long-distance trade, participation in the establishment of the colonial state, involvement in the founding of Christianity, and most significantly in staging the politics of protest against colonial rule.[35] Indeed, African initiative in the colonial era has been projected as being synonymous with the politics of protest. This, however, was intended to establish the indigenous origins of nationalism in Africa with a view to correcting the elitist approach in the study of African politics.[36] More significantly perhaps, emphasis on the importance of 'the groundswell from below' in African politics was intended 'to demonstrate an interplay between European and African initiatives by showing that Africans were not the passive objects of colonial rule, unable to influence their fate or to respond rationally to new situations'.[37]

African response to colonial rule has been perceived as a progression through three stages: rejection, acceptance, and finally the endeavour to control the process of modernization.[38] Further research has facilitated the refining of the notion of initiative. Thus it has been observed that decisions at the level of 'high colonialism' were reserved for Europeans. 'Africans could act only within the context created by these decisions; the options available to them were to some extent determined by forces and people outside their own control.' At lower levels of the hierarchy found in the colonial situation, however, the range of options and opportunities open to talented and ambitious men was wide. Indeed, the options could have been even wider but for the repressive nature of a society 'full of intelligent men living frustrating and unintelligent lives'; but 'opportunities for innovation and leadership did exist'.[39]

This argument is indicative of the ambiguity of the notion of the political as employed in most colonial and postcolonial studies of Africanist history. Double-faced like Janus, the political is considered oppressive but not totally so. Thus 'politicking' does take place under the colonial regime, despite views to the contrary. The political is therefore regarded as something neutral which is responsive to all kind of groundswells from below. 'Colonial administration is thus seen to be essentially similar to other forms of government, concerned to resolve conflict – sometimes by means of active development planning – rather than to impose a preconceived design on virgin territory.' Here, colonial and postcolonial historiography converge. The empiricism of the colonial Leviathan is vindicated.[40]

On Resistance to Colonialism
Initial African initiative in the colonial era comprised primary resistance. This began the era of politics of protest which, it is claimed, subsequently

culminated in 'mass nationalism', the most important condition for the attainment of constitutional independence. Primary resistance engaged 'only the power structure of traditional societies'. This, it has wrongly been alleged, amounted to the 'instinctual attempt of an unmodified traditional structure to extrude a foreign body'.[41] Primary resistance failed, but this was soon displaced by the period of colonial rebellions; colonial grievances did not end with the initial assertion of the African voice.

Colonial rebellions represented an enlargement of the scale of commitment and participation, as well as a sharpening of political focus, as compared with primary resistance. This theme can be illustrated with the help of oral history collected from the Matumbi people of Southern Tanzania in East Africa. Collectors of this history have written that, having occupied the Matumbi country, the Germans, who were the first batch of European colonizers in Tanganyika, imposed their control over the area by appointing subordinate officials called *akidas* empowered to collect taxes from the local people. The taxes were intended to finance the machinery of colonial administration. Harsh methods were employed to collect taxes, a situation worsened by the fact that the *akidas* were paid according to the amount they collected. In 1897 the Matumbi refused to pay these impositions. The revolt which ensued was swiftly put down with the help of a German punitive expedition.[42]

Harsher conditions followed with the introduction of an oppressive scheme to grow cotton and with the institutionalization of forced labour to build public works. These grievances contributed to the circumstances which caused the Maji Maji Rebellion in 1905. Compared with previous revolts in Southern Tanzania, the Maji Maji involved many ethnic communities. It was precipitated by a diviner called Kinjitikile who claimed to be possessed by the spirit of Kolelo, a religious cult dominant in the region. Kinjitikile preached that 'Africans were one and that . . . his medicine – the *maji* – was stronger than European weapons.' The news of this medicine spread among the people living around the Rufiji. It reached the Matumbi through a whispering campaign called *njwinywila*. Kinjitikile preached that Africans had been defeated in their former struggles against the Germans because of disunity. He preached that unity was important if the struggle against imperialism were to succeed. This unity was made possible by the discovery of the *maji* medicine.[43]

As a mass movement, the Maji Maji Rebellion 'originated in peasant grievances, was then sanctified and extended by prophetic religion, and finally crumbled as crisis compelled reliance on fundamental loyalties to kin and tribe.' As with other colonial rebellions, the Maji Maji was confronted with 'the central historical problem . . . between the ideology of revolt and economic, political and cultural realities'.[44] Even so, its occurrence is adequate testimony that social structure alone did not determine the type of African response to colonial rule. The size of a society, too, 'whether one is referring simply to social size or social organization [was] . . . of little significance'. This has been reinforced by a study of 'the complex range of responses of the

Khoisan to the Dutch' which 'seem to suggest that there are few societies, however small-scale, that have not responded to colonial conquest by at times collaborating and at other times resisting, though undoubtedly the nature of collaboration or resistance has to be related to social structure'.[45]

It has been argued that Africans managed to assert their will against colonial rule because the colonial balance of power was in many cases in their favour. Where the balance was unfavourable, Africans used passive resistance, a technique which was to become dominant in the inter-war years and after. The variety of African response to colonial rule therefore seemed overwhelming. It included active positive resistance, active negative response, passive positive response, and passive negative resistance.[46]

By asserting their will against colonial rule, Africans, it has been argued, secured many reforms from the colonial state. These ranged from educational and administrative to economic, religious and social reforms. It has been said that the manner of resistance also influenced subsequent assertions against colonial rule.[47] It has therefore been possible to trace connections between the initial stages of African resistance to colonial rule and the modern phase of mass nationalism. The alleged hiatus of the 'vital middle years' between the two sets of movements has thus been nullified. At no time during the colonial era were Africans passive. Liberals, missionaries and anthropologists have complained that, for too long a time, it befell them to speak on behalf of Africans, who were politically passive; but historical reality shows that Africans were always active in movements which in many cases oscillated between integration with and separatism from colonial rule. These movements kept alive the memories of early resistance until the advent of the more sophisticated politics of modern nationalism. In this way the 'African factor' in Africanist history has been asserted by professional Africanist historians. Thus, too, it has been concluded that African history was made in Africa, and that colonial proconsuls and the like were more influenced by what was happening in the African continent than in Europe. This assertion has been toned down here and there, but the central theme, the African factor in the making of history, has firmly been maintained.[48]

The Concept of Local Initiative: A Critique

To assert the importance of African initiative in the making of African history is one thing; to ascertain the historical and social content of this phenomenon, quite another. The meaning of African initiative in the making of history, as far as professional Africanist historiography is concerned, is still elusive. It has been concluded in one critical study of postcolonial Africanist historiography that, in terms of status, the real bearer of initiative is hard to locate. The search for initiative therefore turns out to be a search for form. In its content, instead of having a specific initiative for a specific instance, the same categories provide the basis of interpretation, and thus violence is done to the facts in order to fit them into some preconceived mould. From this juncture, speculative abstraction takes over. Serious scholarship is suddenly reduced to scholasticism, in which safe questions of how many angels can stand on the head of a pin take precedence over those of exploitation and oppression.[49]

For postcolonial Africanist historians, the term, *initiative*, has a wide range of meanings. To some it means commitment to the idea of social change. To others it includes the notion of enlargement of scale and the sharpening of political focus. There appears to be no explicit criterion to help determine the content of colonial protest. This could be due to the philosophy of pragmatism dominant in postcolonial Africanist historiography. There have, therefore, been arguments about whether movements of resistance like the Maji Maji can actually be called rebellions (since in any case Africans generally did not accept colonial rule), or whether Africans were also on the offensive rather than merely reacting to colonial stimuli, and so forth. Such are the realms of linguistic philosophy;[50] no wonder some Africanist historians have turned to the study of economic history under the new banner of the notion of the development of underdevelopment. Even so, there has also been an attempt to assess the impact of colonial rebellions upon colonial regimes. This can be illustrated with the help of material drawn from the contrasting history of two parts of the German empire in Africa during the first decade of this century – Tanganyika and South West Africa. These cases show up the problems that arise with any simplistic notion of 'local initiative'.

Its Analysis of the European Response to African Resistance

The assessment, in the case of the colonial history of Tanzania, that the Dernburg Reforms introduced in the aftermath of the Maji Maji Rebellion were the European response to which the Rebellion constituted the African initiative has been criticized for being one-dimensional.[51] It has been argued that the forces operating in German East Africa included the German Imperial Government and the metropolitan audience, and that these might have been of paramount importance in determining the nature of the Dernburg Reforms. Moreover, whereas the Maji Maji might have forced the German imperial authorities to relax their grip on German East Africa, this was not so with South West Africa, where German imperialists were faced with a similar kind of rebellion.[52] In South West Africa, rather than giving in to the groundswell from below, the Germans, together with the settler community, eventually routed the rebellious Africans and placed them in a weaker position than before. If there were reforms favourable to Africans in German East Africa, therefore, that was not so in the case of South West Africa, where the settler population, given its South African connections, was stronger. Thus, it might be argued further, the conditions prevailing in German East Africa constituted a peculiarity of their own. The concrete conditions prevailing there cannot, therefore, be compared with those dominant in South West Africa. But it seems proper at this juncture, nonetheless, to emphasize that, in terms of ownership and control, there were two fractions of capital dominant in most colonial situations competing for control of the colonial state with a view to determining its structure. Where metropolitan capital was dominant, peasant commodity production was encouraged, for in such a case the sheer availability of a cheap source of raw materials took precedence over the manner of production. In most cases, too, peasant commodity production was cheaper than settler farming.[53] On the other hand, where, owing to peculiar historical circumstances, the settler element was too strong to be controlled fully by metropolitan capital, settler plantation agriculture prevailed. For instance, in South West Africa, Southern Rhodesia and Kenya, peasant agriculture was destroyed and Africans forced to become migrant labourers. Otherwise, settler agriculture could not have survived side by side with peasant commodity production.

In German East Africa, with the Dernburg Reforms, agents of metropolitan capital acquired hegemonic control of the organization of the colonial state. As an ideology of the colonial state, paternalism was orchestrated more loudly than before.[54] Where, on the other hand, the fraction of settler capital remained dominant, as in South West Africa, colonial enlightenment was left in settler hands. Here the nature of articulation of precapitalist modes of production under imperialist hegemony was mediated differently, compared with social formations where peasant commodity production became dominant. Alienation of land was more pronounced in settler colonies, the demand for surplus labour more crude, and the niceties of paternalism less articulate. In settler colonies and colonies of partial settlement, therefore, the reproduction of precapitalist institutions under conditions determined by imperialist control was less marked. Compromise with chiefs and other precapitalist institutions was not as pronounced as in colonies where peasant agriculture was dominant. Consequently, if reforms in German East Africa meant recognition of the place of chiefs in the colonial hierarchy, then the Maji Maji scored some points in favour of the African peoples; but, as has been observed about reforms in the metropolitan countries of the North Atlantic Basin, such measures have been carried out at the instigation of capital. In most cases it has also been discovered that authoritarianism is tightened with the institutionalization of the reforms. Reforms are merely intended to conceal the other face of Janus, force.[55]

Where, then, does that leave us with regard to the impact of the Maji Maji on German colonial policy? The influence of the Maji Maji in forcing the Germans to re-examine their position in East Africa cannot be gainsaid. The crucial question, however, is whether the content of this sort of 'African initiative' was similar to the 'concessions' made by the Germans in the form of the Dernburg Reforms. We shall return to this question later. However, the Rebellion revealed an important feature of settler power in German East Africa: its weakness *vis-à-vis* local forces and, more significantly, *vis-à-vis* the German metropolitan bourgeoisie. During the earlier Abushiri Revolt of 1888-9, the German Imperial Government had been forced to come to the rescue of the German East Africa Company which, together with its thirty sub-companies in the colony, had proved unable to contain the wrath of the Arab aristocracy on the East African coast. In 1890 the German imperial

Government assumed formal control of the colony. The Maji Maji was similarly a demonstration of the weakness of settler power in German East Africa. Subsequently, the dominance of metropolitan control unmediated by settler power was institutionalized by the Dernburg Reforms. Reproduction of African precapitalist social formations under conditions determined by the capitalist mode of production became more pronounced. So a situation which was brought about in reality by a peculiar balance of social forces in German East Africa has been viewed simplistically by postcolonial African historiography as the sole product of African initiative. Indeed, men do make history but not under conditions of their own choice. The particularities of German East Africa as determined by the alignment of the prevailing social forces were different from those prevalent in German South West Africa. The outcome of the revolts in the two colonies could, therefore, never have been similar.

Its Analysis of African Rebellions: Form, Not Content
The impact of colonial rebellions on imperial policy aside, postcolonial Africanist historians have shown a great deal of interest in the forms of organization which the rebellions assumed.[56] This area of analysis, it has been observed by some critics of postcolonial Africanist historiography, constitutes another of the School's great weaknesses and has been attacked time and again.[57] However, concern with the organization and ideology of African protest movements is indicative of the purpose for which postcolonial Africanist historiography was constituted: first and foremost as an ideological rejoinder to colonial historiography. In this enterprise, too, it remains trapped.[58]

The concern with the organization of African protest movements has arisen from the belief that tribal aggregations are the natural form of African social organization, a phenomenon which necessitates rigorous investigations of any deviation from this norm. Interest in the organization of colonial rebellions, however, has of late been considered by this School as too formalistic. Besides the organization of colonial rebellions, therefore, it has been found fruitful to investigate their patterns of participation. But to pay so much attention to types of participation in colonial rebellions with a view to establishing the role of the colonized as subjects of history in the colonial situation should not be undertaken at the expense of considering a very important factor, observed with regard to the history of Vietnam, that 'while the entire Vietnamese people took part in [the making of history] at all times, the political line adopted, like the methods of action and the prospects for the future, differed from one stage to another according to the social classes, personalities, organizations and parties at the head of the national movement.'[59]

It has also been underlined with regard to European history that, in its struggle to control society, the bourgeoisie 'finds itself involved in a constant battle. At first with the aristocracy: later on, with portions of the bourgeoisie itself, whose interests have become antagonistic to the progress of industry;

at all times, with the bourgeoisie of foreign countries. In all these battles it sees itself compelled to appeal to the proletariat, to ask for its help, and thus, to drag it into the political arena.'[60] A great deal of blood was shed in the struggles between the European bourgeoisie and feudal lords, but these conflicts were not of the same nature as those between the feudal lords and the peasantry. In the latter struggle, the bourgeoisie and the aristocracy joined hands against the peasantry. But the other struggle, between bourgeoisie and aristocracy, was a struggle for a 'share-out' of surplus once it had been expropriated from the basic producers. This conflict was secondary; it was not fundamental. The bourgeoisie dragged the proletariat into the battlefield, in its endeavour to have a finger in the pie – a share-out of the surplus. There was, however, a world of difference between the bourgeoisie and the proletariat, as was shown once the bourgeoisie had won its battle against the aristocracy. Commonsense has it that a rich man's war is a poor man's fight.[61]

There is a big difference between the bourgeoisie and the proletariat, notwithstanding the involvement of the two classes in the same battles. Participation neither confirms similarity of aims nor equal control of the movement by the two classes. So the use of terms like *mobilization, integration* and *participation* in analyses of social movements should not be taken for granted. Yet this is precisely what postcolonial African historiography has done. Those who have studied these rebellions have, it would appear, concentrated on form rather than content; the problem they have posed has been how the rebellions occurred rather than why – as if the two were separable; form has been seen as a sort of jar into which all sorts of ideas can be poured.[62]

In his discussion of the causes of the Maji Maji Rebellion, John Iliffe observes that most German colonial administrators believed that the Rebellion was instigated by local conspirators, peddlers of the *maji* medicine. The 'natives' easily followed the conspirators because of superstition. The German Left, however, believed at the time that Maji Maji was caused by colonial maladministration. This, they argued, was shown in the way that the 'natives' were forced to grow cotton for export.[63] The German Left pleaded for colonial paternalism, which they confused with benevolence. In this, they were not different from British Liberals like Morel who campaigned against King Leopold's policies of plunder in the Congo.[64]

Iliffe, however, argues that, while the Rebellion may be explained solely in terms of German maladministration, grievances against colonial rule were *not* restricted to Southern Tanzania. German colonial policies in Northeastern Tanzania, where plantation agriculture had been introduced, were equally vicious. Iliffe therefore resurrects the importance of the medicine, *maji*, in mobilizing the 'natives' to rise above their narrow peasant and tribal loyalties. Had it not been for the cult of *hongo*, Iliffe's argument implies, there would have been no Maji Maji, however intense the maladministration. On one level Iliffe rejects the efficacy of the *maji* medicine as an explanation for the Maji Maji Rising – at least in the manner in which colonial administrators saw it. On another level, he accepts it; only in doing so he invokes the tin god, rationality. *Maji* becomes a jar into which the colonial administrators could pour the notion of superstition, and into which Iliffe has poured the idea of rationality.[65] However, one is left wondering whether the 'natives' as well did not pour their own ideas into this jar.

Professional historians have resorted to the comparative method whenever the spirit of a particular age has refused to reveal itself in a given set of facts. That seems to be the case with Iliffe's attempt to explain the Maji Maji in terms of the *hongo* cult. But this assumes that there were no similar cults elsewhere in Tanzania. As for Northeastern Tanzania, it should not be forgotten that prevalent here was the plantation system of agriculture whose organization, and thus control of labour, was completely different from that of areas under peasant commodity production. Here many of the early labourers came from as far away as Tabora. They were strangers isolated from the local population. The possibilities of such strangers joining hands with the local population against the Germans were minimal. Their protests took a form different from that of the Maji Maji. It has been argued very admirably, in the case of the tin miners of Northern Nigeria for example, that 'theft and other individualized types of resistance to the iron rule of private property dominated early forms of proletarian class consciousness, but gave way subsequently to collective organization and more challenging industrial and political struggle.'[66] Eric Hobsbawm has argued similarly with regard to European bandits and *mafiosi*, a social category he has chosen to term 'primitive rebels'.[67] In the nineteenth century, Engels made an equally penetrating observation about the 'bold men who robbed from the rich':[68]

> The revolt of the workers began soon after the first industrial development, and has passed through several phases . . . . The earliest, crudest and least fruitful form of this rebellion was that of crime. The working man lived in poverty and want, and saw that others were better off than he. It was not clear to his mind why he, who did more for society than the rich idler, should be the one to suffer under these conditions. Want conquered his inherited respect for the sacredness of property, and he stole. We have seen how crime increased with the extension of manufacture; how the yearly number of arrests bore a constant relation to the number of bales of cotton annually consumed.
> The workers soon realized that crime did not help matters. The criminal could protest against the existing order of society singly, as one individual; the whole might of society was brought to bear upon each criminal, and crushed him with its immense superiority.[69]

In just such a way the proletariat and semi-proletariat in Africa protested before the advent of trade unionism. Small wonder then that complaints of theft by the rich were so frequent. Similarly, laws to restrict free movement of the poor were passed by those at the helm.[70]

So much for 'primitive rebels'. Too much emphasis on the form of revolts as opposed to their content, where the oppressed classes are concerned, serves to divert attention from the social conditions of the downtrodden as well as from the content of their actions. Bourgeois scholars increased their concern with the form of revolts with the advent of the proletariat as a force to reckon with in the political arena. The Paris Commune, in particular, demonstrated for the first time to the European ruling class the determination of the French working class to live under a state of their own creation. Bourgeois confidence was shattered. Such shocks also penetrated the ivory towers of scholarship. Nihilist tendencies began to be revealed in academic treatises of various kinds. It was under such conditions that Max Weber discovered the idea of *charisma* in the latter part of the nineteenth century.[71] *Charisma*, it is now taken as an article of faith, is 'a certain quality of an individual personality by virtue of which he is set apart from ordinary men and treated as endowed with supernatural, superhuman, or at least specifically exceptional qualities'. *Charisma*, it is said, is found in abnormal situations which legitimize the role of the 'anointed'. But why, it could be asked, should abnormal conditions be problematic and not the converse? For Weber, capitalism constituted the normal order of things. Workers revolted because they were abnormal, or were led into doing so by demagogues exploiting abnormal times.[72]

As has already been shown, postcolonial historians have declared colonial revolts rational rather than abnormal. Maybe they were so since, as is implied in most assertions by these professionals, with the attainment of independence, African countries began to undergo the bourgeois revolution. If this was so, the revolution was shortlived because it was not long before postcolonial historians like Low and Shepperson called for the use of Weberian ideas, like *charisma*, in the study of African history.[73] In any case, the assertion of the rationality of African colonial protest was most probably made as an attack on the 'spasmodic view of history' dominant in the study of such events. Many questions still remain unanswered. Why should the 'natives' behave mainly as tribes? What is so special about tribal organization? Is there something peculiar about peasants which makes their movements so ephemeral?

Separation of form from content is indicative of the tendency to view reality through the prism of dichotomies: myth versus reality, theory versus experience, ideology versus facts, and so on.[74] This approach, however, tends to discount the possibility of a dialectical relationship between dichotomies. Reality is reduced to one or other pole of the dichotomy, but not the whole. If for some reason one of the poles is found realistic, the other is declared mythical. Thus, too, the medicine used in the Maji Maji Rebellion becomes superstitious or rational depending on whether one was writing during the colonial period, when the *telos* of colonial historiography was civilization as defined by the 'Lords of Human Kind', or in the postcolonial era, in which the destination of African history – in the view of postcolonial African historiography – has been reduced to the establishment of the postcolonial state.

Ideas, myths, superstitions and the like are part of social reality. In scholarly enterprise, it does not help to declare such entities irrational or otherwise, however vehemently. To study them in the context of their time is more useful. This, at least, is how some of the impressive studies of the oppressed have been conducted. Whether postcolonial professional historians of Africa have followed in the footsteps of such a method, as is claimed, is another matter. 'Ideas and the language in which they are expressed,' it has been observed, 'are more than a simple reflection of "reality": they are as much a part of social reality as the institutional and class structure of a society.'[75] 'The American and French Revolutions,' Eric Hobsbawm has written, 'are probably the first mass political movements in the history of the world which expressed their ideology and aspirations in terms of a secular rationalism and not of traditional religion.' Besides, 'what men think about the world is one thing, the terms in which they think about it is another'. Except for the Chinese, men have for a long time thought about the world in religious terms; so much so, that in some parts of the world *Christian* was synonymous with Man himself.[76]

It was observed in the middle of the last century that 'all facts and personages of great importance in world history occur, as it were, twice ... the first time as tragedy, the second as farce'. Martin Luther 'donned the mask of the Apostle Paul, the Revolution of 1789 to 1814 draped itself alternately as the Roman Republic and the Roman Empire .... Cromwell and the English people had borrowed speech, passions and illusions from the Old Testament for their own bourgeois revolution.'[77] The English working class, before the advent of trade unionism, expressed their discontent in religious terms.[78] So, too, the fighters in the Maji Maji Rebellion donned the cloak of the spirit of Kolelo, but the social context in which it was invoked should not be ignored because of its glittering appearance. What gave 'life and vigour' to the idea of the spirit of Kolelo was the class struggle touched off by the Germans in the course of presiding over the articulation of the precapitalist social formations in Southern Tanzania under imperialist hegemony, through the institution of peasant commodity production and exchange, and under the banner of the White Man's Burden. The ideas used by the Maji Maji fighters, as has been observed with regard to the English Revolution, were 'second-hand; the passion behind them is not'. Kinjitikile the diviner, like radicals of other countries and epochs, claimed to have received his truth from the spirit of Kolelo. Perhaps he deceived himself, but he 'gave form and shape to vague ideas that were in the air'. The 'form and shape' were his own; but the ideas were 'drawn from the experience of daily life' in Southern Tanzania of the early colonial period.[79]

The Material Basis of Colonial Violence and Resistance

'In connection with the investigation of imperialism', it is necessary that 'every feature of world economy', in fact every feature of life, 'be taken in its

Emphasis on the African spirit of enterprise, as well as on the dominance of individual activities in the formation of the African past, ushered in the talismanic notion of progressive change. The idea of progressive social change was considered seminal in the endeavour to confirm the historicity of the past. African history did not commence with the arrival of European proconsuls whom imperial historians raised to the level of deities, neither did the colonial period constitute the golden age of African history – such was the predominant mode of thinking of the so-called African historiographical revolution.

But facts are stubborn things; they can be ignored, but not denied completely. The African historiographical revolution did not last long. Following the crisis which now haunts postcolonial Africanist historiography, colonial historiography has re-emerged in a refurbished form. The colonial period might not have constituted a golden age, it has now been asserted, but neither did the precolonial period of the African past. It has also been argued that the colonial period was not as bleak as has been portrayed by postcolonial Africanist historians. This is so, it has been alleged, because the benefits brought about by the building of railways, hospitals and schools, the establishment of an efficient administration, and the teaching of the dignity of labour cannot be gainsaid. Injustice may have been perpetrated in the course of realizing these aims, the argument runs, but this was committed in the course of fulfilling a 'noble' task. On balance, then, colonialism was beneficial to Africa.[7] At this point, however, a new school inspired by the development-of-underdevelopment theorists took over.[8]

The birth and popularization of postcolonial Africanist historiography constituted an ideological response to its colonial predecessor. Its strength was grounded in the efforts to show the ideological content of colonial historiography by the use of nationalist and moralist counter-ideology. Imperial and colonial history was declared racist. The question of why racist stereotypes have managed to survive in African Studies for so long, however, was not even reconnoitred. It should be remembered that the endeavour to establish the African past as an independent area of study amenable to the historian's professional vigour did not begin in 1945: as early as the first half of the eighteenth century Anthony William Amoo, an African philosopher who studied in Germany and taught at the Universities of Wittenberg, Jena and Halle, was forced by the prejudices levelled at that time against Africans, with a view to defending slavery and the Altantic slave trade, to come to the defence of Africa.[9] In his philosophical treatise *On the Nature of the Human Mind* he wrote:

> Great once was the dignity of Africa, whether one considers natural talents of mind or the study of letters, or the very institutions for safeguarding religion. For she had given birth to several men of the greatest pre-eminence by whose talents and efforts the whole of human knowledge, no less than divine knowledge, has been built up ... though in our times, indeed, that part of the world is reported to be more

organic relation with *capital*, not as a separate sphere, the development of which can be abstracted, to be treated in isolation from the rest.'[80] This injunction by Pilling has not been heeded, especially with regard to the study of violence in colonial societies, despite various studies of the state, as well as the observation that the oppressed make their feelings known when they 'rudely' make an intrusion on the stage of history. Thus there has been a tendency, on the one hand, to show how colonial societies heroically resisted colonial rule, without showing the content of the resistance; and on the other to argue, somewhat glibly, that it was foolhardy for colonial societies to resist colonial rule since the colonial state was so powerful.

In the case of Oriental history, for example, it has been argued that there were only a few colonial revolts on the Indian subcontinent because of the Indian genius for bearing grievances with patience and indifference characteristic of Oriental people'. The few examples of resistance which occurred, therefore, were a deviation from the normal evolution of colonial history in India. They represented a surrender 'to the primitive human instinct of violent reaction against injustice . . . without any thought of . . . [the] consequences'. The backlash which followed in the aftermath of the protests, it seems, was too much for the natives, 'misled' as they allegedly had been into revolting against the might of the colonial state.[81] Many books have been written on why people revolt, commit violence, suicide and so on, but such studies have not gone beyond reproducing the beliefs of the petty-bourgeois scholars involved in writing them. Torn between the primary classes of oppressor and the oppressed, such scholars have merely revealed their own simultaneous 'potential for heroic acts and for dastardly deeds'.[82]

Some professional historians have alleged that 'natives' went on the rampage merely to kill each other, because there was an element of violence inherent in them.[83] Equally crude has been the discussion of colonial violence which reduced the study of imperialism to its acts of violence. Perhaps this is intended as counter-ideology to imperialist paternalism, but it seems that many professionals have made a fetish of it. For Fanon the dividing line between the colonized and the colonizer in a colonial society was 'shown by barracks and police stations. In the colonies it is the policeman and the soldier who are officials, instituted go-betweens, the spokesmen of the settler and his rule of oppression.' 'In the capitalist countries a multitude of moral teachers, counsellors and "bewilderers" separate the exploited from those in power.' Here evidence is cushioned with some form of ideological stratum. In the colonies, according to Fanon, it is not.[84]

The colonial situation, says Cesaire, could not be otherwise. Colonial officials were 'sweepings from the metropolitan gutter': people who were prepared to commit murder at the slightest provocation, but who were restrained from doing so in the metropolis because of prevailing 'civilized ethics'. Hence in 1907 Carl Siger said:

> The new countries offer a vast field for individual violent activities which, in the metropolitan countries, would run up against sober and

orderly conceptions of life, and which in the colonies have a greater freedom to develop, and consequently, to affirm their worth. Thus to a certain extent the colonies can serve as a safety valve for modern society.[85]

Some settlements were actually founded as penal colonies. But colonial atrocities were not restricted to the initial stages of the establishment of European overseas empires.

In South West Africa, the Herero as well as their cattle were exterminated. 'In the Belgian Congo', Ho Chi Minh observed, the 'population fell from 25 million in 1891 to 8.5 million in 1911'. The survivors, many of whom were disabled, were even then not left in peace. 'Their land was robbed, while traditional industries were destroyed.'[86] Where the 'natives' were apparently left in peace, 'villain complicity' was woven between 'local tyrants' and colonial despots to create colonial despotism. 'They talk to me,' Cesaire remonstrates, 'about local tyrants brought to reason; but I note that in general the old tyrants get on very well with the new ones, and that there has been established between them, to the detriment of the people, a circuit of mutual services and complicity.' Colonialism 'grafted modern abuse onto ancient injustice, hateful racism onto old inequality'. As children of two worlds, the 'natives' got the worst of both.[87]

It may well be, as has been suggested with regard to some postcolonial regimes, that since the colonial state was an imposition from without, and since, like an army of occupation it lived on the local population without developing organic links with it, the security of the colonial administration was tenuous. To break down the potential of the people to unite against the alleged universality of colonial rule, therefore, the colonial state had to rely more on its repressive than ideological apparatus. But it should not be forgotten that the establishment as well as the reproduction of such politics of alienation was in the last analysis intended to clear the way for creating the conditions necessary for extracting surplus labour subject to the dominance of capital. To make unnecessary mystique out of violence without relating it to the content of colonial rule may blur the issue of exploitation in colonial societies.[88] The rest of the discussion here is intended to tackle this issue in relation to the debate on African resistance to colonial rule.

Capitalist Penetration and the Colonial State

The middle of the nineteenth century witnessed an unprecedented construction of railways in colonial societies like India, the development of telegraphic communications, the opening of the Suez Canal, and similar events. This improved communication on a global scale sounded the knell of *laissez-faire* capitalism. It also ushered in the dominance of monopoly capitalism.[89] The accumulation of capital could no longer be based largely on mechanisms of the economic instance of the capitalist mode of production. The political instance gained the upper hand in breaking into new areas intended for capitalist exploitation, as well as ensuring their monopoly by particular imperialist countries. So emerged the interventionist state. It has, therefore, been said that the purpose of establishing colonial rule was 'to reap advantages from the colony over and above what could have been gained within the framework of market relationships'.[90]

The demand for cheap raw materials through the process of exploiting cheap labour power has been regarded as the spring behind the imperialist move to carve out Africa and Oceania into colonies. The process which followed the imposition of colonial rule has variously been called plunder, super-exploitation, and so on: terms which imply the extraction of absolute surplus value. However, what is clear about the establishment of colonial social formations is that the wages paid to migrant labourers were only sufficient for their maintenance. Their reconstitution and reproduction were not taken into account. The exploitation of peasants was conducted on similar lines. This has been termed 'systematic exchange below value', because in addition to the 'appropriation of surplus value there is also value-transfer derived from that part of the production of use-value by the domestic community that is consumed in the maintenance and replacement of labour-power.' Besides the unpaid labour time of those actually involved in production in capitalist enterprises or for the capitalist market, there is the unpaid labour of the community which goes into the maintenance of the former as well as the reproduction of labour.[91]

Two things are required of the colonial state in the endeavour to reproduce cheap labour power: the destruction of the simple reproduction cycle of precapitalist social formations under its control, and the reproduction of truncated and transformed precapitalist social relations of production under capitalist hegemony. The colonial state, therefore, has to perform the function of capital. It has also to carry out the equivalent of the liberal democratic state's 'welfare statism' by maintaining what is normally called the traditional sector of the colonial social formation. What are in appearance two sectors of the colonial social formation, however, are on closer examination found to be an articulated combination, subject to the domination of capital.[92] Thus the two are not 'given essences which enter into external relations with each other, but constitute an articulated combination in which each presupposes the other.'[93]

The role of the colonial state in reproducing precapitalist social relations comprises its paternalist claims which have been confused with benevolence. As we shall see, the ruthlessness with which people were driven out of their houses and made to work in plantations and public works, and subsequently the violence which was used to drive the labour reserve out of towns so as to locate it in rural areas where it apparently 'belongs', hardly justify the use of the term *benevolence*. On closer examination, however, paternalism and violence are in practice not mutually exclusive notions, despite claims by liberals, missionaries, and colonial officials. Paternalism was used to justify the use of violence in the endeavour to extract surplus labour from the 'natives'. *Prima facie*, there is harmony in capitalist social formations. In reality, there are all sorts of conflicts caused by the coercive power of capital.

The colonial state was intended to reproduce cheap labour power. This state, moreover, had to be run cheaply through the mediation of precapitalist superstructures articulated to it. The situation was not that of independent entities allied to each other, or that of superimposition and subordination. In a colonial situation, imperial authority and local power were mutually implicit, from whatever angle they were perceived. This was clear during periods of rebellion when the oppressed treated both as enemies to be eliminated.

But the very processes of articulating precapitalist social formations under imperialist hegemony and reproducing them under conditions determined by the capitalist mode of production constitute 'a contradictory movement which brings conflict between different classes and factions within classes'. There was a conflict between the metropolitan bourgeoisie and white settlers over the control of the colonial state; in its fetishized form this was posed as a dilemma of peasantisation versus proletarianization. There was conflict between the covenanted and subordinate staff of the colonial administration over the restructuring of the relations of exploitation, which is normally known as primary resistance. There was also the fundamental conflict between the forces of exploitation and the oppressed classes. The path taken by such conflicts determined the contours of a given colonial social formation together with the relative positions of the economic, political and ideological instances within it.

To dampen colonial conflicts, especially the fundamental ones, the colonial state sought to divide the mass of the people, and place them against one another through the reproduction of precapitalist ideological and political divisions. Economic policies of the colonial state which resulted in the creation of new classes or the polarization of old ones were also intended to divide the mass of the people against one another. The colonial state wielded tremendous economic power; this was shown by the fact that even the allocation of land which supposedly belonged to the 'natives' was controlled by its paid functionaries. Armed with this enormous power, the colonial state was able to interfere with all spheres of the life of the colonial population in the interest of capitalist accumulation.

As we have already said, the initial stage, laying the foundations for the exploitation of the precapitalist social formations, was accomplished by destroying the simple reproduction of peasant societies. These societies were in the main self-sufficient. They therefore had to be disarticulated by separating their agricultural functions from manufacture. Subsequently, the former were commoditized and the latter destroyed so as to facilitate the extraction of surplus labour. Excessive violence was employed in the initial stages of the process of articulation, for in most cases taxes did not constitute a weapon powerful enough to force peasant households to part with their surplus labour.[94] When settler plantation agriculture was established in Kenya, for example, the Kamba, among other ethnic communities, were required to go to work on settler farms. Taxes were imposed to ensure that the Kamba did what was required of them. The Kamba, however, were prepared to sell their goats and cattle so as to pay the colonial taxes required rather than leave their reserves and go to work on the settler farms. Subsequently, more pressure was brought to bear on them, in the belief that it was out of sheer laziness that they refused to comply with colonial labour ordinances. Most colonial officials considered the Kamba a drunken and lazy lot who needed to be shaken out of their drunken stupor by *'kiboko, kiboko* and more *kiboko'*. The Kamba reacted to these oppressive measures by staging all sorts of resistance like the Ndonye-wa Kauti movement.[95]

The Kikuyu aside,[96] the Giriama were also not left in peace following the establishment of colonial rule in Kenya. Even so, turning the Giriama country into a labour reserve was not easy. In 1912 A.M. Champion was appointed Assistant District Commissioner of Giriama Station to take charge of destroying the Giriama's natural economy in accordance with the labour demands of the sisal and coconut plantations on the coast of Kenya. Champion's task, as shown by one of his letters to the Provincial Commissioner of Mombasa, was not enviable:

> In reply to your Circular No. 38/126/14 . . . I have been trying every expedient in order to advise the elders to send out the young men to work.
> It is no exaggeration to say that I have held the elders for hours arguing with them and advising them for the good of the tribe to fall in with Government wishes. At distant places which are seldom visited, they adopt the usual custom of agreeing, knowing well that I would be leaving on the following day and that the Government Station is far off – whilst nearer home they have given me a flat refusal and any attempts to get hold of the young men have been frustrated by their disappearance. I do not consider myself justified in resorting to more active measures to obtain labour.
> On several occasions attempts to obtain porters have been opposed by violence and bows and arrows have been produced. Quite recently, a headman was sent round to get some men to carry flour to the station when a father and son in one village threatened to kill the messenger – supporting their threats, the one by drawing a knife the other by notching an arrow. Under these circumstances I cannot see my way to taking any active steps to obtain labour nor can I hold out the slightest prospect of obtaining one man for work in Mombassa and I think it is in the best interest to say so at once.[97]

Champion was surprised by the refusal of the Giriama to go to work on the settler plantations. However, one wonders how such a crude alienation of their labour could have been liked by the Giriama.

In 1912 famine occurred in the Giriama country. But it was observed that, although the Giriama were obliged to seek work outside their reserve, they would not go to work on the plantations. They would rather work for other ethnic communities, usually for short periods, than submit to the routine of plantation labour, which they found too exacting. The colonial government of Kenya exploited the desperate situation engendered by famine in the Giriama country by increasing poll tax. The Giriama responded by selling the few domestic animals which had survived the drought to pay their taxes rather than work on the settler plantations as migrant labourers.[98] Further coercion forced the Giriama to rebel, and so began the Giriama War in 1914. The rebellion was put down ruthlessly the following year.[99] Two hundred and fifty Giriama were murdered; '70 per cent of their huts were set on fire, 600 goats were captured, a collective fine of Rs 100,000 was imposed out of which compensation for damage done in burning private and Mission buildings, huts of friendlies' and so on was to be paid. On the official side, colonial administrators hastened to show that 'casualties were small; one Sudanese private in the K.A.R. was killed and three others were wounded.'[100] It would be proper to add that the Giriama War was not caused by maladministration alone, nor was maladministration the ultimate cause. The new demands imposed on African societies by the penetration of capital seem to provide a more plausible explanation.

According to the British liberals, Edmund Morel and Roger Casement, colonial demands were at their worst in King Leopold's Congo Free State. For quite some time the Congo seems to have been a travesty even of European imperialism. The capitalist Centaur failed to balance its viciousness with any humanitarianism. Here, the system worked as follows. An agent of King Leopold would arrive in an area and establish an 'out-station' to act as the centre from which to raid the surrounding villages. Women, children and domestic animals would then be seized as hostages until their men delivered enough rubber to Leopold's agent to secure their dependents' release. The wild rubber was collected in the forest, which was exacting and time-consuming. Failure to deliver the required quantity and quality of rubber was viciously punished, normally by mutilation. 'Villages were burnt to the ground and there were skeletons everywhere.' Colonial enlightenment became an embarrassment in the Congo, and in 1908 Leopold was forced to give up the colony to the Belgian Government.[101]

Elsewhere in Africa colonial exploitation seems to have been less vicious. Even so, it placed an extra burden on African precolonial superstructures articulated with colonial administration. The articulation of the precolonial superstructures under colonial hegemony necessitated their transformation. This entailed interference with the previous methods of appropriating surplus labour, which were now centralized under the colonial administration to the detriment of the erstwhile political segmentation.[102] Transformation of the precolonial authorities into functionaries paid by the colonial state alienated some factions of the old ruling classes who, faced with impoverishment, rose against colonial rule. It may be, as has been maintained by many postcolonial Africanist historians, that this was a matter of choice. But people faced with the possibility of ruin have a very narrow 'political market' on which to base their choice. It has been argued by others that these rebels were committed to principles. But given the social hierarchy they wanted to perpetuate, their commitment was not a mystery. It has been asserted by yet another group of professional historians that the difference between local colonial functionaries and rebels was not very marked, since today's colonial friendlies could become tomorrow's enemies. This was so, for example, with Kabaka Mwanga of Buganda.[103] But if colonial officials behaved as crudely as Lugard did in Kampala when breaking down local solidarities by exploiting secondary contradictions within the Buganda social formation, those who were alienated in the course of such penetration, however eccentric, could certainly not have remained friendly to the British.[104]

Initial response to colonial rule has been called primary resistance because it only employed the coercive apparatus of the precapitalist superstructures. There were many examples of primary resistance in Tanzania. As well as Abushiri's resistance, Lubetsky writes that:

> From 1890 to 1907 the Germans confonted a series of rebellions covering almost the entire area of Tanganyika. Between 1889 and 1894 Siki, Chief of the Wanyamwezi, tried to drive the Germans out of Tabora District. Siki was defeated when Tabora was occupied by the German forces in 1890. In 1890 Wagogo raided the Tabora area, and a German expedition had to be sent out to subdue the Wagogo. Kalmera, Chief of the Usarimbo, fought against the Germans in 1890, while between 1890 and 1898 Sinna of the Kibosho conducted a campaign to rid his area of the Germans. In 1894 Kilwa erupted under the leadership of Hassan bin Omari, who was defeated the following year. Between 1891 and 1898 Mkwawa fought against the Germans until he was finally defeated and committed suicide in 1898. Between 1892 and 1893 Meli, Chief of Chagga, fought the Germans when they tried to establish hegemony in the Kilimanjaro region. In 1894 Machembo, the Yao chief southwest of Lindi, led an unsuccessful tax protest which was ended in 1899 when he fled to the Portuguese territory of Mozambique and his followers were imprisoned. During the 1890s the Germans also clashed with the Masai, the Hehe, and the Ngoni. In 1902 Mkoto Mkulungwa, from Kitangari, led a tax protest which was quickly ended when he was hanged, while from 1902 to 1904 a rebellion occurred in the Matengo area of Tanganyika.[105]

There were many more resistances of this kind, which have been recovered, through the tireless efforts of postcolonial Africanist historians, from the oblivion to which imperial historians had relegated them.

From the Age of Resistance to the Age of Improvement?

After primary resistance, as has already been observed, followed the age of rebellions. It has been asserted that rebellions involved greater commitment by larger sections of the population. Such a clear distinction, however, is hard to locate in practice since ordinary people have always been involved in various kinds of struggles, whether between the oppressed and the dominant classes, or among the latter themselves. The degree of social stratification which determined the nature of control by the dominant classes, however, seems to have been more influential in shaping the form of participation adopted by the classes involved in the struggle. Nevertheless, involvement by the oppressed on their own terms was caused by the imposition of new methods of exploitation or the radical transformation of the old. Colonial rebellions like the Maji Maji were opposed not only to colonial rule, but also to the new kind of exploitation being imposed under the whip of capital. The preceding movements, the so-called resistance movements, aimed to secure a different distribution of surplus labour rather than to wipe out exploitation itself. There was a sharp difference between the two types of opposition. This needs to be reiterated. The difference between the two types was not merely one of ideology or intensity of participation. Rather, while the primary resistance movements struggled to enable traditional rulers to continue to control the conduits for the extraction of surplus labour, which were being brought under stricter and closer control by the colonial state, the secondary resistance movements were intended to abolish all kinds of exploitation. Where the oppressed intervened in the political arena on their own terms, the latter point seems to have been more at stake than the former.

Protests mounted by local dominant classes, old and new, were intended only to reform the colonial structure. Rebellions by the exploited classes had the aim of overthrowing the colonial system together with all it stood for: the capitalist exploitation of labour. Their stance *vis-a-vis* the colonial administrative structure, from the village level upwards, as well as their wrath against its ideological paraphernalia, was symbolic of the aims of the rebels. For them, and as far as the Maji Maji was concerned, the covenanted and subordinate colonial staff, together with missionaries and white settlers, were all 'friends of cotton' who deserved to be eliminated.[106] The aims of the rebels were not articulated in what would be considered a modern political language, but this is immaterial. The actions adopted were more significant than the subsequent political language of nationalist reformism. The medicine of the Maji Maji rebels – the *maji*, as they called it – should be comprehended within this context. The fetishizing of its form common among African postcolonial Africanist historians must be avoided.[107]

It has been normal to see colonial rebellions as a puzzle because of their religious overtones. In some cases the rebellions have been dubbed aberrant. As we have also already seen, and within the prism of dichotomies, myth is considered to be as different from reality as night from day. Whether the consciousness of God or a survival from the past, it above all constitutes the obverse of reality. Yet myth is not a given in which people must participate in one form or another. Myth, together with its millenarian tinge, comprises the very act of creating. Those who create it want to transcend the given order of things. In social matters, they want to undertake the Promethean task of storming the heavens. Such radicals want to return to the fundamentals of society and so explain it from a new perspective. Kinjitikile, a radical at the forefront of the Maji Maji, compared the Germans to red clay. He called them ugly fish of the sea and assured his supporters that they were not invincible.[108] The white man's bullet could break the black man's head into pieces, but not when the latter was fortified with the conviction that he could overcome his oppressive conditions. Kinjikitile encouraged the oppressed people of Southern Tanzania to seize the time; to transcend the prevailing oppressive conditions. Such is the creative potential of the oppressed classes in the course of making their own history.[109] The very act of severance from the given arrangement of reality constitutes the importance of the Maji Maji. The given situation, in this context, was imperialism and all it stood for. This, however, is what postcolonial Africanist historians have glossed over, in various ways, in the interest of past and present dominant classes. The ideology which these historians share with the ruling classes prevents them from seeing reality from the perspective of the oppressed. The constraints placed on them by the ruling classes reinforces this tendency to distort reality. More of this will be shown in Chapter 4.[110]

That said, any connections drawn between the activities of the rebels and 'modern mass nationalism', as the latter has been called by postcolonial Africanist historians, are artificial. The few 'learned' Tanzanians at the time of the Maji Maji Rebellion refused to join the rebels, apparently on the pretext that the ideology of the latter was too primitive.[111] This was not to be the last time that the petty bourgeois were to commit their dastardly deeds against the oppressed, whom they also regard as their 'kith and kin'. Kinjikitile's aims, however, have yet to be vindicated. The concept of exploitation continues to be distorted in the interest of the dominant classes in postcolonial societies. Like Paul Bogle in Jamaican history, however, Kinjikitile can no longer be ignored. Thus the metropolitan bourgeoisies, in conjunction with the petty bourgeoisies of postcolonial societies have decided to honour him in their speeches and writings. But they also insist that what he did 'he had to do, but what he did no longer must be done because everything he fought for has already been won.'[112] The artificiality of such a statement is clear. Kayamba, a leading spokesman of the Tanzanian petty bourgeoisie in the 1920s and 1930s, and Kinjitikile, the radical, were not committed to the same principles. Kayamba was a reformer interested in Africanizing the colonial state.[113] Kinjitikile was a revolutionary committed to discovering the fundamentals of the Tanzanian social formation. To draw parallels between the two is to indulge in a distortion of history with a view to hiding the objective reality of postcolonial societies.[114]

This distortion and reductionism becomes even clearer if we take cognizance of the kind of periodization which has been recommended for the transition from the age of resistance to that of 'mass nationalism'. A leading Africanist and specialist on the modern history of Tanganyika, John Iliffe, has, for example, observed that in the aftermath of the age of colonial rebellions followed a period of improvement and differentiation, when colonial societies laid down their spears in preference for the hoe, the plough and the bible. There has been a tendency to view African history as a succession of local assertions against colonial rule which increased in sophistication from rejection to acceptance, and subsequently to the endeavour to control modernization. It has been said that this periodization was similar to that the proletariat went through in Europe. The age of improvement falls within this process of increasingly sophisticated responses, and appears to be similar to Asa Briggs' 'age of improvement' among the English working class which followed in the aftermath of the period of Chartism.[115]

To discuss concepts like improvement and development is to enter on to extremely slippery ground. Both terms are ideological;[116] and, as has been said, 'Ideologies are world-views which, despite their partial and possibly critical insights, prevent us from understanding the society in which we live and the possibility of changing it. They are world-views which correspond to the standpoints of classes and social groups whose interests in the existing social system and incapacity to change it makes it impossible for them to see it as a whole.'[117] However, it may well be that conditions for some of the local African population did 'improve' in the so-called age of colonial improvement. It may also be that such people wanted to improve their lives and believed very strongly that they were doing so.[118] But beliefs on their own are not sufficient as an explanation of an historical process. For example, one would like to know at whose expense the improvement occurred. In this manner it becomes possible to situate the conflicts prevalent in a given social formation. Moreover, if there was an age of improvement in Tanganyikan history, as has been claimed by some distinguished postcolonial Africanist professional historians, there was not much of it for migrant labourers, the *manamba* or 'numbers' (as they were normally called), who laboured on the plantations,[119] nor for the middle and poor peasants who were constantly subjected to the coercion of capital. For the *manamba* and poor peasants, in particular, this was an age of *impoverishment*, as was shown by the many protests which they staged. The protests of the *manamba* were mirrored in the series of complaints of laziness and theft made by their exploiters, the European settlers. Protests by the peasantry were expressed in their so-called negative reactions to 'agricultural improvement'.[120]

The 'laziness of the natives' as depicted in colonial literature is proverbial. It appears strange, however, that these very 'natives' should have contributed to the coinage of the phrase 'to work like a nigger'. Nevertheless, a 'Machakos settler' in colonial Kenya wrote about the Kamba thus: 'Either through possessing wealth in the shape of cattle or through laziness acquired by their womenfolk doing all the manual work required throughout the past centuries, these Akamba men are at the present time indolent, useless members of the community and the only course open to us settlers to train them the way to go, and to teach civilization and advancement, is to take them from their reserve, cattle and children and teach them to understand and to trust the white man.'[121] Africans, according to Wrigley, were 'economically illiterate'. In his opinion, 'Pastoral people whose sole thought was the increase of the herds, cultivating people who left most of the labour of cultivation to their womenfolk and were unfamiliar even with the iron hoe – these were not likely to respond quickly or effectively to the kind of economic opportunity ... theoretically open to them' by the imposition of colonial rule.[122]

Even when dragged out of their homesteads, and forced to work on plantations, it has been said, Africans remained lazy. They did not know the value of money so the argument ran, and so remained reluctant to sell their labour. And when they did agree to sell their labour, they did not uphold contractual agreements for long. Colonial officials and settlers explained African laziness variously: that it was due to tribal instincts, that it was a psychological problem, and so forth. Either way, *Africans* were posed as the problem: they did not understand the dignity of labour.

The laziness of the *manamba* has of late been considered to be mythical by leading historians such as Alatas.[123] Africans worked hard in their own gardens. And they knew how to work hard long before the imposition of colonial rule. Even those exported to the New World as slaves worked hard on their kitchen gardens, and on Sundays when they were paid.[124] What was written about the laziness of African slaves, however, is not untrue in one sense; for it has been argued that it was in fact a form of resistance against oppression under the slave regime.[125] But it has also been argued that not all acts of defiance constitute resistance. This is so because, while resistance movements are political, acts of sheer defiance are not necessarily so.[126] Even so, the precise meaning of both acts of defiance and of resistance continues to be difficult to pin down.

Laziness and the Work Ethic
For many medical scientists in nineteenth-century America the laziness of black slaves constituted a disease peculiar to people of African origin. This disease was called by the Louisiana doctor, Samuel W. Cartwright, *Dysaethesia Ethiopica*.[127] Du Bois, however, argued that the disease should be explained in terms of African cultural values, which were different from those of Europeans. Blacks, he said, were communalistic while Europeans were individualistic. In America, therefore, black slaves remained 'tropical animals'. Europeans, on the other hand, maintained the Protestant Ethic.[128] But, to cite a case from the initial stages of English overseas migration, 'Mr. Peel ... took with him from England to Swan River, West Australia, means of subsistence and production to the amount of £50,000. Mr. Peel had the foresight to bring with him, besides, 3,000 persons of the working class, men, women and children. Once arrived at his destination, Mr. Peel was left without a servant to make his bed or fetch him water from the river. . . . Unhappy Mr. Peel, who provided for everything except the export of English modes of production to Swan River.'[129] If the Protestant Ethic for the labouring classes meant the ability to part with their surplus labour cheerfully, then (to use Du Bois's phrase) Europeans were also 'tropical animals'. Not many Europeans involved in the colonization of America possessed the Protestant Ethic. Moreover, as has been demonstrated so admirably with regard to English

history during the Industrial Revolution,[130] 'the English working class itself had arisen from the countryside amidst the bitter contention of rival value systems in general and work ethics in particular.'[131] It should not be forgotten either, that many of the early white settlers in America and other colonies were forcibly transported there for alleged laziness, criminal instincts, begging, and so on.[132]

The American philosopher, Santayana, has written that 'certain moralists, without meaning to be satirical, often say that the sovereign cure for unhappiness is work.' Work, above all, should be done for its own sake. One should love it. 'Unhappily, the work they recommend is better fitted to dull pain than to remove its cause. It occupies the faculties without rationalizing life.'[133] More people continue to hate work than to love it. In the colonies it has been observed that the capitalist regime 'everywhere comes into collision with the resistance of the producer who, as owner of his own conditions of labour, employs that labour to enrich himself, instead of the capitalist.' For the sake of ostensible civilization, modernization or improvement, therefore, the capitalist establishes artificial means 'to ensure the poverty of the people'. Here the paternalist armour 'crumbles off, bit by bit, like rotten rouchwood'.[134] Benevolence gives way to violence, and the *manamba* are hauled like stones on to the plantations, there to work and create wealth for the capitalist. Small wonder then that migrant labourers are called *manamba*, nameless people referred to only in terms of numbers – 1, 2, 3, and so forth. More euphemistically they are called 'natives', a term whose meaning in practice has been defined most vividly by Toynbee thus:

> When we Westerners call people 'natives', we implicitly take the cultural colour out of our perception of them. We see them as wild animals infesting the country in which we happen to come across them, as part of a local flora and fauna and not as men with passions like ourselves. So long as we think of them as 'natives' we may exterminate them or, as is more likely today, domesticate them and honestly (perhaps not altogether mistakenly) believe that we are improving the breed, but we do not begin to understand them.[135]

This, in a nutshell, is what constitutes the 'cultural encounter' in which, it is said, the 'natives' are gripped by 'cultural shock' and so behave in ways unintelligible to the civilized races. In this encounter the 'natives' are treated as mere tribes, never as individuals or classes.[136]

Whether as *manamba* or 'natives', it was their surplus labour which mattered. The *manamba* had to be fitted into plantation work rather than the other way round. Men can be distinguished from animals by their consciousness, religion, ideas and so on, but they themselves make the distinction when they begin to produce their means of subsistence. In the course of production men make not only material products, but their own selves. It is in the course of production that people develop their own consciousness. Work is, therefore, central in the development of men. Depending on the work they do, men derive satisfaction from it and also develop their creativity. However, work becomes painful when its end is to ensure the extraction of surplus labour. Here it is no longer the worker who matters but surplus labour. All sorts of methods and ideas will be used to extract the worker's surplus labour. Alienation of surplus labour from the worker makes labour external to him. Labour becomes something which merely happens to the workers, like changes in the weather, to be shunned like the plague. In this case labour is no longer integrated but alienated. The labour process becomes a battlefield, a protracted struggle between those who labour and those who exploit. Thus while workers want to do as little work as possible, their expropriators force them to do as much work as they can extract. The former destroy the means of production (for if work stops, so much the better for them), 'steal' the products of their labour, assault overseers and so on. The latter adopt more stringent measures intended to pin down the worker and sit on his neck.[137] In such a situation, the idea of loving work for its own sake is intended to camouflage the social relations of exploitation.

Relations between the *manamba* and *wanyapara* (overseers) were so bitter and the behaviour of the latter so arrogant and ruthless that they have carved an indelible niche in the hoard of Tanzanian legends. The whip (*kiboko* or *sjambok*) was used wantonly against the *manamba*. It found its way into all walks of life in colonial social formations, especially in the schools. To be sure, colonies were not the only places where authoritarian relationships in their fetishized form were reproduced in everyday life.[138] Nevertheless, in colonial social formations, this relationship penetrated even into the peasant household, where like a *mnyapara* or he-goat, the head bossed his family around. In many cases the head of the household even wore a moustache or goatee to put up an appearance proper to this role. In India members of the lower classes were refused this privilege and forced to remain contented with their position of super-exploitation like 'women'.[139] Even biological differences were to be exploited in the process of fleecing the oppressed. This chauvinism *par excellence* was also extended to men of the lower classes.

The Colonial Reign of Terror

Terror was rampant in the colonial era. This was particularly true when agents of labour recruitment paid a visit to the countryside. The amount of force they used was incredible. When these caricatures of human beings were seen moving in the villages like demons with the intent to kidnap workers for the plantation system, people fled into the bush. These caricatures were taken for ghosts who sucked human blood, *mumiani*.[140] Indeed they were bloodsuckers, or agents of such creatures. Among the Iraqw of Northern Tanzania, the labour recruiters were called *boi lik lik* – people always on the move while molesting others. Even after kidnapping the required number of people, these caricatures would return to the villages to molest unarmed children, women, and the aged. Such was the 'mission to civilize'.

In the colonial situation, therefore, there was neither benevolence nor choice. Paternalism amounted to colonial despotism. It existed only at the level of appearance, and quickly receded into the background whenever labour became the central issue. Indeed, it is not labour which was pampered; rather it was capital. If we (wrongly) view the relationship between capital and labour in the colonial social formation as an exchange of equivalents, with the colonial state as the referee empowered to help labour *vis-a-vis* capital (since 'natives' were still regarded as backward and thus on the weaker side), colonial violence becomes hard indeed to explain.[141] But a lot becomes clearer when the issue of capital is brought in. It is therefore proper to note that, in the field of production, coercion was used wantonly. From the point of labour recruitment to the plantation, the *manamba* were coerced. The agents responsible for recruiting the *manamba* were no different from the slave kidnappers of the nineteenth century. One of the early colonial officials in Tanzania found the method of labour recruitment terrifying:

> In Tabora we found that . . . recruitment officials had burned down entire villages and had taken men to the Coast in chains in order to supply labour for the Usambara plantations and collect their commission from the same. These agents often described themselves as colonial officers. Sometimes, however, recruitment was done through a local ruler who was normally induced, through sham presents of trinkets and other commodities, into alliance with recruitment agents.[142]

So violent was the recruitment that, rather than continue to live under the Pax Colonia, the Luguru of Morogoro withdrew to the mountains.[143] Evidence of forced labour survived in Morogoro to the 1920s when it was still 'virtually impossible to engage any labourer for wages, unless he was ordered to go to work by his headman; men so obtained were most unsatisfactory workers, and required perpetual supervision'.[144]

Perpetual supervision, in turn, necessitated deployment of the *kiboko*. Settlers of all kinds for ever insisted on 'the advisability of recourse to the *kiboko*'.[145] This was not restricted to Africa, for as a colonial official in Malaya, Clifford, wrote towards the end of the nineteenth century:

> He [the Malay] never works if he can help it, and often will never suffer himself to be induced or tempted into doing so by offers of the most extravagant wages. If, when promises and persuasion have failed, however, the magic word *Krah* is whispered in his ears, he will come without a murmur, and work really hard for no pay, bringing with him his own supply of food. *Krah*, as everybody knows, is the system of forced labour which is a state prerequisite in unprotected Malay countries, and an ancestral instinct, inherited from his fathers, seems to prompt him to comply cheerfully with the custom, when on no other terms whatsoever would he permit himself to do a stroke of work. When so engaged, he will labour as no other man will do. I have had Pahang Malays working continuously for sixty hours at a stretch, and all on a handful of boiled rice; but they will only do this for one they

know, whom they regard as their Chief, and in whose sight they would be ashamed to murmur as to the severity of the work, or to give in when all are sharing the strain in equal measure.[146]

Thus it was rationalized that the use of forced labour was natural to the Malay, and that, if relieved of terror, he would not work.

The belief that the use of violence in colonial societies was natural was not restricted to the recruitment and exploitation of labour. It was also felt to be efficacious in the political sphere, where it was used extensively.[147] When the German Secretary of State for Colonies, Dernburg, visited Tanganyika in 1907 he found that almost every European was armed with a whip, and that all officers, from the highest to the lowest, were well stocked with them. 'In Dar es Salaam', he wrote, 'every white man walks around with a whip; I saw one on the table of the main revenue office; in the station office of the Usambara railway there was one right next to the inkpot - and thus almost every white indulges in thrashing any black man he wants.'[148] Such violence was employed to ensure tight control of the colonial labour force. Since it was subjected to super-exploitation, and to prevent it from uniting against its exploiters, it was kept migrant (to limit the possibility of any labour reserve congregating in urban areas). Ethnic divisions within the migrant labour force were also amplified to forestall possibilities of unity on a broader social base. Measures of this kind constituted the policy of divide and rule which, although an integral part of colonial rule, has been neither demonstrated nor elaborated adequately. When this policy subsequently proved inadequate to contain the colonial labour force, trade unions were imposed from above as a joint venture between the nascent petty bourgeoisies and the colonial state.[149]

It has been said that the colonial state was faced with the dilemma of proletarianization versus peasantization - indicative of the fact that colonial idealists did not all think alike.[150] As well as the usual demands placed on peasant commodity production, it would perhaps be proper to note that peasantization was insisted upon to check the process of proletarianization, a process which would have proved dangerous in colonial social formations based on the production of cheap labour power under precapitalist social relations articulated with the capitalist mode of production. If there was a dilemma here, it was symptomatic of the contradictions prevalent in the colonial social formation.[151] As migrant labourers resorted to striking more frequently, and as the conventional methods of controlling this labour force became less effective, besides introducing trade unionism, the ideology of paternalism was put aside so as to allow the idea of nationalism to loom large as a new strategy for controlling the oppressed.[152]

The dilemma of migrant labourers has been discussed at length. David Livingstone, the nineteenth-century missionary explorer, urged European nations to colonize Africa with a view to replacing the slave trade with 'legitimate trade'. If the introduction of legitimate trade was intended to increase the choice of opportunities open to Africans as individuals and as social groups, these hopes were never realized. True, with colonialism the era of plunder came to an end; but it was superseded by the period of super-exploitation. Moreover, even in the sphere of selling and buying, where choice is supposed to prevail, violence was very much in evidence; the more so if labour happened to be the commodity in question. Even by liberal standards, exploitation persisted.[153] The kidnapping of blacks from their homesteads did not end with the rise of colonialism as the successor to the slave trade — not even when the market forces became pronounced in the 1920s.[154] This phenomenon seems to have arrived in Africa too late; for the state was already interventionist and potentially totalitarian by the last quarter of the nineteenth century.

The harassment to which the *manamba* were subjected is beyond imagination. Relatives left behind in the reserves by the *manamba* were not left in peace either. They were pestered in all sorts of ways — now to grow more food crops, now to participate in building public works. Where they were allowed to produce commodities, peasants were also pushed around a great deal by functionaries of the colonial state, admittedly not to the same degree as the *manamba* who worked in the plantation system. We have already alluded to the initial stages of articulation of the African natural economies under imperialist hegemony in relation to the resistance movements of the colonial era.[155] In the second quarter of this century imperial governments appealed to their colonies to produce more in order to rescue the metropolitan economy from the economic doldrums into which it was thrust. This period falls into what has been called the era of 'colonial development', when economic planning was adopted by the colonial state.[156] It is the period which has also been called the 'age of improvement' by postcolonial professional historians of Africa.

Various colonial development schemes were started during this period by the colonial state, and imperial governments did give loans to colonial administrations to stimulate colonial development in sectors considered of importance for the recovery of the *metropolitan* societies. Even in this endeavour the coercive apparatus of the colonial state was invoked in order to fulfil its newly appointed tasks. In this effort overcropping, hasty cultivation and the like caused an ecological crisis which forced the colonial state to adopt measures to curb it. There followed 'the reaction to agricultural improvement . . . during the enforced colonial period'.[157] These reactions have been perceived variously. Colonial functionaries dubbed them irrational, thinking rationality to be their own preserve. Resorting to administrative measures in an attempt to contain the 'reactions', colonial functionaries claimed to be representatives of the 'rational choice'. Development in the form of the so-called agricultural improvement was considered neutral and beneficial to all who participated in it.

With the rise of nationalism and the search for its roots in the countryside, however, it has been considered proper to idealize the mass of the peasantry. The new view was to consider their reactions rational, and to declare colonial agricultural policies, accordingly, irrational. It has been alleged that many of the colonial policies were meaningless if considered from the perspective of the local situation. Local experience was neglected for the sake of agricultural improvements, planned in most cases by metropolitan specialists.[158] Problems, therefore, were bound to occur when the policies were exposed to local realities. Colonial authorities in turn resorted to highhanded methods to implement these unrealistic policies.[159] Mistrust followed and the 'peasant problem' was reduced to a competition between two traditions, each of which could be considered rational depending upon the perspective 'chosen' when perceiving the problem.[160]

Yet to view as the legitimate subject of history either the accumulation of capital, which in this context was manifested in the agricultural improvements of the colonial state, or the peasantry, obfuscates the relationship between the two sides in which peasant production was a crucial precondition in the process of capitalist exploitation.[161] The administrative innovations in agriculture were intended to facilitate the accumulation of capital. In this process the neutrality of the innovations was purely hypothetical, since they were intended to facilitate the extraction of more surplus labour from the peasantry. This, in any case, was the content of the apparent rationality of colonial agricultural policies. The harshness with which the policies were implemented was also geared towards this end. For the peasantry, the introduction of more agricultural innovations required more labour time, which, it should be noted, was not inexhaustible. Moreover, as well as implementing the colonial agricultural policies, the peasants had to produce their own food, unless the process of commoditization had been completed. It has also to be noted that peasants are not capitalists, but people who produce commodities to be exchanged for other commodities required for their own maintenance. This is the position into which they have been forced by capital. Lastly, for the peasantry to resist exploitation, whatever form this takes, seems irrational only to those who perform the function of capital. However, to explain the reactions of the peasantry in the epoch of imperialism without relating them to the process of the accumulation of capital to which they are tied is to indulge in idealism.[162]

Transcending Africanist Historiography

This chapter has attempted to show some of the salient features of postcolonial Africanist historiography. Implied in this analysis is the assumption that, despite the efforts by a previous generation of black professional historians in America, and African observers in Africa, to assert the historicity of the African past, a new breed of postcolonial professional historians found it worthwhile to go over the already traversed ground once again, admittedly more thoroughly. The manifesto, however, remained the same: to liberate the African race from the stigma imposed on it by the imperialist world. Thus postcolonial Africanist historians locked horns with imperial scholars to put the African record straight.

Professionalization of the study of the African past, it should also be remembered, commenced in the imperialist countries. There also, it was institutionalized before it found its way into Africa under metropolitan tutelage. Africanization of the profession did not begin seriously until the 1960s. In this process West Africa was ahead of East and Central Africa, for reasons which are best explained in terms of the backwardness of the latter's petty bourgeoisie.[163] Metropolitan concern with the development of postcolonial Africanist historiography, in the case of Britain, was shown in a most pronounced form in the 1950s, when the Syndics of Cambridge University Press explored the possibility of canonizing the endeavour to recover the African past with the idea of writing a *Cambridge History of Africa*. The task was found too ambitious at this early stage and so the Syndics were advised to undertake the more modest task of publishing a journal in which the findings of 'original research' could be published. Thus the *Journal of African History* was launched in 1960.[164] This journal served as the combined manifesto, charter, programme and shop-window for the field of professional Africanist history.[165] However, Africanist history was soon inundated with publications which, in the words of Lalage Bown, have changed the discipline 'from a cottage industry to a multinational enterprise'.[166] In 1966 the Syndics of Cambridge University Press returned to their original idea and commissioned the founding editors of the *Journal of African History* to undertake the general editorship of the *Cambridge History of Africa*, a 'multi-volume work ... of history, with chapters written by experts on a particular topic, and unified by the guiding hand of volume editors of senior standing'.[167] Thus professional Africanist history was accorded a place among the Cambridge Histories which have since the beginning of the century been compiled on 'various aspects of respectable history'. The original idea of the Cambridge Histories as planned by Lord Acton was to write ultimate history.[168] Whether this was also the ambition for writing the *Cambridge History of Africa* is not clear. The anticlimax which postcolonial Africanist historiography in the event resulted in will however be discussed in the next chapter.

An important aim of postcolonial Africanist historiography has been to establish the continuity of African history. This aim, which is evident in many resolutions passed in conferences on professional Africanist history, is not antithetical to the quest for recovering the idea of change in the African past. Rather, it is intended to show the originality inherent in that past.[169] Studies of African empire building and the establishment of connections between medieval African culture and ancient Egyptian civilization are two instances which have been used to show the historical continuity of the African past. But as Yusufu Bala Usman has argued in one of his papers, the purpose of history 'is not simply to assemble a lot of data, and thus demonstrate scholarship. We feel the purpose of historical scholarship is to penetrate the data, to transcend it, to surpass it and get to the essence of the historical process in question.' This entails a struggle against the dominant ideas normally taken for granted in history.[170] Some of the dominant ideas which

The African Factor

postcolonial Africanist historians use carelessly – as Lenin says, 'without at all understanding their serious significance, giving no thought whatever to the fact that *words commit one to deeds*'[171] – are in our view those of continuity, modernity, tradition, transition, and revolution.

A closer examination of the notion of tradition, as undertaken by Usman for example, shows that it is in reality 'mythical and imaginary'. Indeed, it is a recent creation – not something that existed in the past. 'It is essentially what has existed in the colonial and neocolonial present, and only elements of it are taken up and used for particular political ends.' This he illustrates with the aid of the history of Katsina in Northern Nigeria. Usman maintains that, if one wants to call Katsina society traditional, one has the option of choosing from the social organizations of five epochs each separated from the other by a fundamental transformation. These are the epoch of the autonomous Garuruwa, the period of the Sarauta system, the times of the Jamals, the years of the Emirate system and, lastly, the period of the Native Authority system. Each of these was overthrown in a drastic manner, contrary to the 'prevalent notion in Nigeria nowadays that the only form of historical change is gradual evolution'. This, too, can be said about the extablishment of the Native Authority system, despite what has been maintained by imperial historians that the colonial encounter was not catastrophic.[172]

What is crucial is not merely to show change or continuity in African history but also the social and historical content of that change. The nature of social change in precapitalist Africa was different from change in the continent under imperialist domination. To talk about continuity of African history during the colonial era seems dangerous if the content of the continuity is not shown. This is also the case with change, for, as has been maintained by some critical historians, there is no neutral or inevitable change. Continuity and change should be studied in their historical as well as their social contexts. In this way it will become clear that history is not the study of 'neutral and inevitable change, but of exploitation and resistance, of values lost and values gained'.[173]

The farrago about the age of improvement under imperialism should be placed in this context. This seems a more fruitful approach than the idea of 'opportunities' open to Africans in the epoch of imperialist exploitation; in this way the meaning of people's resistance to colonial 'improvement schemes' will become clear. It was also pointed out by the initiators of the age of improvement that, from the 1920s, more people in colonial Africa were willing to offer themselves as *manamba* on plantations or to grow crops for sale than was the case formerly. Such a willingness, however, has to be placed within the context of the coercive measures which had been undertaken by the colonial state in laying the foundations for the imperialist super-exploitation of African basic producers. If there was progress, it was achieved at a price.[174] If the African petty bourgeoisie progressed, the African basic producers paid for it. Iliffe, for example, has measured the growth of various African countries' economies in terms of the size of their petty bourgeoisies, and has argued that there could have been more growth had the petty bourgeoisies been bigger.[175] Perhaps the options offered to the petty bourgeoisies were not many; perhaps they did not take serious advantage of those opportunities that were open to them. But the nature of the opportunities themselves needs to be determined within the context of imperialism. The petty bourgeoisies, too, had to be maintained with the help of resources involuntarily extracted from African basic producers. Africans had to be turned into *manamba* and peasants, and kept that way, if a few others were to enjoy their age of improvement. In this, we obviously assume that the source of wealth is labour power, not entrepreneurship or capital (that dead labour which has to be increased constantly at the expense of the living).

It is this fundamental process of accumulating dead labour at the expense of the living that should be the concern of the new 'critical school' of African history. This school should re-examine postcolonial Africanist historiography and question its role in legitimizing the present arrangements of everyday life, which it has done by creating false connections between the history of the oppressed classes and their oppressors. Struggles against imperialism have been confused with struggles against colonialism, and the two have been presented as similar. By the same token the precolonial and colonial histories of Africa have been discussed under the same rubric using the talismanic notions of change and continuity, as if the motor of development in the two periods were the same. Indeed, although it has been claimed that Africanist history is an integrated whole, it lacks an intrinsic quality of its own. It is hard to distinguish Africanist history from bourgeois history as a whole, for example, apart from the claim that Africanist history is concerned with the African past or a part of it. Even in this case, there are still problems. Does the African past consist of everything that happened in the continent, for instance, or only of everything that can be attributed to internal factors, whatever they are?

Africanist history appears confusing, but this confusion is itself historically determined. It concentrates on describing the appearance of the movement of history and so avoids analysing its meaning. Such is the hallmark of bourgeois scholarship, which is given to taking things as they present themselves rather than as they really are, and so helps to oil the machinery of capitalist exploitation. The capitalist system presents itself as a system of market relations in which exchange takes the form of 'equivalent' entities changing hands. This exchange is said to be fair, and the only thing said to distinguish the rich from the poor is that the former work hard and save while the latter do not. In practice, however, it is the poor who work more; this can be seen in any factory or on any farm. And so we are then told that it is because the rich have capital and the poor have not. But from where did the rich get this dead labour? Moreover, labour power rather than capital is the source of wealth. The poor have to be worked hard, paid less, and kept that way if the rich are to get richer. Thus what is on the surface an exchange of equivalents is in reality not so, especially if one of the commodities happens to be labour power itself.

We are told in history books that during the era of merchant capital the kidnapping of slaves from Africa was trade. Later on, however, this transaction became illegitimate, and so 'legitimate trade' was introduced. To start with, and especially in colonial historiography, this took the form of the mission to civilize. Since 1945, however, racism has been removed from the 'objective' history of Africa. The term, modernization, has become fashionable and has been nationalized with the introduction, once again, of the talismanic notions of social change and continuity. Terms like class and exploitation are outlawed from professional African history on the grounds that Africa is communalistic. From here intellectual McCarthyism takes over. We shall have more to say about this, especially in the last chapter. But the ideological content of Africanist historiography, colonial and postcolonial, should be underlined. Colonial historiography was intended to idealize the colonial state and justify its endeavour to 'civilize' the precapitalist African economies with a view to articulating them under imperialist hegemony. Postcolonial historiography has concerned itself with idealizing the realization of the African nation state. In the latter endeavour, 'African origins' of the nation state have been shown. In this way its connections with the colonial state and the reforms hatched in the course of its establishment have been obscured. The imperialist moorings of the African nation state have to be hidden for the sake of maintaining the class alliances forged in the aftermath of the Second World War. Small wonder, then, that side by side with the development of postcolonial Africanist historiography has developed a crescendo of intellectual McCarthyism.

References

1. J.D. Hargreaves, 'Biography and the debate about imperialism', *Journal of Modern African Studies*, 2, 1964.
2. The term was coined by Eric Stokes, S. Marks, 'South African studies since World War Two', in C. Fyfe (ed.), *African Studies Since 1945*, London 1976, p. 187.
3. T. Hodgkin, 'Some African and Third World theories of imperialism', in R. Owen and B. Sutcliffe (eds.), *Studies in the Theories of Imperialism*, London 1972, p. 103.
4. R.E. Robinson and J. Gallagher, *Africa and the Victorians*, New York 1961.
5. T.O. Ranger, Lecture given to African History Teachers' Seminar, Dar es Salaam, 31 December 1965, mimeo.
6. K.O. Dike and J.F.A. Ajayi, 'African historiography', in D.L. Shils (ed.), *International Encyclopedia of the Social Sciences*, New York 1967.
7. L.P. Gann and P. Duignan, *The Burden of Empire*, New York 1967.
8. W. Rodney, *How Europe Underdeveloped Africa*, London 1972.
9. M. Craton, 'Searching for the invisible man: problems of writing on slave society in the British West Indies', *Historical Reflections*, I, 1974.

10. Quoted by R.U. Nwala, 'Anthony William Amoo of Ghana on the mind–body problem', *Présence africaine*, 108, 1978, p. 159.
11. *Ibid.*
12. E.E. Thorpe, *Negro Historians in the United States*, Baton Rouge 1958.
13. Quoted by O. Onoge, 'The counter-revolutionary tradition in African studies: the case of applied anthropology', *The Nigerian Journal of Economic and Social Studies*, 15, 1973, p. 326.
14. L. Kapteijns, *African Historiography written by Africans 1955–1973: The Nigerian Case*, Leiden 1977, pp. 7-10.
15. M. Shaw, *Marxism and Social Science*, London 1977, pp. viii-ix.
16. L. Baxendall (ed.), *Radical Perspectives of the Arts*, Harmondsworth 1973.
17. M. Perham (ed.), *Ten Africans*, London 1934.
18. T.O. Ranger, 'The historiography of Southern Rhodesia', *Transafrican Journal of History*, I, 1971. J.F.A. Ajayi, 'The continuity of African institutions under colonialism', in T.O. Ranger (ed.), *Emerging Themes of African History*, Nairobi 1968.
19. T.O. Ranger, *The Recovery of Local Initiative in Tanzanian History*, Dar es Salaam 1969.
20. J.F.A. Ajayi, 'The place of African history and culture in the process of nation-building in Africa south of the Sahara', in I. Wallerstein (ed.), *Social Change: The Colonial Situation*, New York 1966.
21. T.O. Ranger, 'Towards a usable African past', in Fyfe (ed.), *African Studies Since 1945*.
22. J.F.A. Ajayi, 'West African states at the beginning of the nineteenth century', in J.F.A. Ajayi and I. Espie (eds.), *A Thousand Years of West African History*, Ibadan 1965.
23. J. Depelchin, review I. Wilks, *Asante in the Nineteenth Century: The structure and evolution of a political order* (Cambridge 1975), in *Africa Development*, II, 1977. See also D.A. Low, *Lion Rampant*, London 1974.
24. F.M. Mutibwa, *The Malagasy and the Europeans*, London 1974.
25. *Ibid.*
26. Bonaventure Swai, 'Trade and politics in eighteenth-century Malabar', Dar es Salaam 1979, mimeo.
27. The phrase is adopted from A.L. Basham, *The Wonder that was India*, London 1971.
28. C. Wilson, *Before the White Man in Kenya*, London 1952, p. 18.
29. W. Rodney, *The Groundings with my Brothers*, London 1970, pp. 35-6.
30. W. Rodney, *How Europe Underdeveloped Africa*, p. 42.
31. C.A. Diop, 'The cultural contributions and prospects of Africa', *Présence africaine*, 8-9, 1956, p. 348. Walter Rodney, *How Europe Underdeveloped Africa*, p. 42.
32. R.G. Armstrong, 'The development of kingdoms in Negro Africa', *Journal of the Historical Society of Nigeria*, II, 1960.
33. I.N. Kimambo, *A Political History of the Pare to 1900*, Nairobi 1969.
34. K. Buttner, 'New methods and forms of imperialist ideological diversion against the people of Africa', K. Buttner (ed.), *Theories on Africa and Neo-colonialism*, Leipzig 1971.
35. J.F.A. Ajayi, *Christian Missions in Nigeria 1841–1891*, London 1965.

D.E. Barrett (ed.), *African Initiatives in Religion*, Nairobi 1971. T.O. Ranger, *The African Churches of Tanzania*, Nairobi 1972. A.J. Temu, 'Tanzania societies and colonial invasion 1875-1907', Dar es Salaam 1974, mimeo.
36. J.M. Lonsdale, 'Some origins of nationalism in East Africa', *Journal of African History*, IX, 1968.
37. J. Iliffe, *Tanganyika under German Rule, 1905-1912*, Nairobi 1969. See also his *A Modern History of Tanganyika*, Cambridge 1979.
38. T.O. Ranger, 'African attempts to control education in East and Central Africa 1900-1939', *Past and Present*, 32, 1965.
39. Introduction in J. Iliffe (ed.), *Modern Tanzanians*, Nairobi 1973.
40. J. Iliffe, *Tanganyika Under German Rule 1905-1912*.
41. E. Stokes, 'Traditional resistance movements and Afro-Asian nationalism: the context of the 1857 mutiny rebellion', *Past and Present*, 48, 1970, p. 104.
42. G.C.K. Gwassa and J. Iliffe (eds.), *Records of the Maji Maji Rising*, Nairobi 1968.
43. *Ibid.*
44. J. Iliffe, 'The organization of the Maji Maji rebellion', *Journal of African History*, VIII, 1967. See also his *A Modern History of Tanganyika*.
45. S. Marks, 'Khoisan resistance to the Dutch in the seventeenth and eighteenth centuries', *Journal of African History*, XII, 1972. See also her larger work, *The Reluctant Rebellion*, Oxford 1970.
46. G.N. Uzoigwe, 'The Kyanyangire 1907: passive revolt against British overrule', University of East Africa Social Science Conference 1969, mimeo. See also G.C.K. Gwassa, 'The German intervention and African resistance in Tanzania', I.N. Kimambo and A.J. Temu (eds.), *A History of Tanzania*, Nairobi 1969.
47. T.O. Ranger, 'Reactions to colonial rule', L.H. Gann and P. Duignan (eds.), *Colonialism in Africa 1870-1960*, I, Cambridge 1969.
48. T.O. Ranger, 'Connections between primary resistance movements and modern mass nationalism in East and Central Africa', *Journal of African History*, IX-X, 1968. See also his *The African Voice in Southern Rhodesia 1898-1930*, London 1970.
49. Bonaventure Swai, 'The contradictory past: historians and African history' and 'Cacus and imperial history: India and Africa', Southern African Universities Social Science Conference 1979. Albeit in a different context, see also A. Kozharov, *Monism and Pluralism in Ideology and in Politics*, Sofia, n.d. L. Seve, *Man in Marxist Theory*, Hassocks, Sussex, 1978. K. Buttner, 'Historical aspects of the bourgeois concept of colonialism', *Asia, Africa and Latin America*, 2, 1977.
50. M. Cornforth, *Marxism and Linguistic Philosophy*, London 1970.
51. J. Iliffe, 'The effects of the Maji Maji rebellion of 1905-1906 on German occupation policy in East Africa', P. Gifford and W.R. Lewis (eds.), *Britain and Germany in Africa*, New Haven 1967.
52. H.P. von Strandmann, 'The German role in Africa and German imperialism', *African Affairs*, 69, 1970. H. Bley, 'Rebellions in colonial Africa: the case of South West Africa', Dar es Salaam 1971, mimeo.
53. J. Banaji, 'Modes of production in a materialist conception of history',

Dar es Salaam 1975, mimeo.
54. D. Williams, 'Law and socialist rural development', Dar es Salaam 1973, mimeo. K.F. Hirji, 'Colonial ideological apparatus in Tanganyika under the Germans', Dar es Salaam 1974, mimeo.
55. Seve, *Man in Marxist Theory*. S. Bowles and H. Gintis, *Schooling in Capitalist America*, New York 1976.
56. D. Beach, 'The rising in South Western Mashonaland', PhD thesis, London 1971. J. Cobbing, 'The Ndebele under Khumalos', PhD thesis, Lancaster 1979. T.O. Ranger, *Revolt in Southern Rhodesia*, London 1979; and 'The people in African resistance', *Journal of Southern African Studies*, 4, 1977.
57. J.R. Mbwiliza, 'Resistance and collaboration or the struggle and unity of opposites', *Utafiti*, 4, 1979.
58. Swai, 'Trade and politics in eighteenth-century Malabar'.
59. Nguyen Khac Thien, *The Long Resistance 1858-1975*, Hanoi 1975, p. 5.
60. K. Marx and F. Engels, *The Communist Manifesto*, Harmondsworth 1973, p. 90.
61. R. Hilton, 'Warriors and peasants', *New Left Review*, 83, 1973.
62. Ranger, 'Connections between primary resistance movements and modern mass nationalism in East and Central Africa'. In his PhD thesis, 'The outbreak and development of the maji maji war 1905-7', Dar es Salaam 1973, G.C.K. Gwassa has argued that the use of the ideology of Maji showed that African institutions and ideas could be adapted to meet new demands. Such is the concentration on form, omitting to show clearly what it represents.
63. Iliffe, *Tanganyika under Colonial Rule 1905-1912*.
64. I.P. Hulten, *An Episode of Colonial History: The German Press in Tanzania*, Uppsala 1974. J. Harris, 'The end of red rubber', *Journal of African History*, XVI, 1975.
65. Iliffe, 'Organization of the Maji Maji rebellion'.
66. W. Freund, 'Theft and social protest among the tin miners of Northern Nigeria', Dar es Salaam 1979, mimeo.
67. *Ibid*. E. Hobsbawm, *Primitive Rebels*, Harmondsworth 1968.
68. Freund, *op. cit.*, p. 1.
69. Quoted by Freund, *op. cit.*
70. I. Shivji, 'Semi-proletarian labour and the use of penal sanctions in the labour law of colonial Tanganyika 1920-1938', Dar es Salaam 1979, mimeo. D.V. Williams, 'The interaction of legal superstructure and economic basis in the process of colonization', Dar es Salaam 1978, mimeo.
71. H.S. Hughes, *Consciousness and Society*, St Albans, Herts. 1974.
72. S.N. Eisenstadt (ed.), *Max Weber*, Chicago 1968, p. xviii.
73. Low, *Lion Rampant*.
74. H. Harris, *Beliefs in Society*, Harmondsworth 1971.
75. E. Foner, *Tom Paine and Revolutionary America*, London 1976, p. xv.
76. E.J. Hobsbawm, *The Age of Revolution 1789-1848*, New York 1962, p. 253.
77. K. Marx, *The Eighteenth Brumaire of Louis Bonaparte*, Moscow 1967.
78. G.S. Jones, 'Class struggle and the industrial revolution', *New Left Review*, 90, 1975.

79. C. Hill, *The World Turned Upside Down*, Harmondsworth 1975, pp. 363-4.
80. Quoted by H. Bernstein, 'Capital and the peasantry in the epoch of imperialism', Dar es Salaam 1976, mimeo.
81. R.C. Majumdar, A.K. Majumdar and D.K. Ghose, *History and Culture of the Indian People*, IX, Bombay 1970, pp. 435-6.
82. See the editorial on South Africa in *Review of African Political Economy*, 7, 1976.
83. M. Twaddle, reviewing R.I. Rotberg and A.A. Mazrui, in *Journal of Commonwealth Political Studies*, 9, 1971.
84. F. Fanon, *The Wretched of the Earth*, Harmondsworth 1976.
85. A. Césaire, *Discourse on Colonialism*, New York 1957.
86. Quoted by G.T. Mishambi, 'The mystification of African history: a critique of Rodney's *How Europe Underdeveloped Africa*, Dar es Salaam 1976, mimeo.
87. Césaire, *Discourse on Colonialism*.
88. M. von Freyhold, 'On colonial modes of production', Dar es Salaam 1977, mimeo.
89. E. Mandel, *Marxist Economic Theory*, London 1971, Ch. 13.
90. Freyhold, 'On colonial modes of production'.
91. H. Bernstein, 'Capital and the peasantry in the epoch of imperialism', Dar es Salaam 1976, mimeo. See also an abridged but updated version of this paper, entitled 'Notes on capital and peasantry', Dar es Salaam 1978, mimeo.
92. See Bonaventure Swai, 'The colonial state: a study of the initial stages of its establishment in Zanzibar', E. Ferguson and A. Sheriff (eds.), *Zanzibar Under Colonial Rule*, London forthcoming; 'Colonial Leviathan and Kenya', A.J. Temu and Bonaventure Swai (eds.), *Kenya Under Colonial Rule*, London forthcoming.
93. This phrase is borrowed from N. Abercrombie, B. Turner and J. Urry, 'Class, state and fascism: the work of Nicos Poulantzas', *Political Studies*, XXIV, 1976.
94. L. Cliffe, 'Rural class formation in East Africa', *Journal of Peasant Studies*, 4, 1977.
95. E.S. Atieno-Odhiambo, 'Some reflections on African initiatives in early colonial Kenya', *East African Journal*, 8, 1971.
96. R.M.A. van Zwanenberg, *Colonial Capitalism and Labour in Kenya 1919-1939*, Nairobi 1975. A. Clayton and D.C. Savage, *Government and Labour in Kenya 1895-1963*, London 1974.
97. Brett's memorandum 14 September 1912, Kenya National Archives CP4/308.
98. For a similar example from Ukambani see S.B. Stichter, 'The formation of a labouring class in Kenya', R. Sandbrook and R. Cohen (eds.), *The Development of an African Working Class*, London 1975.
99. A.J. Temu, 'The Giriama war 1914-1915', Dar es Salaam 1970, mimeo.
100. Annual Reports of 1914-15, Vol. I, Kenya National Archives CP16/49.
101. B. Williams, *Modern Africa 1870-1970*, London 1970, pp. 10-14.
102. Bonaventure Swai, 'On myth and reality of the empiricism of colonial empires', Dar es Salaam 1977, mimeo.
103. D.A. Low, *Buganda in Modern History*, London 1971, pp. 7-8.

104. J.A. Rowe, 'Lugard at Kampala: a reassessment', Universities of East Africa Social Science Conference 1968, mimeo.
105. R. Lubertsky, 'Sectoral development and stratification in Tanganyika 1890-1914', Universities of East Africa Social Science Conference 1972, mimeo.
106. J. Iliffe, 'Organization of the Maji Maji Rebellion'.
107. J. Depelchin, 'Towards a problematic history of Africa', *Tanzania Zamani*, 18, 1976.
108. B.C. Ray, *African Religions*, Englewood Cliffs, NJ, 1976, Ch. 6.
109. R. Garaudy, *Marxism in the Twentieth Century*, London 1970.
110. J. Depelchin, 'Inequality and the fetishization of African history', Dar es Salaam 1978, mimeo.
111. Hirji, 'Colonial ideological apparatus in Tanzania under the Germans'.
112. Rodney, *The Groundings with my Brothers*, p. 9.
113. Iliffe, (ed.), *Modern Tanzanians*, Ch. 4.
114. J. Depelchin, 'Class formation, class structure, class consciousness in Zaire', Dar es Salaam 1976, mimeo.
115. T. Nairn, 'The English working class', in R. Blackburn (ed.), *Ideology in Social Science*, London 1973.
116. B. Davey, *Economic Development of India*, Nottingham 1975.
117. M. Shaw, 'The coming crisis of radical sociology', in Blackburn (ed.), *Ideology in Social Science*, pp. 33-4.
118. Iliffe (ed.), *Modern Tanzanians*.
119. W. Rodney, 'Migrant labour reserves in the Tanganyika colonial economy', University of London, School of Oriental and African Studies 1976, mimeo.
120. L. Cliffe, 'Nationalism and the reaction to agricultural improvement in Tanganyika during the enforced colonial period', Makerere 1964, mimeo.
121. Quoted by Low, *Lion Rampant*, p. 79.
122. C.C. Wrigley, 'Kenya: the pattern of economic life, 1902-1945', in V. Harlow and E.M. Chilver (eds.), *History of East Africa*, I, Oxford 1965.
123. S.H. Alatas, *The Myth of the Lazy Native*, London 1977.
124. O. Patterson, *The Sociology of Slavery*, London 1977.
125. K.M. Stamp, *The Peculiar Institution*, New York 1956.
126. G.M. Frederickson and C. Lasch, 'Resistance to slavery', in A. Weinstein and F.O. Gattell (eds.), *American Negro Slavery*, New York 1973.
127. Stamp, *The Peculiar Institution*, p. 105.
128. E.D. Genovese, *Roll, Jordan, Roll*, New York 1974, p. 306.
129. K. Marx, *Capital*, I, Moscow 1974, p. 717.
130. E.P. Thompson, *The Making of the English Working Class*, Harmondsworth 1968.
131. Genovese, *Roll, Jordan, Roll*, p. 306.
132. C.H. George, 'The making of the English bourgeoisie, 1500-1750', *Science and Society*, 35, 1971. Marx, *Capital*, I.
133. Genovese, *Roll, Jordan, Roll*, p. 311.
134. Marx, *Capital*, I.
135. Quoted by W.A. Jerome, *National Agrarianism*, I, Nairobi 1973, p. 60.

136. M. Perham (ed.), *Ten Africans*, pp. 9-10.
137. S. Bowles and H. Gintis, 'Class power and alienated labour', *Monthly Review*, 26, 1975.
138. A. Wolfe, 'New directions in the Marxist theory of politics', *Politics and Society*, 4, 1974.
139. K.C. George, *Immortal Punnapra-Vavala*, Delhi 1975.
140. S. Mesaki, 'Mumiani', Dar es Salaam 1977, mimeo.
141. For a definition of neutrality (which should not be confused with impartiality or detachment) see A. Montefiore (ed.), *Neutrality and Impartiality*, London 1975, Part I.
142. Quoted by G.C.K. Gwassa, 'On colonial labour force and labour market in Tanzania', Dar es Salaam 1974, mimeo.
143. J.R. Mlahagwa, 'The Uluguru land usage scheme: crisis in colonial production', Dar es Salaam 1977, mimeo.
144. Freyhold, 'On colonial modes of production'.
145. Zwanenberg, *Colonial Capitalism and Labour in Kenya 1919-1939*.
146. Quoted by Alatas, *Myth of the Lazy Native*.
147. Bonaventure Swai, 'The British in Malabar 1792 to 1806', DPhil., University of Sussex, Brighton, 1974.
148. Quoted by Freyhold, 'On colonial modes of production'.
149. The case of India has been argued by H. Alavi, 'India and the colonial mode of production', *Socialist Register*, 1975. Bonaventure Swai, 'Notes on the colonial state with reference to 18th and 19th century Malabar', *Social Scientist*, 7, 1978.
150. C. Ehrlich, 'Some social and economic implications of paternalism in Uganda', *Journal of African History*, IV, 1963.
151. For the problem of controlling mining labour in a situation where a permanent proletariat located in an urban complex seemed imminent see E.L. Berger, 'Government policy towards migrant labour on the Copperbelt 1930-1945', *Transafrican Journal of History*, II, 1972.
152. Bonaventure Swai, 'Native labour under colonialism', *Tanzania Zamani*, 21, 1979.
153. Williams, 'Law and socialist development'.
154. G. Arrighi, 'Labour supplies in historical perspective: a study of the proletarianization of African peasantry in Rhodesia', in G. Arrighi and J.S. Saul, *Essays in the Political Economy of Africa*, New York 1973.
155. See also D. Barnett, *Peasant Types and Revolutionary Potential in Africa*, Richmond, BC, 1973.
156. G. Kay, *Development and Underdevelopment*, London 1975.
157. Cliffe, 'Nationalism and the reaction to agricultural improvement in Tanganyika during the enforced colonial period'.
158. *Ibid.*
159. *Ibid.*
160. E.R. Wolf, *Peasant Wars in the Twentieth Century*, London 1969. I. Sheiner, 'The mindful peasants: sketches for a study of rebellion', *Journal of Asian Studies*, XXXII, 1973.
161. For a discussion of the fallacy of viewing the peasantry as absolute objects or subjects of history see H. Bernstein, 'Concepts for the analysis of contemporary peasantries', Dar es Salaam 1978, mimeo.
162. G. Lee, 'Commodity production and reproduction among the Malayan

peasantry', *Journal of Contemporary Asia*, 6, 1976.
163. This excludes North Africa (which belongs to the Arab world, notwithstanding Diop's endeavour to reclaim Egypt) and South Africa. S. Marks, 'South African studies since World War Two', Fyfe (ed.), *African Studies Since 1945*.
164. See the preface in R. Gray (ed.), *The Cambridge History of Africa*, 4, Cambridge 1975, p. xi.
165. Ranger, 'Towards a usable past', Fyfe (ed.), *African Studies Since 1945*.
166. *Ibid.*, p. 2.
167. Gray (ed.), *The Cambridge History of Africa*, 4.
168. *Ibid.*
169. Kepteijns, *African Historiography Written by Africans 1955-1973: The Nigerian Case*.
170. Y.B. Usman, 'History, tradition and reaction: the perception of Nigerian history in the 19th and 20th centuries', public lecture at Ahmadu Bello University, 27 April 1977.
171. V.I. Lenin, *On Imperialism and Opportunism*, Copenhagen 1974, p. 87.
172. Usman, 'History, tradition and reaction: the perception of Nigerian history in the 19th and 20th centuries'.
173. Quoted by A. Marwick, *The Nature of History*, London 1970.
174. D. Thompson, 'Progress at a price', *New Society*, 6 November 1975.
175. J. Iliffe, *Agricultural Change in Modern Tanganyika*, Dar es Salaam 1971.

3. Local Initiative: The Crisis from Within

Postcolonial Africanist history was posed as a critique of the reminiscences of colonial empire-building in Africa. It was also intended to establish the primacy of African agency in the making of history. Learned articles and monographs were published and the field of African professional history was transformed so much that even African historiography, 'the history of African historical research', has now become a viable academic enterprise.[1] The dominant themes of African history were recovered and researched. Patterns of change and continuity were debated vigorously, but, like vogue words which are intended to improve an image and increase credibility, the notions of change and continuity were so mesmerizing that they actually succeeded in concealing the underlying social reality which needed to be investigated.[2] Upon this an illusion was created. On this mystifying base, whole schools of professional Africanist history were founded. Although this claim has been gainsaid by some professional Africanist historians, for example the defenders of the Dar es Salaam School of New Historiography,[3] it is unwise to discuss and dismiss an allegation so nonchalantly.[4]

The cluster of ideas embodied in radical European social history can generally be termed Marxist, a distinction shared by a small segment of the growing band of what professional Africanist historians have called the radical pessimists of Africanist history.[5] This group of historians has constantly been subjected to intellectual ostracism and academic harassment.[6] However, this kind of intellectual Trotskyism aside, the radical historians stand for change rather than for the glorification of the past for its own sake.[7] The latter is tantamount to intellectual masturbation; the former has kindled a spark of hope for the oppressed peoples of Africa.

In professional Africanist history, ideas are sparse. Its limits are the inner organizational possibilities of the facts under investigation rather than their setting in space and history.[8] Postcolonial Africanist historiography demands that African history should be explained in terms of its own facts. In this endeavour it is colonial history which has been regarded as being problematic rather than professional metropolitan history, which has been viewed as unproblematic and a model to be emulated conscientiously.[9] In this belief it has been forgotten that colonial historiography and professional metropolitan history share the same empiricist method,[10] and that imperial history branched off from metropolitan history in conformity with the empiricist parcellization of knowledge.

Since colonial and postcolonial Africanist historiography have both operated within the empiricist method, it is largely on this basis that they have been judged. Assessments of this kind have been arrived at by the process of counter-questioning, which has tended to elicit counter-factualization. But as has been observed about this procedure, what is specifically deficient about it is that if 'the original question, which is under attack, is mistaken, then its basic assumptions are probably faulty.' What is more, 'a counter-question, in its reflexive inversion of the original, tends to repeat the original assumptions, faults and all, and thereby to perpetuate the error.' 'Counter-questions repudiate conclusions but reiterate premises. The resultant revision is objectionable not because it is revisionist but because its revisionism is incomplete and superficial.'[11] It is perhaps for this reason some scholars have observed that the only way to criticize a position is to repudiate it and so shift 'the focus of inquiry to its proper location, namely the production of social knowledge, whether concerning the past or the present.'[12] Moreover, the crisis of colonial and postcolonial historiography should not merely be viewed as a crisis of data. For as has been observed in the case of Africanist anthropology, when facts are consistently 'misinterpreted', there must be more to the problem than meets the eye.[13] The crisis should be analysed in conjunction with the terrain in which the facts are constituted and interpreted. Short of this, the search for an objective history of Africa becomes perpetually elusive.

An analysis of the terrain of production of historical knowledge is undertaken in Chapter 4. In this chapter, we attempt to examine the criticisms which have been levelled against the 'initiative school' of Africanist historiography within the empiricist framework. The emergence of the 'initiative school' together with the techniques of data collection which it introduced was initially termed a historiographical revolution. It is now clear, as was implied in the previous chapter, that Africanist history has not had any such revolution. Rather, the emergence of the initiative school has merely meant the imposition of bourgeois historiography upon Africa. This chapter attempts to give reasons for the crisis which has ensued in postcolonial Africanist history, as well as for the failure to realize the revolution which the 'initiators' of Africanist historiography had promised. In the previous chapter a good deal of attention was given to African resistance movements against colonial rule, in order to amplify the main arguments embedded in Africanist historiography and their weaknesses. In this chapter precolonial trade, especially the slave trade, will be used to illustrate the arguments which will be made. Africanist historians have used the example of precolonial trade to demonstrate African initiative in the making of history. This the critics of the 'initiative school' operating within an empiricist problematic have termed an historicist enterprise. The main problem with this critique, however, is that its proponents have not come up with any new ideas to resolve the impasse prevalent in Africanist history. Towards the end of this chapter, therefore, Marx's notion of merchant capital is used to show how the impasse could be resolved. Examples are drawn from nineteenth-century Eastern African commercial history to illustrate this point.

From the Golden Age of African Historiography to Pessimism

The 1960s witnessed the high noon of postcolonial Africanist historiography. These were the years of the 'golden age of consensus' in professional Africanist history. 'Anyone who served even as a foot soldier, in the armies that fought and won these battles', it has been observed by one of the pioneeers of professional Africanist history, 'can remember the sense of solidarity and commitment.' Thus it has been remarked:

> I can remember myself my admiration for the coherence and vigour of strategy for research embodied in the issues of the *Journal [of African History]*; my gratitude for the first synthesizing works which made undergraduate teaching possible: my even greater gratitude for the essential demonstrations of the respectability of oral history or a historical linguistics. I can remember the exhilaration of being part of the small but active historiographical communities which developed in East and Central Africa. And I can remember the sense that historians of Africa everywhere were engaged in the same task of *demonstration* of the possibility and viability of the field.[14]

It is proper that a pioneer who was active in the forefront of establishing professional respectability for Africanist history should look 'back at all this' with 'emotions of admiration and excitement'. But as with a number of other pioneers of postcolonial Africanist historiography, Ranger now realizes that 'the harsher climate' has come. The golden age has been displaced by an iron age; the age of consensus has been superseded by a period of confrontation. The flabbiness of professional African history is being exposed more than ever before.[15]

Ranger's present stand resembles the professional confession of a sepoy, a sort of *Ars Poetica*. For lack of rigour in professional African history, Ranger blames the 'African public' for its 'very ready and flattering interest shown', following publication of the results of the historiographical revolution. 'When our customers were so satisfied with what we gave them, there was not much incentive to examine more closely how related to African realities it really was.' Africa was interested in cult heroes, and these it got. In so doing, it seems, Africanist historians divested themselves of their professionalism.[16]

Indeed, it has been said that, if professional Africanists intended to emulate and reproduce the tenets of professional history, the attempt was a fiasco. Perhaps this is due to the fact that there still persists 'an unspoken assumption that serious and important decisions must always be made outside Africa', that Tarzan's role has not yet ended.[17] But it has also been argued that many studies produced by professional Africanist historians do not measure up to the standards of professional history as practised in the metropolis. Professional Africanist history is 'a kind of committed history – sometimes even a thesis to be defended'. 'It embodies a passionate approach, like the Soviet School'. It is not rich in information. Its practitioners are careless. They pay little attention to 'standards as applied to European history'.[18] For this reason, imperial historians like Robinson and Gallagher at Cambridge University found it necessary to maintain some sense in this area of study by writing their *Africa and the Victorians*, which shows 'in a most brilliant manner the British Government's concern with the hard, cold realities of imperial strategy when annexing vast areas of Africa', and avoids 'either censure or praise'.[19]

Professional Africanist historians rejected colonial historiography because it was mythical and aberrant; it paid no attention to *facts*. But it appears that Africanist historians are being accused of the same faults of omission and commission – that is, flagrant violation of professional standards. Colonial historiography denied the existence of the African past so as to idealize the colonial era. African postcolonial historiography has instead distorted the past so as to glorify the precolonial era, and by implication the postcolonial era.[20] Overemphasis on the politics of protest its critics have now dubbed mythical, since such efforts were interspersed with the activities of modernizers and improvers.[21] Furthermore, the focus on connections between the heroism of colonial resistances and the cult of independence has been considered unrealistic, since (notwithstanding attempts to overstretch their meaning)[22] there were colonies which witnessed few or no colonial rebellions, but which obtained independence from colonial rule nonetheless.[23] The colonial rebellions have not been analysed satisfactorily either. Many of their precedents have been neglected. As in most revisionist work, too, many of the faults found in colonial historiography have been repeated by Africanist professional historians.[24]

The act of studying the past with a view to establishing patterns of change and continuity intended to glorify current political trends has been labelled historicist.[25] Studying the past with the intent to discover patterns of progress or otherwise has vehemently been disputed by metropolitan historians ever since the First World War, when bourgeois confidence was shattered. It occurred earlier on the European continent.[26] Since then professional historians like H.A.L. Fisher have staunchly maintained: 'The fact of progress is written plain and large on the page of history; but progress is not a law of Nature. The ground gained by one generation may be lost by the next. The thoughts of men may flow into the channels which lead to disaster and barbarism.' Confidence has given way to nihilism.[27]

Pessimism in professional African history commenced with the onset of a crisis in the discipline. But this was only symptomatic of deeper crises within postcolonial African social formations. Overemphasis on the indigenous origins of change in the African past was considered a travesty of scholarship. It was also argued that concern with the politics of change in postcolonial historiography had been at the risk of neglecting a terrain of facts which constituted the politics of survival. Similarly, that research on the politics of protest during the colonial era had been one-dimensional, since it overlooked the politics of collaboration which embodied 'imperialism in practice'.[28]

'Among historians,' D.A. Low has written, 'there is now a growing literature' about resistance and revolt. But 'what of the long intervals when there was next to none such?' Questions of imperial authority as determined by initial imperial situations, its establishment, and intensity of power are just as valid as those of 'the groundswell from below'.[29] It has also been observed that a society 'cannot consist only of gentlemen and slaves. There must be a sufficiently large free population of lower ranks who identify themselves with the gentlemen and enable them to keep the slaves in order.'[30] It has been asserted with equal emphasis that 'it is a characteristic of empires that they turn their victims into their friends'.[31] Collaboration, or 'the non-European foundations of European imperialism', it seems, played an important role in establishing colonial rule.[32] Indeed, collaborative mechanisms, it has been argued, were not restricted to the political sphere. They were also dominant in the economic and cultural spheres.[33]

Collaborative mechanisms, the politics of survival and so on were indicative of the pragmatism of colonial empires, whose policies were more empirical than imperial.[34] Under imperial authority, it seems, even the term, policy, was a misnomer unless the very absence of policy is itself regarded as a policy.[35] There appears to be no other way of explaining the vast variety of colonial control mechanisms, colonial 'development' projects, and the different kinds of local situations which resulted from imperial pursuits. Indeed, for Professor Sir Keith Hancock, the variegated plethora of colonial situations demonstrates the importance of the empiricism of the colonial empire, which was highly adaptive to local pressures.[36]

Conditions which developed under colonialism were varied and complex. However, these have been blurred by the stimulus-response approach which dominates postcolonial historiography. This interpretation takes no account of the intensity of the stimulus nor the disposition of its target nor the nature of the response. There was not one colonizing power, but many, each with a different approach in the 'civilizing mission'. Moreover, the societies colonized were not on an equal level of development.[37] What is more, even in the same society not all its social constituents were affected equally by the onslaught of colonial rule.[38] The conditions under which the colonial equation was struck, therefore, were extremely complex.[39]

Arguments of this sort are a pointer to the effect that there exist other terrains of facts to be investigated. This apart, it has also been observed that postcolonial historiography developed from the too-naive assumption that history consists of nothing more than past politics. Man, it has now been realized, is not merely a political animal. According to liberal philosophers, modern man seems to be more of an economic animal than ever before.[40] There are also other 'Cinderella' subjects like intellectual and social history, and public administration, which have been neglected by the founders of postcolonial African historiography.[41] These have to be attended to if the parcellization of historical knowledge about Africa is to acquire the subtlety of professional metropolitan history.

Economic history was introduced into postcolonial historiography at a time when development-of-underdevelopment theory was gaining currency. Economic history was therefore now studied but with the purpose of showing *How Europe Underdeveloped Africa*. The main exponent of the study of underdevelopment in Africa was Walter Rodney. He observed that the imposition of 'international' trade on Africa turned its inhabitants into mere objects of exploitation. International trade was intended to promote unequal exchange between Africa and Europe. It was a dialectical relationship in which what was lost by Africa was gained by Europe. Commonsense also shows that 'no Chinese junks reached Europe, and if any African canoes reached the Americas (as is sometimes maintained) they did not establish two-way links. This meant that what was called international trade was nothing but the extension overseas of European interests.'[42]

The controversies over the validity of the nihilist approach, which sees no pattern in the making of African history, and over the development-of-underdevelopment theory as an alternative to the assertion of African agency in the making of history, seem to have continued unabated. Indeed, even contemporary history has been posed as an alternative in postcolonial Africanist historiography.[43] Professional Africanist historians continue to put their faith in the collection of more facts as the precondition for a breakthrough in professional African history. But this may simply turn the craft into a mindless accumulation of facts which would result in the production of dry-as-dust history. Perhaps that is the ultimate goal of professionalism: to produce specialists, who like the 'Cabots of Boston may end up with no-one to talk to but God'.[44] The rest of the discussion in this chapter aims to assess the viability of the nihilist approach and the development-of-underdevelopment theory as alternatives to the ideas of change and continuity articulated in postcolonial Africanist historiography.

The Nihilist School as an Alternative

The previous discussion has shown that the golden age of postcolonial Africanist historiography, during which the supremacy of the African factor was asserted, soon gave way to pessimism. With the onset of pessimism it was asserted there were no patterns or progress in Africanist history, and that historians should merely be concerned with describing the past with the aid of facts accumulated for this purpose. Thus was born the nihilist school of Africanist historiography, which has also been put forward now as the conscience of the historian's craft as far as the African past is concerned.

Professional Africanist historians who are nihilists have dismissed efforts to establish patterns in the African past as historicist. Opposition from this standpoint has been directed against this or that particular 'school of historical studies', parochially known by different names. The depth of the roots of this school overall, which emphasizes the primacy of African initiative, have varied from one area to another depending on the strength of its petty-bourgeois moorings. A summary of the achievements of this school in East and Central Africa is available in Ranger's 1969 Dar es Salaam inaugural lecture,[45] and in Ajayi's study of the initiative of Africans in the 'establishment of their own church' in West Africa.[46] Some of the weaknesses, on the other hand, of this endeavour to establish the primacy of African agency in the making of history were discussed in Chapter 2; Denoon and Kuper have in addition argued that too much stress on the African voice is extremely nationalistic because it disregards the consideration of factors which operated outside the boundaries of the continent, and that this approach is therefore one-dimensional and unrealistic.[47]

Emphasis on local factors, especially on the politics of protest during the colonial era, has also been selective. Protest is not the same thing as resistance, and both strategies existed together in the face of colonialism. Both types of politics constituted 'a unique response to the local situation, a weighing of interests and a calculation of odds'. A detailed picture of this sort 'is already emerging for the Shona uprising in Rhodesia'. Rational as people are, they could not have been driven either to collaborate with or to resist colonialism on the spur of the moment. As calculating individuals, they took sides, bearing in mind the implications and consequences of such action. Situations of collaboration were just as important as those of resistance. While each 'protest had its own nature, its own movement, its own cause and its own aim', each protest also 'had some counterpoise in groups who either remained aloof from protest or who participated against revolt, sometimes turning the scales to favour the colonial administrator'. As long ago as 1861, John Stuart Mill observed that 'such a thing as government of one people by another does not and cannot exist'. Recent colonial history has proved him right.[48]

Nationalist history, it has been argued, is weak because it is committed and subjective. That too was the case with European nationalist history, which has been on the decline since the Second World War. Professional European history before the War was extremely patriotic. Professional historians praised the 'pursuit of the world mission abroad' and the intensification of conservative politics at home. Patriotism induced historians like Treitschke to view the state 'as the highest personality in historical life, which needed maximum power for self-realization'.[49] Inter-war European politics shattered this kind of patriotic history and even ushered in attitudes which were anti-nationalistic. State policies praised before the War now began to come under penetrating and critical scrutiny. However, this was not the case with professional African history, which was in the ascendant in the post-war period. Nevertheless, many of the mistakes made by European professional historians could have been avoided had the founders of postcolonial Africanist historiography been less rash. This is how nihilist historians have viewed postcolonial Africanist historiography, as shown in their criticism of the way that the precolonial African slave trade has been discussed, especially in relation to its impact on the political development of precapitalist African social formations.

Professor Wrigley has been at the forefront of the nihilist approach in professional Africanist history. To start with, Wrigley's criticism is presented as a critique of Professor Fage's interpretative essay on the impact of the Atlantic slave trade on West African precapitalist social formations.[50] In his essay, Fage has argued that not so many Africans were sold into slavery and that only the surplus African population was thus disposed of.[51] Thus the population remained dense in areas like Eastern Nigeria and Malawi, from where slave-traders obtained most of their merchandise.[52] Furthermore, although perishables and luxuries like whiskey, gin and trinkets were exchanged for human beings, slaves were bought from willing sellers. The exchange was therefore fair. The African slave trade was, in the last analysis, trade, and thus amenable to economic analysis. The laws of supply and demand should be employed in the 'clinical' study of the African slave trade with a view to writing without prejudice or censure. These are the lengths to which academic objectivity in this view should go.[53]

In commercial exchange like the slave trade, both sides are bound to gain in one way or the other. Thus Fage argues that West Africa enjoyed a noticeable degree of economic and political development during the years of the overseas slave trade. In fact, he maintains, development may even have been stepped up during the time of the slave trade, as evidenced by the many complaints made by Africans that its abolition meant their ruin. In addition, there was the positive relationship, so the argument runs, of the slave trade to political development. This was not restricted to the formation of large political groupings like the West African empires of Mali, Songhai and Ghana, or the Arab commercial empire of East Africa. Unomah has argued that even obscure areas like Unyamwezi in Western Tanzania witnessed an unprecedented period of prosperity;[54] and this enlargement of scale in African commercial activities was translated into the political arena.[55] Even the *Mfecane*, which for a long time has been regarded as having had a destructive impact, in fact contributed positively to the development of East and Central Africa. Indeed most historical events, however destructive, seem on balance to have had positive influences.[56]

The issue of development aside, Wrigley seems unhappy with the manner in which Fage treats Africans as collectivities rather than as individuals who suffered in various ways from the unfair demands of the slave trade. Wrigley repeats this point in his review of E.A. Brett's *Colonialism and Underdevelopment in East Africa*. He writes that, as with all 'neo-Marxist' works, the argument in Brett's book is 'forceful and admirably organized, yet the question presents itself: how is it that a passion for human freedom and dignity can create a lunar landscape of language from which all signs of human life have vanished, leaving only "strata" and "structures" and "social formations"?'[57] Man, it appears to Wrigley, as an individual and a possessor of himself, is important for the survival of freedom, of the right to choose.[58] Those who have resorted to discussing man as part of a collectivity, in his view, have in most cases paved the way for totalitarianism.

The major danger facing professional African history and society, writes Wrigley, is the 'drastic simplification of the old political diversity':

Despite a number of ambiguities the term, economic development, does contain some approximate definable commonsense meaning. It is much more difficult to know what to make of the concept of political development, for the benefits which people seek from a political system are extremely varied and often contradictory, so that it is hardly possible to determine whether a new system provides more satisfaction than that which it has replaced. Fage, however, clearly has no doubts. For him political development means the creation and enlargement of states.[59]

Here, students of Africanist history, it might be said, will find themselves in familiar terrain. For just as social scientists have concentrated on nation-building, the sociology of development, and the politics of integration, historians have found antecedents of these processes in the African past. Notions of modernization and social change have proved useful tools for analysing not only current events in Africa but also the African past.

Terms like enlargement of scale, sharpening of political focus, convergence, initiative, and so on have been deployed by historians to show how African history has progressed from simple to complex and bureaucratized political, economic and social entities. This conception of the idea of complexity has also been used to show how African societies invariably progressed to the stage of the nation state, which apparently seems to be the ultimate goal of African dynamism.[60] The professional Africanist historians' concern to prove that African societies progressed from simple to complex entities has been dismissed by Wrigley as crude and deterministic, on the grounds that, firstly, it is hard to prove that all African societies traversed the same path — that is, 'from tribe to state, from segmentary to centralized political system'; and secondly, it is hard to sustain a convincing argument that large-scale organizations are necessarily better than small ones in providing the 'better life'. Moreover, what about the violence committed in the course of realizing this enlargement of political scale? Should that be called necessary sacrifice? These, according to Wrigley, are important questions that have not yet been tackled by professional Africanist historians.

The obsession with progress in professional Africanist history, which is also a powerful European intellectual tradition, is regarded by Wrigley as 'a crude form of what Popper identified as historicism'. An important feature of historicism, according to Wrigley, 'is its ethnocentricity. Historicist schemata, like that of Marx, are abstractions from the historical experience of Western Europe which are then generalized as laws of development for the entire human race . . . It might be better to be less confident about the nature of Africa's past in order that we may be less limited in our prescriptions for the present and its future.' The African past is unique, and so are its facts. More attention, therefore, should be paid to the unique and the particular in the African past than to applying to this past crude laws drawn from elsewhere. It is also necessary to resist the temptations of a preoccupation with the present if the professional Africanist historian is to be faithful to his craft, and so study the past for its own sake.[61]

Professor Omer-Cooper has advanced a similar argument about the relationship between precolonial African kingdoms and overseas trade. He writes that, while it is untrue that in a bid to control external trade African kingdoms expanded or contracted in relation to the intensity of commercial transactions, there is evidence to show that kingdoms along the coast disintegrated in order to give room for more entrepreneurs to participate fully in overseas trade. This was especially true of the kingdoms of Angola and the Congo.[62] However, if all that is necessary in history is to match one set of facts against another, it might be of interest to note that the Zanzibar empire did not disintegrate with the internationalization of the East African ivory and slave trades in the nineteenth century.[63]

The 'cult of empiricism and pragmatic conservatism' got a new lease of life in 1945 when Karl Popper published his work, *The Poverty of Historicism*, which he dedicated to those 'men and women of all creeds or nations or races who fell victims to the fascist and communist belief in Inexorable Laws of Historical Destiny'. This work was prompted by the intellectual crisis precipitated by the rise of Fascism and Nazism in Europe in the inter-war years.[64] According to E.H. Carr, the term historicism as used by Popper is 'a catch-all for any opinion about history which he dislikes'. Formerly, the term meant the tendency to view history as a science. Now it has been confused so much that it even includes the notion of relativism. For Popper, 'everything is possible in human affairs'. Since the totality of human affairs is its province, history cannot be a science.[65]

Popper maintains that it is impossible to predict man's future, because development is influenced by the growth of human knowledge, which is unpredictable. Unlike the physical sciences, it is hard to have theoretical history because history depends on the occurrence of events, which rules out the possibility of prediction. The historicist 'approach in the social sciences which assures that historical prediction is their principal aim, and which assumes that this aim is attainable by discovering the "rhythms" or the "patterns", the "laws" or the "trends" that underlie the evolution of history', therefore, promises more than is attainable. Thus the historicist approach is dangerous to the social sciences and to society. To the social sciences, historicism holds out the hope of a theoretical study of human beings comparable to theoretical physics. This, however, is an impossibility; yet it has encouraged scholars to shy away from empiricism, a method which emphasizes the importance of the observable fact as the basis of social investigation. Historicism encourages deference towards great theoreticians like Plato, Hegel and Marx, all of whom were determinists whose notions were the fountain-head of ideas inimical to our open society.[66]

Determinism has encouraged revolt against the open society; it has dissuaded people from making the transition from the closed society, which is traditional and totalitarian, to the abode of civilization, the open society. Unlike the closed society, says Popper, the open society encourages the free development of the individual. The ethics of the open society should, therefore, be defended by fighting determinism with the help of the empirical method.⁶⁷ Thus, to return to Wrigley, who has espoused the Popper approach, the empirical method should be brought to bear in the study of African history, since the dark clouds of totalitarianism are on the verge of engulfing the continent. The density of these clouds is increasing day by day, in part precisely because of the efforts to look for patterns, themes and internal factors in African history. The point, however, – so this nihilist approach argues – is that there is *no* pattern in the development of African history. There are only unique events to be studied one at a time. Thus the professional Africanist historian, as has been observed by Lord Bullock in the case of contemporary history, should concern himself with 'the concrete world of the experience itself, undifferentiated and unstructured, precisely the sort of world in which a creature like Hitler can burst through the walls of probability'.⁶⁸ There is no other way in which the multi-layered and complex past can be understood. The past has to be approached on its own terms and studied for its own sake.

The New Breed of Imperial Historians

The original endeavour by postcolonial African historiography to portray the African past as dynamic was intended, as we have seen, as an ideological intervention against colonial historiography. But even if the African past was dynamic, its nature should still be determined. It is necessary to be precise with notions like change and continuity. Moreover, the character and sources of change should be studied more carefully. This is particularly so with the self-appointed tasks of colonialism. Postcolonial Africanist historiography has to be more subtle if it is to enjoy professional respectability. Such is the way in which the new breed of imperial historians has viewed the results of postcolonial historiography.

Much as we can talk about the indigenous origins of change in Africa, it has been acknowledged that there is also something to be said for the contribution of external factors. This is also the case with the sources of continuity of African institutions. Hence the importance of studying the 'empiricism of colonial empires'. Most imperialists were practical. They had no overall system of colonial governance. There was much imperial adaptation to local circumstance, in which considerable local initiative was possible.⁶⁹

The British have long regarded themselves as the greatest empiricists of them all. They believe that they muddled through the English Revolution of the seventeenth century which ushered in the capitalist era in a kind of fit of absent-mindedness.⁷⁰ It is said that the Revolution did not bring about a decisive victory for the English bourgeoisie, since it was not until the enactment of the Corn Laws in the 1840s that the doctrine of *laissez-faire* was accepted as part of normal English life.⁷¹ The slow development of the English bourgeoisie, it is said, was also reflected in their intellectual tradition, especially the obsession with empiricism. Thus as late as 1937 the Prime Minister, Stanley Baldwin, is reported to have boasted that 'one of the reasons why our people are alive and flourishing, and have avoided many of the troubles that have fallen to less happy nations, is that we have never been guided by logic in anything we did'. For Baldwin, empiricism was the hallmark of British life.[72]

This tradition, it has been argued, also influenced the policies pursued in the British colonial empire. Thus Asa Briggs has observed that:

> The British Empire remains the most difficult of all empires to study in that it was neither extended nor restricted on the basis of one single theory of empire or even of a single set of generally accepted presuppositions. Those who tried in its later phases, like Smuts, to climb to the top of a high mountain and survey the scene from above were all too easily lifted into the clouds: those who pushed pens in Whitehall or even in offices overseas often saw no further than the end of their own noses.[73]

Even the term, empire, might have been a misnomer because, from the viewpoint of policy-makers in London, the British Empire was 'an embarrassment rather than an asset'. Perhaps it could not have been otherwise, for as H. G. Wells wrote in 1916: 'Politically, the British Empire is a clumsy collection of strange accidents. It is a thing as little to be proud of as the outline of a fruit or the shape of a potato. For the mass of the English people India and Egypt, and all that side of our system, mean less than nothing; our trade is something they do not understand, and imperial wealth something they do not share.'[74]

Apart from administrative policy, the behaviour of the British as a nation of empiricists was also shown in the manner in which they acquired their colonies.[75] Colonies were acquired rather slowly. There was no period, as Robinson and Gallagher have maintained, which could be characterized as constituting the imperialist leap in the acquisition of colonies.[76] The slow process of acquiring colonies, as well as the caution which accompanied the assertion of imperial authority, accounts for the variety of colonial situations.[77] Various forms of imperial authority were found not only in the colonial empire as a whole but also within a single colony. Such variety was amplified by the various imperial situations out of which colonies arose, of which there were three: situations of displacement, of creation, and of domination.[78] Thus, as well as direct colonial control, there were other forms of domination like extraterritorial jurisdiction, the residency system, chartered companies, protectorates, paramountcy, and indirect rule. This, McIntyre has asserted, was the hallmark of British empiricism. The situation, both in terms of the ways in which the British pursued their acquisition of colonies and the great variety of local circumstances within the colonial empire, was so complex that 'a simple either-or' explanation of annexation or withdrawal would not suffice. 'Refusals to annex are not proof of reluctance to control. But willingness to control is no proof of desire .... The question', says McIntyre, 'should be: what sort of control and to what purpose?'[79] Like McIntyre, most of the new imperial historians would suggest that colonialism as well as the local forms it acquired must be explained in terms of circumstances prevailing in the colonial societies. In this way colonialism is dissociated from its imperialist moorings. Colonial expansion is thus explained in terms of metropolitan humanitarian instincts coupled with the 'turbulent frontier in the tropics'. Such considerations constitute 'the complex irrationality' of the processes by which decisions to expand were made.[80]

Empiricism, it has been argued, was not only shown in the process of colonization and imperial control but also in the endeavour by empire builders to behave like ruling authorities. In most cases imperial powers tried to introduce only those changes that were essential. This, in practice, meant only a modicum of interference with the traditional order. In fact, imperial powers adopted much of what was considered traditional. Colonial proconsuls were therefore more practical than idealistic; more preservationist than developmentalist.[81]

In this complex situation, colonial survivals were possible. They ranged from political, social and cultural institutions to social strata like the peasantry. Thus it becomes difficult 'to judge whether in retrospect the colonial period will appear as an earthshaking era of irreversible change', or merely as a half-century of an episode like others which preceded it.[82] What is certain, however, is that this is not an 'either-or' question. To be sure, attempts have been made to explain the phenomenon of colonial survivals. But this, as undertaken by the pioneers of postcolonial Africanist historiography, cannot be restricted to the 'originality' of the African genius alone.[83] The preservationist tendency of imperial authority cannot be discounted. Imperial proconsuls were also conscious of this role. Governor Hugh Clifford observed in the case of peasant cultivation in the Gold Coast, for example, that it was more than a mere 'economic agglomeration created for the pursuit of profit. It substitutes itself for the primitive societies which in sickness and in health sustain their members.'[84] Humanitarianism aside, the perpetuation of peasant cultivation was a form of welfare-statism.

By pointing to the precolonial survivals, the new imperial historians have sought to establish that imperial authorities had no single strategy of development, and that even if they had, there was no guarantee that all colonial societies would attain the same level of development. This thinking conforms to the Social Darwinist philosophy of predestination which saturated colonial policies.[85] Colonial societies developed, in terms of this view, according to their own inherent abilities. If they remained stagnant, they themselves were to blame. Imperial rule, which was paternalist, merely tried to enforce the rules of the game during the period of colonial enlightenment. Thus colonialism is cleared of its crimes. Yet the problem of how to account for both social change and continuity remains.

Change, like revolution, has been discussed a great deal. Change in history comprises experiences or events whose meaning is defined in terms of its destination. 'To venture a statement about the meaning of historical events is possible only when their *telos* becomes apparent.'[86] It would therefore seem hard to have a history without a pattern. As with the notion of social change, the difficulty of this argument is that the basis of the *telos* which determines the pattern of history is not shown. This is also the case with historical facts, about which we shall have more to say in Chapter 4.

The failure to locate the motor of change, whose basis lies in our view (as we shall show later) in the contradiction between the forces and relations of production, results in perceiving the process of historical development in a non-dialectical manner. Change is regarded as synonymous with evolution or diffusion, in which even the survival of the fittest does not necessarily ensure success.[87] Adaptation, survival and change (whether cumulative or substitutive)[88] become meaningless unless perceived as an ideological demand of the prevailing order of everyday life. Thus in his discussion of continuity in history, Gerschenkron observes that continuity does not mean absence of change, but, rather reveals the nature of change itself. Change amounts to continuity where there is constancy of direction in the evolution of historical events, where the periodicity of events is cyclical, or where the source of change is endogenous. While continuity may be regarded as periodicity or as 'a long causal chain' which is directional, Gerschenkron also argues that 'at all times and in all cases, continuity must be regarded as a tool forged by the historian rather than as something inherent and invariantly contained in the historical matter. To say "continuity" means to formulate a question or a set of questions and to address it to the material.' However one wishes to view continuity, at all times it is the ordering hand of the historian that creates continuities or discontinuities.[89]

This kind of pragmatism is also being revealed in the study of Africanist history. History becomes what historians write and tell us, rather than a product of the social relations of a specific social formation. In place of the confidence of the early 1960s, pessimism has bombarded the professional study of African history. The pioneers asserted that theirs was an endeavour to recover the truth about the African past. In their sober moments, however, they confessed that they took the African past too lightly and that their audience was too credulous. Amidst this controversy was issued the call for a serious consideration of other aspects of African history.

From Africanist Economic History to the Notion of Development of Underdevelopment

> Yet political history, however varied and exciting, gives only a part of the picture of the past .... And in order to understand how political history came about, why things happened as they did and not in some other way, we have to look beyond the big events, beyond the high traditions and the rulers of magnificence and power. We have to listen behind the deep drum-beats of history, behind the din of armies on the march and the bitter crash of battles. We have to observe, if we can, how ordinary people lived and worked and organized their lives. This is the business of economic and social history.[90]

Towards the end of the 1960s it was becoming obvious that, besides the weaknesses in professional Africanist history already mentioned, there was overconcentration on the political aspects of both the precolonial and colonial African past.[91] It was felt that all the various facets of the African past had to be researched rigorously if professional Africanist history was to attain the maturity of the other respectable branches of the discipline. There was a particularly urgent need in the area of economic history. Besides precolonial trade, a call was made for 'serious experimentation with agrarian history at area level'. 'From the viewpoint of the administrator, social scientist, or teacher,' it was felt, 'what is most needed from the historian . . . at present was painstaking and detailed economic history at regional or district level - a transfer of energy from area politics to area economics similar to the transfer from national to area politics that took place soon after independence.'[92] In the words of Basil Davidson, 'those who want to grasp the fuller meaning of history in Africa must also . . . manage to catch the clink of the farmer's hoe, the thump of the housewife's pounding stick, the iron-smelter's bellows'.[93]

The perception of the need to study economic history came at a time when the development-of-underdevelopment theory was being popularized beyond its cradle in South America.[94] African economic history came therefore to be studied in the context of the underdevelopment of the continent, and this approach was posed as an alternative to the notion of African agency hitherto dominant in postcolonial Africanist historiography. Thus Rodney argued in his most famous book that Africans lost their initiative with the onslaught of colonialism, and that this was only regained with the attainment of independence. This was so because African responses in the colonial era, 'albeit vigorous', 'were simply responses to the options laid down by the colonialist. True historical initiative by a whole people or by individuals requires that they have the power to decide on the direction in which they want to move. That latter aspect had to await the decade of the 1960s.'[95]

Ideologically, it was also felt that the nationalist euphoria of the 1960s had not brought tangible results to the mass of the people. As well as the campaign to seek first the political kingdom as a precondition to restoring the African personality, therefore, it came to be strongly believed that it was necessary to lay the foundations for economic independence. This attitude entailed a search for the roots of African poverty.[96] At the methodological level the Africanist pioneers applying development-of-underdevelopment theory sought to provide a broader 'theoretical' view of African historiography because they felt that, despite the change in method and focus, colonial and postcolonial historiography still had one factor in common, and that was 'empiricism'. As a result, there had been an overemphasis on the study of tribes on an empirical level. As is normal with such studies, researches tended to be small in scale to allow evidence to be accumulated easily and properly. This methodology has been characterized as development 'towards the minute in historical studies' which, we have maintained, is a bourgeois approach. Development-of-underdevelopment theory, therefore, was posed not only as an alternative to the endeavour to seek out and recover local initiative in African history but also as a pointer to the application of the Marxist method in African studies.[97]

Underdevelopment was presented not as an original condition to be explained by the examination of features inherently African, but as an historical characteristic deposited as a condition of Euro-African relations of exploitation. In this regard it has been said:

> *Colonialism* was not simply and merely a conflict between cultures or races, and not even the simple result of a violent policy of certain governments involving bad people with sinister malicious emotions. By no means! It followed from the objective, inherent laws and tendencies of a particular socio-economic system, i.e. capitalism, in a certain stage of its development, and *as* an adequate reaction of this system to the state of its basic contradictions at that time.[98]

This is what the prevailing notions of development, social change and modernization have failed to consider. Social change has been viewed hitherto as a teleological condition to be analysed in terms of its destination, the metropolitan achievements. The point of departure of this process has been understood to be the traditional society. This entity, it has now been realized, is confusing, since it includes too many forms of 'pre-modern' social formations. Professional Africanist historians had nonetheless tried to historicize the notion of traditional society by always asserting that it was dynamic.

Underdevelopment, instead, was 'posed as an object of study . . . more appropriate to the realities of the Third World . . . against prevailing notions of development and modernization held to be ideological'. It was conceived as a dialectical and dynamic process to be analysed within the framework of 'the world system perspective' with a view to showing the international relations of inequality.[99]

An Evaluation of This New Approach

The thesis of unequal exchange, however, has come under vehement attack of late. It has been observed that, while the notion of exploitation has been illustrated at the international level, its articulation within specific social formations has not been revealed. Since the conditions under which underdevelopment obtained have been glossed over, neither the historical stages it underwent nor its forms of realization in various countries have been analysed.[100] In most cases the study of the process of underdevelopment in Africa has been nothing more than a descriptive attempt to show the actuality of an idea — very similar to the earlier endeavour to show African agency in history — both of which approaches are rather ahistorical.[101] For example, recently Mishambi has argued that the use of development-of-underdevelopment theory to explain the growth of African history has to be viewed as in reality a continuation of cultural nationalism notwithstanding the use of radical rhetoric.[102]

Development-of-underdevelopment theorists have conceived the poverty of Africa as problematic, and thus an appropriate object of investigation. The model of comparison, as with the previous pioneers of modernization theories, however, still remains 'the self-centred metropolitan economy . . . which for undeclared reasons is considered nonproblematic'.[103] Bernstein has recently argued that the development-of-underdevelopment theory is populist. It is, he says, intended to legitimize the idea that African poverty would come to a dramatic end if only there were a charismatic leader courageous enough to effect the process of 'disengagement from imperialism'. Indeed, 'the wishes of the romantics are very good . . . . Their recognition of the contradictions of capitalism places them above the blind optimists who deny the existence of these contradictions.'[104] Development-of-underdevelopment theorists have also elaborated in useful ways the 'symptomology' of the uneven development of capitalism on the world scale. 'But their claim that their theory is based on historical materialism has yet to be demonstrated.'[105] Meanwhile, a fresh terrain of facts has been revealed and incorporated into professional Africanist history; that of man as above all *Homo economicus*.[106]

The Cul-de-Sac of Postcolonial Africanist Historiography

Granted that from its inception postcolonial Africanist historiography was intended to be the basis of the writing of a 'history of the people' - a history of 'Africans as agents rather than as passive victims, as migrants, or as statistics'[107] - this object has proved one of the major areas of contention in professional Africanist history. Investigating the history of the people in professional Africanist history is like reading the palimpsest, the ancient manuscript on which generation upon generation wrote without obliterating the writings of their predecessors. While in such an excavation one is bound to discover one layer after another, each full of interesting information, the main problem is whether one will be able to determine which layer belongs to the people. It is all right to talk about history written from above or history written from below, but it is just as important to ask for the criteria for such a pursuit.

The first generation of postcolonial Africanist historians claimed that the results of their enterprise constituted a history written from below. This, however, has been declared 'drum and trumpet history'.[108] The nihilists of Africanist history subsequently restored the importance of history viewed from above as a precondition for understanding 'the history of the people'.[109] But what of the people? Is there a history of the people in general, or even history in general? Perhaps these questions are too obvious to deserve serious attention. But what is the basis of such an assumption?

Indeed, one Africanist considers the question so obvious that in his endeavour 'to restore the *people* as agents of African initiative' he declares: 'There will be no great men in the following pages, where the focus is on man as a doer, husbandman, industrialist and trader. In these initiatives the individual takes on the anonymity of mere numbers and purposeful action becomes that of great masses of people.' For him the activity of the common people takes on the 'anonymity of mere numbers'.[110] Such declarations have become very vulnerable targets of criticism by the nihilist professionals of Africanist history.[111]

For this reason, there have been belated attempts to reintroduce the notion of people's initiative in the making of history. However, as Alpers has cautioned, African initiative in history must be considered in the context of international trade.[112] Alpers feels that there were two types of agencies coexisting within the context of Euro-African international trade: the one, European and the other, African. The European agency was dominant. This meant that 'in the context of world economic history the Africans were being had'. But Africans did not see the inequality embedded in this relationship because of their narrow world-view. Alpers assumes that exploitation existed wherever there was an unfair 'game' and that it could be remedied with the introduction of neutral 'rules', such as occurred later when 'legitimate trade' was imposed upon Africa during the era of Free Trade imperialism, and subsequently with colonial penetration. If Africans were clever, they could avoid exploitation, and so could trade with Europeans on a basis of equality. Thus this view reduces the notion of African agency in the context of international trade simply to the ability to haggle so as to enforce the rules of exchange on an equal footing. Here, therefore, Africans are turned into individual subjects with the ability to enter into a competitive game like the individuals of other races who established commercial relations with Africa. Alpers gives the example of West African traders, who, because they had learnt 'to be rogue as good as white man',[113] were more involved in the making of their own history than the Makua traders of Mozambique, whom European merchants considered savages because they 'could not see that they were compradores in a colonial relationship with Europe, Asia, or their economic systems'.[114]

Two ideas are at stake here: the role of individuals in history, and the meaning of exploitation. Alpers reduces them to the faculty of awareness. He asserts that exploitation takes place during the process of exchange. This seems to be the idea which has also guided Fage and Wrigley in their wrangle over the effects of the slave trade in Africa. It is a common liberal belief that development results from exchange, especially if the rules employed in the transaction are fair. If this notion is applied to the slave trade, however one looks at it, the outcome of the analysis will be that Africans, or a section of them, gained by selling their fellow Africans for gin and whisky. That seems to be 'the cold academic analysis of supply and demand', which steers clear of censure.

Trade, however, is an outgrowth of production. It is in the course of production rather than exchange that wealth is created. What is more, 'the most important wealth in any community is manpower'. Fage and Wrigley 'seem to be telling us that loss of manpower for imported odds and ends meant wealth'. This, indeed, is strange historical objectivity.[115] That said, Africa's precolonial trade with Europe has been conceived as comprising the roots of African underdevelopment. If this was so, there was a qualitative difference between such roots and the subsequent development of underdevelopment realized during the colonial era. The former falls into the era of primitive accumulation when Africa was subjected to the travails of plunder, kidnapping and outright theft. During this period it was not only surplus labour which was extracted, but in many cases the productive forces as well, with the consequent destruction of whole African social formations.[116] We cannot, therefore, talk of exploitation during this period if by that we mean the extraction of surplus labour.[117] We can, however, talk about the period of plunder. The development of underdevelopment under colonialism was intended to effect super-exploitation under the auspices of the colonial state. In this case, the precapitalist social formations were not destroyed, but were articulated with the capitalist mode of production. The colonial state played a decisive role in establishing conditions favourable to this process.[118] Such a distinction seems necessary to avoid the reductionist manner in which the debate about underdevelopment has hitherto been conducted.[119]

Precolonial Euro-African trade was determined by the character of capital dominant during this era: merchant capital. Merchant capital specializes in what is termed the 'carrying trade'. This capital takes no part in the actual process of producing what it circulates. To make a profit, therefore, it has to play on the ignorance of its clients. This ignorance is induced by distance and bad communication between the sellers and the ultimate buyers of the commodities circulated by merchant capital. Through this ignorance merchant capital manages 'to buy cheap in order to sell dear' and makes this its motto. Where conditions are otherwise, monopolistic charters are resorted to in order to protect the motto's implementation. Alternatively, outright force is employed.[120] Thus mercantile companies dominant during the era of merchant capital were fortified with charters which made them political and military authorities. 'In those places', Ramkrishna Mukherjee observes, 'where the [local] governments were weak or where in some way or other these foreign merchants could dominate over the local area, robbery became a distinct feature of their enormous gains.' Where local authorities were strong, on the other hand, merchants played down the methods of kidnapping and piracy and stepped up diplomacy. Either way there was latent or actual plunder.[121]

What replaced the period of plunder was discussed in Chapter 2. The question of initiative, individual or otherwise, and the problem of people's history remain. How should we approach the history of a given area, or the history of a specific group of people, given that it is widely felt among professionals and amateurs alike that the history of the people in Africa has yet to be written? This despite claims by many that they have revealed the secrets of the people's history. Why has a people's history in Africa been so hard to write?

More than a century ago it was observed very clearly and admirably that:

> When we consider a given country politico-economically, we begin with its population, its distribution among classes, town, country, the coast, the different branches of production, export and import, annual production and consumption, commodity prices etc.
>
> It seems to be correct to begin with the real and the concrete, with

> the real precondition, thus to begin, in economics, with e.g. the population, which is the foundation and the subject of the entire social act of production. However, on closer examination this proves false. The population is an abstraction if I leave out, for example, the classes of which it is composed. These classes in turn are an empty phrase if I am not familiar with the elements on which they rest . . . wage labour, capital, etc. These latter in turn presuppose exchange, division of labour, prices, etc. For example, capital is nothing without wage labour, without value, money, price . . . . Thus if I were to begin with the population, this would be a chaotic conception . . . of the whole and I would, by means of further determination, move analytically towards ever thinner abstractions until I arrived at the simplest determinations. From there the journey could have to be retraced until I had finally arrived at the population again, but this time not as the chaotic conception of a whole, but as a rich totality of many determinations and relations. The former is the path historically followed by economics at the time of its origins . . . . The latter is obviously the scientifically correct method. The concrete is concrete because it is the concentration of many determinations, hence unity of the diverse.[122]

Nihilist historians of Africa have complained that the individual as an autonomous entity is being effaced from professional history by those authors who concentrate on writing about 'class' and 'stratum'.[123] The crucial problem, however, is to determine what unites individuals as entities. The tribe, among other unifiers, has been suggested. But it is necessary to emphasize that even the tribal entity was historically determined.[124]

It is for this reason that, while acknowledging the role of individuals in history, it has all the same been emphasized:

> An aggregate of human beings constitutes a society when, and only when, the people are in some way interrelated. The essential relation is not kinship, but much wider; namely, that developed through production and mutual exchange of commodities. The particular society is characterised by . . . that which is necessary; who gathers or produces the things, by what implements; who lives off the production of others, and by what right, divine or legal; . . . cults and laws are social by-products; who owns the tools, the land, sometimes the body and soul of the producer; who controls the disposal of the surplus, and regulates the quantity and form of the supply. *Society is held together by bonds of production.*[125]

In such an approach, epochal questions become just as important as historical ones. Concepts like that of mode of production, which constitute the motor of development of a given social formation, become relevant. A given social formation constitutes the basis upon which the writing of history can be undertaken. But this presupposes the existence of a specific mode of production, an ensemble of historically determined productive and social relations. It is in this context that individuals are situated whose initiatives are determined by historically determined social conditions.[126]

Considerations of this kind appear more convincing than the somewhat banal debate about whether there were patterns in African history or 'mere purposeless change'. If there were patterns, we would like to know their basis. If their basis was the African genius, we would like to see it identified in particular. The same principle applies to the now insipid assertion of patternless history. Thus Kosambi has written: 'To maintain that history has always been made' by the supposedly 'backward, ignorant, common people, and that they, not the high priest, glittering aristocrat, warlord, financier, or demagogue, must shape it better in the future, seems presumptuous formalism. Nevertheless it is true.'[127] To declare that something is true, however, is one thing; to demonstrate and document it convincingly, another. Moreover, the call for new history has to be treated with caution. In most cases this has resulted in the production of history to serve a new class of exploiters.[128] Meanwhile, those for whom the new history has purportedly been written have continued to suffer with bitterness.

Such history, as has been shown with regard to American history, 'is too busy celebrating successful tactics and militant actions, too busy attempting to give "radicals" their own history - which is to say a false sense of accomplishment, and therefore a pious satisfaction with the past . . . . [There is a] one-dimensional glorification of motion'. 'Both in history and in the movement "radicalism" has no content. It is purely formal. It operates within bourgeois categories. If the establishment likes decorum, disruption is radical. If straights wear their hair short, it is radical to wear it long. If the corporations oppose contractual relations with unions, it is radical to fight for these. If establishment historians write history by examining only ruling-class sources - and increasingly the better liberal historians do not - then it is radical to use only lower-class sources.' Such an approach is purely responsive. 'Content is lost in the process of reacting to the initiatives of those in power. The ruling class is left in a position to steer militancy [and radicalism] in the direction advantageous to itself.' This is the main problem with any process of ideological intervention which fails to take account of the basis of the ideology under attack.[129] Even the use of the term, radical, begs the question. In fact it is nothing more than a response to the liberal stand that anything out of the normal, and with leftist tendencies, is radical. As for the context of radicalism, that is another matter.[130]

The same can be said about postcolonial Africanist history. What makes colonial historiography a history studied from above, and postcolonial historiography 'history studied from the bottom up', is hard to determine.[131] Why should history viewed 'from the bottom up' be more relevant than history studied from above? Is it just because of the feeling that it has not been studied in this way before? But African history has been studied before - in the latter part of the nineteenth century by Afro-American professional historians.[132] What then makes the post-1945 professional endeavours a better history studied from the bottom up? Such questions have not been answered. Small wonder, then, that postcolonial Africanist historiography has proved so vulnerable to nihilist assaults.

Postcolonial Africanist historiography has reached a cul-de-sac. This, too, in spite of the expectations aroused by the development-of-underdevelopment theory. To a considerable degree Africanist historiography still revolves around the jejune debate about the importance of internal and external factors in the development of the history of the continent. To that extent the discussion has acquired a metaphysical tinge in which, as well as concepts, 'things are their conceptual images', 'are singular, solid, rigid, objects of examination given once and for all, that have to be contemplated one after the other and in isolation from the other'. Thus it would seem that the professional Africanist historian, like the metaphysician thinks in mere antitheses devoid of reason, and speaks thus: 'Yes, yes; no, no, and what is beyond this comes from the evil: For him a thing does or does not exist: a thing cannot be its own self and something else at the same time.' Metaphysics and dialectics are worlds apart.[133]

The issue of factors within factors is misleading because all factors are part of the same process. One set of factors for better or worse influences the other.[134] Real history has to deal with the dialectical interrelationship between the various factors, and in that way reveal the contradictions and complexities of society, if it is to avoid serving a new set of exploiters.[135] Similarly, histories written from below and those written from above are part and parcel of the same process. To write one sort of history is to assume the existence of the other. The process of revolt by the oppressed was brought about and distorted by the policies of their oppressors.[136] Such policies have to be problematized if the character of the protests of the oppressed is to be comprehended.[137] This will be illustrated with the help of the controversy over the state found in discussions on African precapitalist social formations.[138] The examples we shall take focus on African states and the impact of European merchant capital.

Towards Materialist History: An Example [139]

The State in African History

Many nineteenth-century historians, as has already been shown, argued, at times very vehemently, that their craft was synonymous with change itself. Where there was no change, there could be no history. Moreover, such change had to be 'purposive' if it were not to be relegated to 'mere space as it were'.[140] The place of the state in society was considered crucial in an historical process. According to Robinson and Gallagher, that state which governed least governed best; for development depended, to a large degree, on economic freedom.[141] Such was, *inter alia*, the English liberalism which helped release enterprise from the dead hands of the state and which allowed social energy to follow easily from 'the happy play of free minds, free markets, and Christian morality'. From 'this liberty to think, speak and worship, to inquire and invest, to buy cheap and sell dear, to accumulate and venture capital, to practise thrift and self-help' came the basis for English success at home and abroad.[142]

This mid-Victorian outlook on the world 'was suffused with a vivid sense of superiority, if with very good intentions':

> Upon the ladder of progress, nations and races seemed to stand higher or lower according to the proven capacity of each for freedom: the British at the top, followed a few rungs below by the Americans and other striving, go-ahead Anglo-Saxons. The Latin peoples were thought to come next, though far behind. Much lower still stood the vast Oriental communities of Asia and North Africa where progress appeared unfortunately to have been crushed for centuries by military despotism or smothered under passive relations. Lowest of all stood the aborigines who it is thought had never learned enough social discipline to pass from the family and tribe to the making of a state.[143]

While the Orient was considered stagnant because of its despotic system of government, Africa was regarded in the same way because it was still tribal and thus stateless or acephalous. Where the Hobbesian state of nature was rampant, there could be no progress because, it was assumed, all were against all.[144] Here then, and according to Malinowski, history was 'dead and buried', irrelevant mythology.[145]

For many imperial proconsuls and historians, colonial intrusion into such a 'stagnant pool' was necessary. It was intended to act 'as yeast and leaven the lump'. Such were the origins of jingoism and imperialist chauvinism.[146] The 'unhistorical African past' and the paternalism of the colonial period are among the assumptions which postcolonial Africanist historiography has sought to refute. The state has been considered crucial in restoring history to the hitherto unhistorical precolonial past.[147]

The 'historical sense', Cesaire and Fanon have observed, 'is, in the hands of the oppressed, a powerful tool for revolutionary mobilization'.[148] It was for this reason, then, that African institutions were robbed of their history in the colonial era, and it is for the same reason, it seems, that this history had to be restored following the demise of colonialism.[149] The search for states and their history was of particular importance because it offered 'precedents which justified the capacity and right of Africans to enter Nkrumah's long-awaited "political kingdom".' This search was intended to challenge the 'hamitic myth' which had dominated colonial historiography, and to show that the capacity to rule was not the monopoly of any particular race. Yet many of the unarticulated premises immanent in colonial historiography were incorporated into its postcolonial successor where discussions of precolonial states were concerned. Descriptions of state formations mainly concentrated on their origins, but these were portrayed in terms of cataclysmic processes. The distinction between state and stateless societies continued to be maintained.

State societies received more attention in the belief that they were richer in historical information. Thus whatever could be said for evolutionism or diffusionism, most of these ideas remained a camouflage for the empiricist ideology dominant in liberal historiography.[150]

The Trade Thesis

Studies of the state in precolonial African history have been conducted within the problematic of the enlargement of scale.[151] In this, the trade thesis has played a leading role.[152] Enlargement of scale has been regarded as the process of an increasing awareness of the outside world on the part of members of specific societies. The process varied from one member of society to another, and from one society to the next. The process seems to have been complex, but it is one which brought about differentiation, and so made 'modernization and deprivation . . . two sides of the same process'. 'The resulting tensions', it has been observed, 'provided much of the dynamic of (among others) Tanganyika's modern history, especially in the political sphere.'[153]

The relation of state formation to trade, which in postcolonial historiography has been regarded as synonymous with the economic base of society, was intended to show the ability of African initiative to enmesh outside forces or impositions from without into its own body politic. It was also intended to illustrate what has been called the 'politics of survival'. Thus Iliffe has observed with regard to the history of nineteenth-century Tanzania:

> It is a commonplace of African history that long-distance trade often encouraged large-scale political organization. Trade developed communications and created wealth to support central governments. Rulers used scarce goods to secure loyalty. Traders needed security and backed stability. They often lived in towns, which were relatively easy to govern, and possessed skills, especially literacy, which facilitated administration.[154]

Stability was assured by the fact that, besides the rule of arms, chieftainship in, for example, Tanzania was moving from ritual power towards bureaucratic organization and economic power, as the basis of leadership. Moreover, 'whereas in 1800 men generally obtained political office by birth, the nineteenth-century tendency was towards "emphasis on personal achievement and loyalty rather than kinship as a qualification for political office".' Such were the symptoms of 'bureaucracy and modernity' which have been regarded by historians as the basis for political stability and prosperity.[155]

Iliffe considers trade to have been a source of wealth which helped support central governments in the precolonial era. Two concepts are at stake here: trade (and in particular merchant capital), and the state. The concepts have wide implications. E. P. Thompson has noted apropos the state that, when we make an apparently simple statement like 'King Zed died in 1100', we are in fact offering a whole host of concepts and ramifications - kingship, relations of domination and subordination, functions and roles of office, charisma, magical endowments attaching to this role, and so forth.[156] Concepts have very wide ramifications, and these have to be tackled if the dialectical relationship of theory to reality is to be established. It is intended here to tackle the notion of trade and demonstrate its relationship to the state in East African precolonial social formations. This procedure is significant because there is no other way that the contradictions of appearance, as have been revealed time and again in discussions of the state, can be penetrated so as to reveal the essential contradictions. Empirical contradictions are important only because they are a pointer to reality. However, although the latter is determinant, the two are dialectically united.[157]

The existence of trade in any society implies production beyond the mere requirements of subsistence and reproduction of the conditions for maintaining the exploitative relations of production.[158] The existence of trade - and even more so merchant capital, as well as its personification in the figures of the merchants - 'requires merely that at least a portion of the products should be converted into commodities, and that money with its various functions should have developed along with trade in commodities'.[159] Such conditions, indeed, existed in East Africa. What has been written about African initiative in the commercial sphere together with the existence of entrepreneurship in precolonial East Africa attests to this.[160] Such conditions of commodity production coupled with the existence of merchant classes proved a fertile ground for the penetration of European merchant capital, or the articulation of this with regional and local merchant capital. Local forms of merchant capital, however, were soon subordinated to regional ones, especially Swahili and Arab, due to the credit facilities which the latter could enjoy from the Indian capital which was then based in Zanzibar.[161]

But, as we have seen, merchant capital is trading capital. Its characteristics have been summarized thus:

> Merchant capital, through its own development, cannot lead to industrial capital: 'The independent and predominant development of capital as merchant's capital is tantamount to non-subjection of production to capital, and hence capital developing on the basis of an alien social mode of production which is also independent of it. The independent development of merchant's capital, therefore, stands in inverse proportion to the general economic development of society.'[162]

Merchant capital is penned in the sphere of circulation. It adds nothing to what it circulates. It is dependent on the dominant mode of production. During the Roman period – to take one example – it relied on the slave mode of production; but in Medieval Europe it was attached to the feudal mode of production; and in Moghul India it fattened on the so-called Asiatic mode of production 'like the gods of Epicurus in the Intermundia, or like Jews in the pores of Polish society'.[163]

As trading capital, merchant capital is not rooted in the sphere of production; rather it is parasitical to it. It develops no independent economic or political base, but instead uses what it finds in existence. Since it adds nothing of value to the commodities which it helps circulate, it must 'buy cheap and sell dear' to secure profit. This entails controlling its source of commodities and the markets to which such commodities are destined. This gives merchant capital its monopolistic and monopsonistic character. It is a tendency which entails the establishment of social relations intended to control the social formations with which it trades, especially the state systems and merchant classes it finds *in situ*.[164] In the discussion which follows here, attention is focused on the impact of European merchant capital upon precolonial African state systems.

One characteristic of the precolonial state which has helped the penetration of merchant capital in precapitalist social formations is the fragmented nature of its sovereignty. This has forced leading local potentates to use the personification of merchant capital in the form of individuals or companies to help them control their subordinates – or vice versa, where the former were weak. The crucial point which has been stressed by Fox and Frykenberg in the case of Indian precapitalist social formations, and Southall as far as precolonial African states are concerned, is this:

> Pre-industrial agrarian states were often less than the sum of their parts. During the course of any dynasty, local strong men and disgruntled peasants threatened, or actually dissolved, the thin film of state hegemony which bound them to the central power. Industrial states created high levels of regional economic specialization and necessary interdependence not found in simpler technologies. Industrial states also have major communication and transport webs which cement local areas and regions to the central economic and governmental cores. Preindustrial agrarian states, however, are characterized by economically, and therefore potentially politically, self-sufficient regions – each with its own wider cultural distinctions of kinship, language, ritual observances and beliefs, customs, and 'manners'.[165]

Fox uses the preindustrial-industrial problematic, but the point is well made. Here, one finds that production is split up into small 'household-oriented peasant producers', and so too are the mechanisms of appropriation, as well as the instruments for reproducing such a process. The point to emphasize is that, while the 'state in Western political theory enjoys monopoly of coercive force in the society, and is the centre of administrative decisions and judicial reviews', that was not the case with precapitalist states. In the latter instance, 'administration was dispersed, sometimes resting with virtually autonomous or independent local overlords, and at other times with kin groups or civil servants.' The same argument applies to the process of extracting surplus in that 'many levels of local, regional, and finally central power-holders interceded between the cultivator and state autonomy.' Each power-holder had a share in the 'grain heap' in the village. Such power-holders were not paid for their services by the centre.[166] In industrial societies, on the other hand, local officials depended on the centre for their share of surplus, a condition which was underlined by the fact that the centre (in the Weberian sense) enjoyed a monopoly of coercive force.

Such then is the 'parcellization of sovereignty' – or splitting up of power – that exists pre-eminently in the 'segmentary state system'. The structure of power in precapitalist states was highly localized. This localization of power corresponded to the nature of production as well as appropriation, which was also very parochial. For this reason:

> Feudal kingdoms were precarious alliances; their true locus of power was at the base, in the hands of the local lords. The dialectic between the central authority and local power made it a complex polity. Anderson speaks of this as the 'parcellization of sovereignty'. He writes: 'Political sovereignty was never focused in a single centre. The functions of the state were disintegrated in a vertical allocation downwards, at each level of which political or economic relations were, on the other hand, integrated. This parcellization of sovereignty was constitutive of the whole feudal mode of production.'[167]

This then is the explanation for the instability of the precapitalist state and the alleged struggle for survival with which it has been associated.[168] This weakness was exploited ruthlessly by the agents of merchant capital.

Precolonial African states have traditionally been analysed along the continuum of enlargement of scale. This continuum has of late been dubbed historicist because those who subscribe to it, it is alleged, have failed to take full cognizance of the facts. Indeed it has been asserted that such a continuum was non-existent because while some empires rose, others fell, the more so along the African coast where the competition to participate in overseas trade was more intense than in the interior. But while this was true of the Congo empire, it was not so in the case of nineteenth-century Zanzibar. To be sure, one can go on pointing out such contradictory sets of facts for ever. Crucial, however, is their content: the social relations which constitute their core.[169] Some of these points can best be illustrated with the help of the actual histories of nineteenth-century Madagascar, Zanzibar, and Ukimbu in Western Tanzania.

The Case of Madagascar

The reaction of African rulers to mercantilist imperialism has intrigued many scholars, especially when considered in relation to state formation or political initiative. For many scholars, the period of mercantilist imperialism saw the rise of many states in Africa. This has been regarded as an aspect of political development, modernization and so on. The events of this period have been viewed as a clear indication of the 'African genius' in harnessing outside forces for the development of the continent. Indeed it has been argued that, had it not been for colonialism, the formation of the nation-state could have been realized much earlier, given the already constant tendency towards enlargement of scale within Africa.[170] This phenomenon aside, it is important to note the nature of the states which were formed or consolidated during the mercantilist era of African history, especially those which emerged along the African coast. Nineteenth-century Madagascar is a case in point.[171]

In the aftermath of the Berlin Conference which heralded the Scramble for Africa, the island of Madagascar became a French colony in 1896. This event was preceded by a long history of Franco-Malagasy association which began towards the middle of the seventeenth century. This period of association, which has also been called the era of informal imperial influence, had an extremely chequered history. As was common with European traders elsewhere, the French began their association with Madagascar as interlopers before the French East India Company built the settlement of Fort Dauphin in 1643, which nonetheless was short-lived. Even so, the island of Madagascar was for a long time regarded as a constituent part of the French East India Company's sphere of influence. To support this claim, medals bearing the inscription *Colonia Madagascarica* were issued in Paris in 1665.[172]

The French considered the island of Madagascar important because of its position as an 'external arena' for the plantation economy of the Mascarene Islands.[173] For these islands, Madagascar remained the chief source of slaves and food, commodities which were crucial for the survival of the sugar estates. Following the Anglo-French struggle for global hegemony in the aftermath of the French Revolution, the Mascarenes were brought under British imperial control; and although the Bourbon Island was again transferred to the French in 1815, the sister island of Mauritius remained under British control.[174] British presence in this area of the Indian Ocean increased the chances of the endeavour to abolish the slave trade between Mauritius and Madagascar. The presence also allowed the British to deepen relations of so-called 'legitimate' trade between the two islands, for as we have already noted, Madagascar was the chief source of food for Mauritius. Thus began a new era of Anglo-French rivalry for the domination of Madagascar.

The nineteenth-century history of Madagascar has been viewed as the meeting of two forces: one external and European, and the other internal and indigenous. We have already remarked that colonial historiography paid too much attention to the former type of force. Thus there emerged a postcolonial historiography which tended to stress the latter force. The fashion has become to emphasize the Malagasy point of view in the relations which emerged in the nineteenth century; to focus on 'Antananarivo rather than on London or Paris'. In this context Malagasy reactions have been seen as a series of adjustments and reforms to the growing complexity of 'the foreign structure erected over them'.[175]

The initial stages of permanent connections between Europe and Madagascar were established in the 1810s. In 1817 a 'treaty of friendship' was signed between the British and the Malagasy. The treaty was signed between Radama I, who was the King of Madagascar at that time, and the Governor of Mauritius, Sir Robert Farquhar. The treaty was intended to forestall undue French influence in Madagascar, to abolish the slave trade between Madagascar and the British colonial empire, and to ensure a reliable source of rice and meat for Mauritius.

This was the first treaty ever to be signed between a ruler of Madagascar and a foreign power, and its signatory, Radama I, believed that it would increase his chances of survival; for with it he hoped to obtain British support in his endeavour to bring the whole of Madagascar under his control, as well as to establish a reliable source of foreign aid with which to develop the island. Subsequent to the signing of the treaty, missionaries began to arrive on the island. As well as their evangelizing work, many of these new arrivals proved useful in matters of education and 'in a number of small but important industries'.[176] Radama I died in 1828 and was succeeded by Queen Ranavalona. The Queen was somewhat hostile to the British. In the following year Anglo-Malagasy relations turned sour, and the British agent on the island, James Hastie, was asked to leave the capital of the Merina Kingdom, Antananarivo. Queen Ranavalona was also not happy with the missionary work going on in Madagascar, for 'she noticed that, whenever any of her subjects embraced the new religion, they appeared to renounce their allegiance to her; and, instead they talked about, and every Sunday prayed to, one called "Jesus Christ". As the Queen and her advisers believed that Christ was the white man's ancestor, the government became convinced that, in embracing Christianity, the Malagasy were turning their backs to their own ancestors for the sake of those of the foreigners.' For this reason a decree forbidding the teaching of Christianity was issued in 1835. Many Malagasy Christians fled the island to places as far away as England.

Since relations between Madagascar and Europe (that is, France and England) were worsening, Queen Ranavalona decided to send an embassy abroad in 1836 to resolve the deadlock. Diplomacy, it has been said, was a method Malagasy rulers were to resort to time and again as a means of resolving conflict, since they 'realized that because of their weakness, *vis-a-vis* the great powers, the best way to live in peace with them was to talk, rather than to turn their backs, to their enemies.'[177] Not much, however, was gained by Ranavalona's diplomacy. In 1845 the Malagasy port of Tamatave was bombarded by an Anglo-French squadron on the instructions of the Governors of British Mauritius and French Bourbon. To add insult to injury, in 1857 two Frenchmen, Lambert and Laborde, attempted to overthrow Queen Ranavalona's government with a view to making her son, Radama II, the king of Madagascar.

The Queen died in 1861, and many people, it is said, sighed with relief. Indeed, a missionary called Ellis welcomed her death, noting that 'it has been contemplated by all who were interested in the welfare of the country' as a necessary condition for putting a stop to the 'oppression, cruelty, and fearful destruction of human life which had long afflicted that unhappy land, and had excited profound commiseration of all civilized communities.'[178] Ranavalona was succeeded by Radama II, and it has been asserted that the new King and his ministers could be called 'the men of the Age of Improvement, men who, unlike the older generation who had dominated the early part of

Queen Ranavalona I's reign, were willing to renew contacts with the outside world and accept foreigners in their country . . . . Men of "the Age of Improvement were those who", according to Iliffe, "sought to improve both the society and their own position by utilizing novel opportunities".'[179]

Radama II was anxious to open the country to European influence, and in this endeavour he was helped by Rahamiraka (a Christian convert who had sought refuge in Manchester during the reign of Queen Ranavalona) and a small group of the emerging Malagasy petty bourgeoisie who called themselves 'readers'. These were the product of missionary education, and they lived in and around the Malagasy capital of Antananarivo.

Radama II and his supporters took three measures to ensure increased Western penetration of Madagascar. They lifted the ban on Christians, undertook a diplomatic offensive to normalize relations with Britain and France, and indulged in what has been called an 'open door policy' to step up what in reality amounted to capitalist penetration of the island. The endeavour to intensify missionary activities in the island was an easy one, for since the ban of 1835 missionaries had been hovering in the wings ready to return to Madagascar as soon as conditions proved favourable. The King also sent a 'letter to the Pope, inviting Roman Catholic missionaries to come to Madagascar, and requesting the Pope's support for his government'.[180] To bring about a thaw in the relations between the people of Madagascar and the Europeans, emissaries were sent to England, France, and the islands of Mauritius and Bourbon. The Frenchman, Lambert, was sent to France and England. In France, he asked Napoleon III to declare Madagascar a French protectorate, and spend money to the tune of 200,000 francs so as to enhance French influence in Antananarivo. From Paris Lambert went to London, where he was well received, and Queen Victoria agreed to resume diplomatic relations with Madagascar. Thus 'the King . . . had taken the initiative, and he was now waiting for the response of the two governments and the missionaries. In the meantime, laws for the protection of foreigners were promulgated, and the routes between Tamatave and the capital were improved in anticipation of an influx of Europeans into the capital.'[181]

The British in Mauritius were the first to respond effectively. The Governor, Stevenson, sent Middleton to Antananarivo to restore the former good relations that had existed between the colony and Madagascar. He also urged the Colonial Office to safeguard the independence of Madagascar against French ambitions. Stevenson's initiative was understandable since Mauritius depended so much on Madagascar for 'bullocks, rice and other necessities of life'. Middleton was very well received by the Malagasy king, who told him that 'his whole wish was to extend trade, to know and honour the English, and do all he could to obtain their regard and friendship; that he looked upon the English as his greatest and truest friends, and that he very much wished to encourage English education.'[182]

The French soon followed in responding to the Malagasy overtures, but when they did so they found that the British were already entrenched at the Malagasy King's Court, a move which was not to their liking. The strength of

British influence in Madagascar was shown by the size of the dinner given to the French emissary, which was smaller than that which had been prepared for the British ambassador, Middleton. Nevertheless, both European powers soon appointed consuls to look after their interests. Pakenham was appointed the British Consul and Laborde the French one. Laborde was specifically instructed to pay special attention to the increasing British influence in Madagascar.

The third course of action which Radama II embarked on was that of opening the island to European economic interests. This was done by granting concessions to Europeans, the most important of which was the Lambert Charter. Radama II believed that the granting of such a charter would be of help in 'developing' his country; the concession was granted to Lambert, giving him control of the whole of Northwest Madagascar, and was ratified in 1862. In this Charter, Lambert was authorized to form a company, with

> exclusive rights to exploit all the minerals in Madagascar; to acquire timber; cultivate lands on the coast as well as in the interior; make roads, canals, yard-buildings, and other works of public utility; . . . the right to select and acquire any land anywhere in Madagascar which the Company might desire for cultivation . . . . It would make coins for Madagascar; its exports and imports . . . were exempted from any taxation . . . (and the Company would pay the King 10 per cent of its profits).[183]

The Malagasy Government, on the other hand, agreed to assist the Company in all ways possible, especially in the procurement of labour. This, it was believed by those who favoured the formation of the Company, would 'help the Malagasy in their plans for the amelioration and civilization of their country'. This was what Radama II and his 'readers' understood by the concept of development.[184]

Many Europeans resident in Antananarivo believed that granting such concessions to their kith and kin was advantageous to the people of Madagascar. Thus the British Consul observed that for a 'country such as Madagascar, without the proper capital to develop the resources of the country, one had to look to the introduction of collective European capital and industry, and thereby bringing about material improvement likely to be followed by moral advancement.'[185] Remarks concerning 'mutual advantage' were also made by colonialists with regard to other parts of the world. Thus, in their relations with Brazil, the British time and again pointed out the advantages which allegedly accrued to both sides. The first round of commercial concessions was granted by Brazil to the British in 1808. Even the King of Portugal adhered to the 'balanced view' thesis, and consoled the Brazilians by remarking:

> Do not worry that the introduction of British goods might hurt your industry . . . . For now your capital is best applied to the cultivation of your lands . . . . Later you will advance to manufacture . . . . Experience

> will show you that expanding your agriculture need not totally destroy your manufactures; and if some of them are of necessity abandoned, you may rest assured that this is proof that this manufacture did not rest on a solid base and was of no real advantage to the state. In the end, there will result great national prosperity, much greater than you could get before.[186]

Satisfied with what she considered were just concessions, Britain gave the Portuguese monarch naval protection on his departure for Brazil in 1808. The concessions were ratified in 1810, and British manufactured goods were granted better tariff concessions in Brazil.[187] All this was, in reality, a process through which Brazil, a Portuguese colony, as well as Portugal herself, were being turned into a periphery of the British economy.[188]

Madagascar was worse off than Brazil. As if that were not enough, on Rahaniraka's death in 1862, Radama II appointed 'a crazy, drunken, unprincipled American', William Mark, his 'principal secretary of state for foreign affairs'.[189] Furthermore, Ellis, whom we have already mentioned, was given a bigger role in the administration of the island; and to cap it all, the King appointed the French Consul's son in Madagascar, Clement Laborde, as one of his secretaries for foreign affairs. Even the French government admitted that the King was going too far and ordered the cancellation of Clement Laborde's appointment in the foreign service of the Malagasy Government.

The 'Age of Improvement' proved a cause of frustration to many people in Madagascar, and in 1863 the Prime Minister, Rainivoninahitriniony, masterminded the assassination of Radama II and prepared the way for Queen Rasoherina's accession to the throne. Lambert's Charter was withdrawn, and in the same year, diplomatic missions were again sent to Paris and London to explain the changes in policy being effected in Madagascar. The British Government, the source says, was understanding, but the French Government was not. Eventually, however, there was some *rapprochement* and new treaties were signed with the two European powers. Western penetration was intensified, the Queen and the Prime Minister became Christians in 1869, and although between this year and the French annexation of the island in 1896 there were periods of conflict, this was not an obstacle to the increasing European influence. That was Madagascar's tragedy, notwithstanding her efforts to modernize.

Such it seems was Madagascar's 'urge to survive'. It has been concluded that a number of historical events in its nineteenth-century history showed 'the remarkable tenacity with which the Malagasy leaders pursued the policy aimed at opening their country to foreigners so as to secure benefits for the island', 'the desire and determination of the Malagasy leaders to utilize the knowledge and experience of the Europeans who came to live in their midst for the improvement of their way of life', and so on. But whether 'Madagascar wished to show the foreign powers that she was a "civilized" nation, worthy to be considered a member of the "comity of nations" is one thing';[190] the context within which this was done is another.

Europeans in Madagascar were continually involved in conflicts with the

Local Initiative: The Crisis from Within

Malagasy ruling hierarchy. Observers of the time, like Ellis, blamed the crises on the Malagasy rulers. The Lambert Charter, however, showed what Europeans in Madagascar wanted to see happen. The Europeans, many of whom were merchants, intended to control the Malagasy economy. As merchants they were not involved in actual production but in circulating commodities, an enterprise which entailed constant interference with the political system. Where there was involvement in production, the same proviso is also applicable. Interference in the political system tended to alienate some groups of people within the political hierarchy. This was a cause of friction between the Malagasy and the Europeans, which Ellis blamed on the former.

Modern liberal historians have attempted to counter assertions like those of Ellis by alleging that the Malagasy were as civilized as the Europeans, or that they were, at least, trying to catch up with Europeans. But such allegations tend to avoid the inarticulate premises found in imperialist chauvinism. Moreover, civilization is not an independent entity, like a piece of furniture to be appreciated independent of its surroundings or makers. Civilized or not, it is the context that is important.

To reap profits easily and quickly, the Malagasy kingdom was turned into a client state. The appointment of Europeans into the administration in the name of modernization and the urge to survive is quintessential.

The Case of Zanzibar

The Zanzibar story is not very different from that of Madagascar. Zanzibar grew famous in the nineteenth century, a period of increasing dominance by European merchant capital in the western region of the Indian Ocean basin. The establishment of a plantation economy in the Mascarene Islands intensified the association of those areas with Madagascar. The plantation system also stimulated the establishment of relations with the East African coast, firstly with Kilwa, and later with Zanzibar, which was to remain the centre of the East African slave trade until its abolition in 1873. The plantation system in Zanzibar depended on this kind of trade as well. Such commercial activity was augmented by the trade in cloves, which was largely destined for the Orient, and that in ivory, intended for the same region as well as for Europe.[191]

Around this kind of commercial activity various fractions of capital congregated. Locally, the leading fraction was that controlled by Indians of Bania caste extraction. It is normal practice in conventional textbooks to assert that the rise of Seyyid Said in Zanzibar was related to the class of Banias from Western India who controlled his Customs House and collected revenue with which to finance his administration. It has likewise been alleged that the rise of Zanzibar town depended on the Banias as well as on trade.[192] Suffice it to repeat that merchant capital is not productive capital and that the growth of Zanzibar 'was not the result of wealth accumulated by merchant capitalists resident there. On the contrary, merchants appear to have invested little money in social infrastructure.'

There was little urban development in Zanzibar before 1835, when the 'town' was still essentially a maritime trading post. 'Urban development on a large scale and the erection of substantial stone buildings occurred only with the transition to a plantation economy which took place after 1835.' Only then was surplus labour, appropriated from the countryside by the Arab aristocracy, allowed to finance the rise of 'a life of luxury and ease which occasioned a good deal of building'. Meanwhile merchant capitalists continued to pursue channels of 'unequal exchange' whenever and wherever possible, 'contenting themselves with investing only in the simple tools of their vocation and reinvesting the major part of their wealth into their business'.[193]

To pursue their career of buying cheap and selling dear effectively, the Bania merchants of Zanzibar attempted to control the Zanzibar social formation by their presence in the Customs House, which until 1857 was 'a mere shed (albeit a long one) with a mat roof and supported only by rough tree-stems' 'where hundreds of thousands of dollars changed hands annually'.[194] To the Arab aristocracy the Bania supplied credit. The use of the 'debt-trap' is an old one, and Zanzibar was no exception. True to the ethos of the cash-box, however, the Banias did not want to displace the Arab aristocracy in controlling land, lest their capital turned productive. Trade was still lucrative business. Only with the British colonization of Zanzibar, and the imposition of laws favourable to British merchant capital (laws intended deliberately to tame Indian capital) did the Bania merchants begin to invest in land. They might not have taken to drinking then; 'but now the hard times are with them: the golden age has been displaced by an iron one.'[195] As for the caravans which were sent into the interior of East Africa in search of commodities, the Bania merchants of Zanzibar controlled these by a credit system which proved superior to anything that the Arab and Swahili merchants could offer. Indeed, the latter two groups of traders were eventually subordinated to the Bania merchants.[196]

We have emphasized the primacy of production with a view to showing that it is the determinant sector of the economy. But this is not to depreciate the importance of the sphere of circulation with which production is dialectically united. Circulation or consumption gives 'the finishing stroke to production (and thus produces its opposite)', production.[197] This observation is valid also for the economy of Zanzibar in the nineteenth century. We have already remarked that the prosperity of the Bania merchants was dependent, among other things, on the plantation system established in the country during the nineteenth century. But such activity, and indeed the prosperity of the Bania merchants of Zanzibar, was made possible only by the rise of the capitalist world economy which was dominated by European capital. This capital, which was divided into various fractions (English, French, American, Belgian, and so forth), found its way into Zanzibar in the nineteenth century. Politically, this presence was enforced when the Sultan of Zanzibar was made to sign 'a series of "Amity and Commerce" treaties with the United States of America (1833), Great Britain (1839), and France (1844)'. The treaties were accompanied by the establishment of consulates in Zanzibar town 'for the protection of the above powers' commercial interests in East Africa and in the Indian Ocean'.[198]

But of all European nations, the British were still the leading economic power. This was shown by their dominant position in Zanzibar. Here they wanted to control not only the Bania merchants, who they claimed were British subjects, but also the Zanzibari state. The latter was eventually turned into a client state in order to allow easier penetration by British merchant capital, and later the taming of this fraction in the interest of British monopoly capital.[199] The rise of the Zanzibari empire was accompanied by its subordination to European capital. The Zanzibari state was no longer an isolated entity, but part of a broader world economy and an international division of labour which it was helping to perpetuate.[200]

The Case of Ukimbu, Western Tanzania

It has been asserted, at times vehemently, that nineteenth-century East Africa did not witness a disintegration of political systems, despite the Ngoni invasion and the slave trade. Rather, this period saw the rise of many empires. Research so far conducted attests to this observation. Such investigations were undertaken to dislodge the hitherto prevailing conventional wisdom that Africans were unable to build empires of their own, and also to show that imperial proconsuls did not have an easy task when they were establishing European colonial administration. Instead, they encountered viable African states which offered stiff resistance to colonial penetration and so induced the imperial proconsuls to compromise with a number of local potentates. This situation, it seems, offered many chances for 'local initiative in African history'.[201] Nyungu-ya-Mawe's empire of the *ruga ruga* in Ukimbu, Western Tanzania, has received similar attention, and largely for similar reasons. The following pages discuss this political system.[202]

Nyungu-ya-Mawe's empire of the *ruga ruga*, which was situated to the south of Fundikira's empire of Unyanyembe, and with which it was contemporaneous,[203] was founded in the latter half of the nineteenth century and disintegrated in the aftermath of the German colonial onslaught.[204] Like other nineteenth-century political systems which arose in Africa, Nyungu-ya-Mawe's empire has been interpreted variously. Most significantly it has been used to show 'the [African] intellectual capacity and political acumen to hold a million restive, diverse people together in one state - especially under the limitations imposed by pedestrian transport which characterized most of Sub-Saharan Africa before the twentieth century'.[205] This empire has also been analysed in relation to the long-distance trade of nineteenth-century East Africa, as well as to the Ngoni invasion. But this enterprise, too, was undertaken to show that Africans were not mere victims of their own history.[206] Such an enterprise stood as an example of the endeavour to view history from below. It has now been discovered, that this type of undertaking has many faults embedded in it.[207]

The name of the founder of the empire of the *ruga ruga* sounds somewhat strange. Nyungu-ya-Mawe literally means 'the pot of stone'. His lieutenants, *vatwale*, some of whom commanded his army of the *ruga ruga*, which was an army of mercenaries known as much for their valour as for their allegiance to

Nyungu-ya-Mawe himself, were known by equally fearsome names. These were, *inter alia*, Nzwala Mino ga Vanhu (Wearer of Human Teeth), Pundu ya Mbogo (Bull Buffalo), Nsikine (the Grinder), Kafupa Mugazi (Spitter of Blood), Kunia Vanhu (Vanquisher of Men), Hovela Mbesi (Vulture), Kadela Ka Msimba (Lion Skin), and Huzya (the Pacifier).[208] The *ruga ruga* also looked fearsome: 'On their heads they wore grisly trophies hacked from the bodies of the slain, and round their loins they wore a red cloth to which they pointed in battle shouting to their enemies: "This is your blood!" '[209]

The behaviour and appearance of Nyungu-ya-Mawe's empire of the *ruga ruga* induced contemporary observers to assess him from various perspectives.[210] For some he was 'the famous Nyungu', while for others he remained the 'Brigand Chief, terror of the Ngunda Mkali'.[211] Merchants who were engaged in long-distance trade also viewed him from these two different perspectives. On several occasions Nyungu-ya-Mawe disrupted the long-distance trade route which passed through Tabora. Yet he also depended on the same route for his supply of luxuries and weaponry. It was to merchants along this route that he sold his ivory, a commodity upon whose procurement he had declared a state monopoly.[212] Nyungu-ya-Mawe's ambivalence towards merchants is indicative of their status in African societies of the time. Merchants were still a parasitic lot, dependent on dominant modes of production, and to be persecuted or pampered as prevailing circumstances dictated.[213] The existence of merchants in precolonial societies has been used as indicative of the possibility that Africans might have become capitalist on their own account but for colonialism. The nature and characteristics of merchant capital, however, have already been discussed. In this section, therefore, we shall merely show its impact on Ukimbu social formation.

Nyungu-ya-Mawe controlled the procurement of ivory in Ukimbu. The ivory came in the form of tribute or from the surplus labour of gangs who were organized to hunt for it. The ivory was exchanged for 'firearms and the new forms of storable wealth, chiefly cloth and beads'.[214] Ivory was not the only form of surplus labour which Nyungu-ya-Mawe exchanged for the luxuries offered by long-distance trade. Moreover, most of the luxuries were distributed to his confidants in the army and administration.[215] But neither the army nor the administration could survive on the distribution of such luxuries or plunder alone. There had to be a more stable form of tribute collection directly linked to the mainstay of the Ukimbu economy, peasant agriculture.

To secure a stable supply of tribute, Nyungu-ya-Mawe embarked on a policy of placing the people of Ukimbu into large concentrations under the watchful eye of his administration. 'This new form of settlement facilitated the work of the conqueror, Nyungu-ya-Mawe, who set up in the 1870s an incipient if not actual centralized state system over most of Ukimbu, and exercised a tight economic control of hunting and trade.'[216] With the German occupation of Western Tanzania, Nyungu-ya-Mawe's 'fortified royal villages were dismantled'. 'As a result the Kimbu began to break away from these residential centres' or concentrations. By the 1920s 'the Kimbu were now living in "independent" settlements, breaking away from control of the chiefs, and building "family settlements consisting usually of four male householders at most".' There were attempts to reintroduce the village concentrations in the 1930s but the British colonial government was rebuffed. The concentrations were 'a failure from the start'. The Kimbu resented the constant 'exposure to regulations and control; in 1949 and 1951 there were massive movements away from Kipembawe concentration in protest against enforcement of agricultural and hunting rules'.[217]

The movement away from administrative control was also a phenomenon of the nineteenth century. Shorter has observed that the distribution of new forms of storable wealth caused 'on the one hand, a frequent change-over from matrilineal to patrilineal chiefship when they were successful; and on the other, the formation of more splinter chiefdoms'.[218] The establishment of village concentrations in Ukimbu was intended to intensify the exploitation of the Kimbu peasantry. As in other precapitalist social formations, the producers either owned their own means of production or had fairly easy access to them. The extraction of tribute, therefore, was not mediated by the market but by force coupled with the ideology of dependence: the strange name of the ruler of Ukimbu, Nyungu-ya-Mawe, as well as those of his lieutenants, were cases in point. The use of 'sympathetic magic' under the control of Nyungu-ya-Mawe is a pointer in the same direction.[219] The severe exploitation coupled with coercion to which the peasants of Ukimbu were subjected forced them to revolt. And the disgruntled members of the Ukimbu aristocracy capitalized on this situation by establishing splinter chiefdoms.

Such then was the nature of class struggle in Ukimbu. The founding of splinter chiefdoms did not improve the life of the ordinary people. Rather the movement of history here was cyclical. The poor on their own, however, did not succeed in bringing about a revolution. Even so:

> In modern history . . . all political struggles are class struggles and all class struggles for emancipation, despite their necessary political form (for every class, class struggle is a political struggle), turn ultimately on the question of economic emancipation. Therefore, here the state (the political order) is the subordinate element and civil society (the realm of economic relations) the decisive element.[220]

So it was with Ukimbu. The content of the politics of factionalism and formation of new chiefdoms in Ukimbu have to be related to the desire of Kimbu peasants to emancipate themselves from oppression and exploitation.

Merchant Capital and Violence

It has usually been argued that relations between foreign merchants and East African rulers in the precolonial period were amicable. This was allegedly because the number of Swahili and Arab merchants involved in trading with the interior was small, and the weapons which they could have used in the course of raiding African villages not very effective. But generalizations of this kind are very misleading. They are more ideological than realistic. They form part of the endeavour to humanize capital. *Utani*, a system of joking relationships between tribes which emerged during the mercantilist era and which was maintained in the colonial era due to the intensification of migrant labour, has been used to justify this claim of harmony; but, as it has also been observed, 'goodnatured jesting could degenerate into wholesale raiding for food on the part of the hungry travellers.'[221]

The merchant's heart is in his cashbox, and the merchants who operated in East Africa in the nineteenth century were no exception. Their ruthlessness was shown in the latter part of the century as the demand for ivory became more acute, and ivory itself more scarce. Tipoo Tip in the Manyema country, Eastern Zaire, harassed the people of the area with gangs of armed slaves, and decimated its population. 'Rumaliza copied this strategy around Lake Tanganyika after 1881, constructing a personal dominion by attacking and deposing African leaders, installing compliant successors or slaves, levying tribute, and establishing outposts of armed retainers.' Around Lake Nyasa there was Mwinyi Mtwana who set himself up as 'Chief of Mdaburu in the middle of the central caravan route'.[222] These people plundered the areas under their control and ruined them completely. The Manyema ran away from Eastern Zaire and were soon to be found all over the central route which ran from Ujiji, via Tabora, to Bagamoyo. Such were the origins of what eventually came to be called the 'Manyema slave trade detritus'.[223]

Elsewhere the plunder which ensued was not so detrimental, but authoritarianism was in the ascendant. This authoritarianism led to much instability, which took the form of revolts and secessions.[224] The poor had to part with a larger portion of their labour so as to allow the rulers and their aristocracies to buy some of the luxuries which merchants could offer. At times the latter were also turned into clients of merchant capital. These are some of the issues which must be taken into account when discussing the history of states during the mercantilist era in nineteenth-century East Africa – in particular, the changing of empires into client states of merchant capital and the increasing subjugation of the poor to the whims of their rulers and the machinations of alien traders.

The Failure Summed Up

This chapter has attempted to describe the crisis in what has been termed the African historiographical revolution. There is a sense in which the birth of professional Africanist history has been compared to the establishment of bourgeois scientific historiography in the nineteenth century. But while bourgeois scientific historiography comprised part of the epistemological rupture with scholasticism,[225] the African historiographical revolution was intended to perpetuate the bourgeois historiographical path. In this respect its declared break with colonial historiography is mythical, but it is a myth which has been useful in creating the illusion of independence with which the African petty bourgeoisies have liked to associate themselves. The current African endeavour to make a fetish of formal independence in the present epoch of imperialism is not restricted to the discipline of history. But it is appropriate at this juncture to note that professional Africanist history, on the conceptual level, remains a province of bourgeois history, despite all the pretensions which have so far been mustered in an effort to prove the contrary. It is no wonder, then, that the crisis of bourgeois history has also been felt in professional Africanist history.[226] Major decisions in professional Africanist history, after all, are more often than not made outside the continent.[227]

It has been said that, while departments of history in Africa should concentrate on collecting oral histories of tribes, those of Europe, as in the case of Tarzan and the *griot*, would offer the broad interpretations within which the tribal histories are to be conceptualized.[228] The collection of oral data is claimed to be the *forte* of professional Africanist history. This is so because, it is said, the African point of view cannot be captured otherwise; many Africans were inarticulate.[229] Thus the problem of Africanist history is reduced to a question of oral data, and its collection is made the *sine qua non* of writing this history. A book without a list of *griots* who were consulted is viewed with suspicion. Research in Africanist history becomes synonymous with collecting oral traditions. Problems of writing this history are often reduced to the complications of its collection.[230] European sources are blamed for being Eurocentric, a moralistic stance similar to blaming the poor for not being rich.[231]

If there was an African historiographical revolution, therefore, it is to be found in the reliance on oral history as a basis for professionalism. As usual, this was a reaction to assumptions found in colonial historiography. But it should not be forgotten that this method has been used extensively by the colonial school of anthropology which, some people claim, constituted the dawn of 'the African renaissance'.[232] A pioneer of African history, the Gold Coast missionary C. C. Reindorf, published a book in 1889 entitled *History of the Gold Coast and Asante* which 'covered three centuries and was based upon interviews with over two hundred individuals'.[233] The method of collecting oral traditions as a basis for writing African history does not seem so new after all.

As a technique of 'collecting and evaluating data', Africa has not in all probability offered a new method. Neither has it offered new 'principles of investigation and explanation in scientific practice'.[234] Moreover, there is no hope of such a breakthrough. If, as some of our Nigerian colleagues have maintained, there is no crisis in their craft, then it seems that it is restricted to the countries of the North Atlantic Basin. It has also been argued that there is no crisis in African archaeology, and that 'constant questioning of methodology is not a sign of crisis but of vitality, witnessed by the steadily increasing number of African archaeologists'. Indeed, more branches of African studies are being brought to light. The most recent of these is African public administration, for it has been discovered by scholars like A. H. M. Kirk-Greene that, whereas colonial administrators were born, successors to the colonial empire have to be bred.[235]

If, however, those are the specifics of West African history, the same thing cannot be said about East and Central African history. Here, it has already been admitted, there is a real crisis. The discovery of facts was taken too lightly. It was understood to be synonymous with history itself. Ranger has therefore called for a 'pragmatic response' to the crisis. For him crises are a challenge which, if arrested, help to establish the maturity of a discipline.[236] Even so, it should be noted, pragmatism is opportunistic.[237]

Nigerian professional historians' confidence that there is no crisis in their craft may best be explained in terms of their longer tradition in the field;[238] however, a number of them are beginning to pose such questions as 'How truly Nigerian is Nigerian history?'[239] And certainly, Yusufu Bala Usman's revealing Nigerian history indicates that there is in fact something wrong with the concepts and methodology which have hitherto been applied.[240]

References

1. L. Kapteijns, *African Historiography Written by Africans 1955-1973: The Nigerian Case*, Leiden 1977, pp. 2-3.
2. J. Todd, *The Conjurors*, London 1977, pp. 5-7.
3. D. Denoon and A. Kuper, 'Nationalist historians in search of a nation: the new historiography in Dar es Salaam', *African Affairs*, 69, 1970. T. O. Ranger, 'The new historiography in Dar es Salaam: an answer'; and D. Denoon and A. Kuper, 'The new historiography in Dar es Salaam: a rejoinder', *African Affairs*, 70, 1971.
4. T. O. Ranger (ed.), *Emerging Themes of African History*, Nairobi 1968.
5. T. O. Ranger, 'Towards a usable past', in C. Fyfe (ed.), *African Studies Since 1945*, London 1976.
6. Bonaventure Swai, 'Local initiative in African history: a critique', *Tanzania Zamani*, 19, 1977.
7. T. O. Ranger, 'How should we approach and assess African history?', African History Teachers' Seminar, University of Dar es Salaam, 20 December 1965, mimeo.
8. E. Gellner, 'Class before state: the Soviet treatment of African feudalism', *Arch. Europ. Sociol.*, XVIII, 1977.
9. T. O. Ranger, 'African attempts to control education in East and Central Africa 1900-39', *Past and Present*, 32, 1965.
10. A. Mafeje, 'The problem of anthropology in historical perspective: an inquiry into the growth of the social sciences', *Canadian Journal of African Studies*, 10, 1976.
11. D. H. Fischer, *Historians' Fallacies*, London 1971, p. 29. T. A. Climo and P. G. A. Howells, 'Cause and counterfactuals', *Economic History Review*, XXVII, 1974.
12. H. Bernstein and J. Depelchin, 'The object of African history: a materialist perspective', *History in Africa*, 5, 1978.

13. Mafeje, 'The problem of anthropology in historical perspective: an inquiry into the growth of social sciences'.
14. Ranger, 'Towards a usable past', p. 18.
15. *Ibid.*
16. *Ibid.*
17. Fyfe (ed.), *African Studies Since 1945*, p. 2. R. Olive, *African History for the Outside World*, London 1964. R. Cohen, 'Tarzan and development', *The Pan-Africanist*, 6, 1975.
18. V. Monteil, 'The decolonization of the writing of African history', in I. Wallerstein (ed.), *Social Change: The Colonial Situation*, New York 1966.
19. P. M. Kennedy, 'The decline of nationalistic history in the West 1900-1970', *Journal of Contemporary History*, 8, 1973.
20. J. S. Saul, 'Nationalism, socialism and Tanzanian history', L. Cliffe and J. S. Saul, *Socialism in Tanzania*, I, Nairobi 1972.
21. J. Iliffe (ed.), *Modern Tanzanians*, Nairobi 1973.
22. G. C. K. Gwassa, 'The German intervention and African resistance in Tanzania', in I. N. Kimambo and A. J. Temu (eds.), *A History of Tanzania*, Nairobi 1969. H. S. Meebelo, *Reaction to Colonialism*, Manchester 1971.
23. I. Henderson, 'The origins of nationalism in East and Central Africa: the Zambian case', *Journal of African History*, XI, 1970.
24. M. S. Tsomondo, 'Shona reaction and resistance to the European colonization of Zimbabwe (Rhodesia) 1890-1898: a case against colonial and revisionist historiography', University of New York n.d., mimeo.
25. C. C. Wrigley, 'Historicism in Africa: slavery and state formation', *African Affairs*, 70, 1971. See also J. Omer-Cooper, 'Kingdoms and villages: a possible new perspective in African history', Universities of East Africa, Social Science Conference 1968, mimeo.
26. G. S. Jones, 'History: the poverty of empiricism', R. Blackburn (ed.), *Ideology in Social Science*, London 1972.
27. Quoted by J. D. Bernal, *Science in History*, IV, Harmondsworth 1969, p. 108.
28. A. J. Dachs, 'Politics of collaboration: imperialism in practice'; R. H. Palmer, 'Johnston and Jameson: a comparative study in the imposition of colonial rule'; and M. L. Chanock, 'Development and change in the history of Malawi', all in B. Pachai (ed.), *The Early History of Malawi*, London 1972.
29. D. A. Low, *Lion Rampant*, London 1974, p. 8.
30. J. Robinson, *Freedom and Necessity*, London 1970.
31. E. Hobsbawm, quoted by C. Henfrey, 'The invisible age', *Race and Class*, Vol. VIII, 1976.
32. R. E. Robinson, 'Non-European foundations of European imperialism: sketch for a theory of collaboration', in R. Owen and B. Sutcliffe (eds.), *Studies in the Theory of Imperialism*, London 1972.
33. C. van Onselen, 'The role of collaborators in the Rhodesian mining industry 1900-1935', *African Affairs*, 72, 1973. F. Houtart, 'Non-socialist societies of South and East Asia', *Social Scientist*, 4, 1976. T. O. Ranger, *The African Churches in Tanzania*, Nairobi 1972.
34. R. Heussler, *Yesterday's Rulers*, Syracuse 1963. A. P. Thornton, *The*

Imperial Idea and Its Enemies, London 1965. Although the British have claimed that they were the best imperial empiricists, it has been observed that even the latest comers to the process of colonial enlightenment, the Germans, had no overall system of governance. Togo was predominantly a peasant economy, Tanganyika was dominantly so, and South West Africa a settler economy. L. H. Gann and P. Duignan, *The Rulers of German Africa 1884-1914*, Stanford 1977.

35. R. E. Frykenberg, *Guntur District 1788-1848*, Oxford 1965, p. 10.
36. Quoted by C. Ehrlich, 'Some social and economic implications of paternalism in Uganda', *Journal of African History*, IV, 1963, p. 275.
37. P. A. Cohen, 'Ching China: confrontation with the West 1850-1900', in J. B. Crowley (ed.), *Modern East Asia*, New York 1970.
38. P. H. M. van den Dungen, 'Changes in status and occupation in nineteenth-century Punjab', in D. A. Low (ed.), *Soundings in Modern South Asian History*, London 1968.
39. E. Stokes, review of D. A. Low, *Lion Rampant* (London 1973), in *Journal of Commonwealth and Comparative Politics*, XII 1974, p. 231.
40. However, see I. Meszaros, *Marx's Theory of Alienation*, London 1975.
41. A. H. M. Kirk-Greene, 'Public administration in African studies', in Fyfe (ed.), *African Studies Since 1945*.
42. W. Rodney, *How Europe Underdeveloped Africa*, London 1972.
43. R. H. Davis, 'Interpreting the colonial period in African history', *African Affairs*, 72, 1973.
44. C. W. Williams, 'ANU elitist?' *Woroni*, Canberra 1973.
45. T. O. Ranger, *The Recovery of African Initiative in Tanzanian History*, Dar es Salaam 1969.
46. J. F. A. Ajayi, *Christian Missions in Nigeria 1841-1891*, London 1965.
47. D. Denoon and A. Kuper, 'Nationalist historians in search of a nation: the new historiography in Dar es Salaam'.
48. Dachs, 'Politics of collaboration: imperialism in practice'.
49. Kennedy, 'The decline of nationalist history in the West 1900-1970'.
50. Wrigley, 'Historicism in Africa'.
51. J. D. Fage, 'Slavery and the slave trade in the context of West African history', in J. G. Roland (ed.), *Africa: the Heritage and the Challenge*, Greenwich, Conn., 1974.
52. P. D. Curtin, *The Dimensions of the Atlantic Slave Trade*, Madison 1969. W. Rodney, *West Africa and the Atlantic Slave Trade*, Nairobi 1970. E. A. Alpers, *The East African Slave Trade*, Nairobi 1967.
53. Fage, 'Slavery and the slave trade in the context of West African history'.
54. A. C. Unomah, 'Commerce and political centralization in Unyamvezi: Tanzania 1800-1890', University of Ibadan 1978, mimeo.
55. A. D. Roberts (ed.), *Tanzania Before 1900*, Nairobi 1969.
56. A. M. H. Sheriff, 'Tanzania societies at the time of the partition', University of Dar es Salaam 1974, mimeo.
57. C. C. Wrigley, review of E. A. Brett, *Colonialism and Underdevelopment in East Africa* (London 1973), in *African Affairs*, 74, 1975.
58. C. B. Macpherson, *The Political Theory of Possessive Individualism*, London 1962.
59. Wrigley, review of E. A. Brett, *op. cit.*

60. J. M. Lonsdale, 'The emergence of African nations', in Ranger (ed.), *Emerging Themes of African History*.
61. Wrigley, 'Historicism in Africa'.
62. Omer-Cooper, 'Kingdoms and villages'.
63. A. M. H. Sheriff, 'The Rise of a commercial empire: an aspect of economic history of Zanzibar 1770-1873', PhD thesis, London University 1971. See also W. Rodney, 'European activities and African reaction in Angola', in T. O. Ranger (ed.), *Aspects of Central African History*, London 1968.
64. J. Petras, 'Popperism: the scarcity of reason', *Science and Society*, 30, 1966. c. M. Lightfoot, *Racism and Human Survival*, New York 1972.
65. E. H. Carr, *What is History?*, London 1962. See also A. Bullock, *Is History Becoming a Social Science?*, Cambridge 1976.
66. K. Popper, *The Poverty of Historicism*, I, London 1972.
67. For a critique of Popper see M. Cornforth, *The Open Philosophy and the Open Society*, New York 1976.
68. Bullock, *Is History Becoming a Social Science?*
69. Ranger, *The Recovery of African Initiative in Tanzanian History*.
70. C. Hill, *The Intellectual Origins of the English Revolution*, Oxford 1965.
71. C. L. R. James, *The Black Jacobins*, New York 1963.
72. Fischer, *Historians' Fallacies*, pp. x-xi.
73. A. Briggs, 'High noon and sunset: perspective of empire', *Encounter*, XXXV, 1970, p. 87.
74. *Ibid*.
75. R. Heussler, *Yesterday's Rulers*.
76. R. Robinson and J. Gallagher, *Africa and the Victorians*, New York 1961.
77. Low, *Lion Rampant*.
78. *Ibid*.
79. W. D. McIntyre, *The Imperial Frontier in the Tropics 1865-75*, London 1967.
80. J. D. Hargreaves, 'Biography and the debate about imperialism', *Journal of Modern African Studies*, 2, 1964.
81. Stokes, reviewing Low, *op. cit.*
82. E. S. Atieno-Odhiambo, 'Some reflections on African initiatives in early colonial Kenya', *East African Journal*, 8, 1971, p. 30.
83. J. F. A. Ajayi, 'The continuity of African institutions under colonialism', in Ranger (ed.), *Emerging Themes of African History*.
84. Quoted by Ehrlich, 'Some social and economic implications of paternalism in Uganda'.
85. S. Marks, *Reluctant Rebellion*, Oxford 1970. For an admirable discussion of Social Darwinism in the era of monopoly capitalism, see G. M. Fredrickson, *The Black Image in the White Mind*, New York 1971.
86. K. Lowith, *Meaning in History*, Chicago 1960, pp. 1-6.
87. H. Tinker, 'Continuity and change in Asian studies', *Modern Asian Studies*, 3, 1969.
88. P. Ehrensaft, 'The political economy of informal empire in precolonial Nigeria', *Canadian Journal of African Studies*, IV, 1972.
89. A. Gerschenkron, *Continuity in History and other Essays*, Cambridge, Mass., 1968.
90. B. Davidson, *East and Central Africa to the Late Nineteenth Century*,

Nairobi 1970.
91. J. Iliffe, 'The recent historiography of 19th and 20th century Tanganyika', SOAS 1972, mimeo.
92. I. N. Kimambo, 'Historical research in Tanzania', University of Dar es Salaam, 1968, mimeo.
93. Davidson, *East and Central Africa to the Late Nineteenth Century*.
94. P. J. O'Brien, 'A critique of Latin American theories of dependency', in I. Oxaal, T. Barnett and D. Booth (eds.), *Beyond the Sociology of Development*, London 1975.
95. Rodney, *How Europe Underdeveloped Africa*, p. 243.
96. E. Isichei, 'The development of underdevelopment: some relevant debates among historians', Universities of East Africa Social Science Conference 1970, mimeo.
97. R. M. A. van Zwanenberg, *Colonial Capitalism and Labour in Kenya 1919-1939*, Nairobi 1975, p. xv.
98. T. Szentes, *Underdevelopment and Socialism*, Dar es Salaam 1970.
99. H. Bernstein, 'Sociology of underdevelopment vs sociology of development', in H. Bernstein, D. Cruise O'Brien and W. Nafziger, *Development Theory: Three Critical Essays*, London 1978.
100. G. Kay, *Development and Underdevelopment*, London 1975.
101. A. M. H. Sheriff, 'The development of underdevelopment: the role of international trade in the economic history of the East African coast before the sixteenth century', University of Dar es Salaam 1973, mimeo.
102. G. T. Mishambi, 'The mystification of African history: a critique of Rodney's *How Europe Underdeveloped Africa*, University of Dar es Salaam 1976, mimeo.
103. S. Amin, 'Accumulation and development: a theoretical model', *Review of African Political Economy*, I, 1974.
104. Quoted by Bernstein, 'Sociology of underdevelopment versus sociology of development'.
105. *Ibid.*
106. H. Kjekshus, *Ecology Control and Economic Development in East African History*, London 1977.
107. Ranger, *The Recovery of African Initiative in Tanzanian History*, p. 12.
108. Chanock, 'Development and change in the history of Malawi'.
109. Palmer, Johnston and Jameson, 'A comparative study in the imposition of colonial rule'.
110. Kjekshus, *Ecology Control and Economic Development in East African History*.
111. Wrigley, review of E. A. Brett, *op. cit.*
112. E. A. Alpers, 'Rethinking African economic history: a contribution to the discussion of roots of underdevelopment', *Kenya Historical Review*, I, 1973.
113. Quoted by Rodney, *How Europe Underdeveloped Africa*.
114. E. A. Alpers, *Ivory and Slaves in East and Central Africa*, London 1975.
115. W. Rodney, review of R. Gray and D. Birmingham (eds.), *Precolonial African Trade* (London 1970), in *Transafrican Journal of History*, 2, 1972.
116. For the so-called development brought by the Portuguese slave trade in Congo see J. Depelchin, 'African history and the ideological

reproduction of exploitative relations of production', *Africa Development*, II, 1977.
117. C. Keyder, 'Concepts and terms: surplus', *Journal of Peasant Studies*, 2, 1975.
118. H. Bernstein, 'Concepts for the analysis of contemporary peasantries', University of Dar es Salaam 1978, mimeo.
119. A. M. H. Sheriff, 'The development of underdevelopment in the economic history of the East African coast before the sixteenth century'. See also C. Leys, *Underdevelopment in Kenya*, London 1975.
120. K. Marx, *Capital*, III, Moscow 1975, pp. 232-7.
121. R. Mukherjee, *The Rise and Fall of the East India Company*, Berlin 1958. See also I. Wallerstein, *The Modern World System*, New York 1974.
122. K. Marx, *Grundrisse*, Harmondsworth 1973, pp. 100-101.
123. Wrigley, *op. cit.*
124. Bonaventure Swai, 'The colonial Leviathan and Kenya' in A. J. Temu and Bonaventure Swai (eds.), *Kenya under Colonial Rule*, London forthcoming.
125. D. D. Kosambi, *An Introduction to the Study of Indian History*, Bombay 1975, p. xiii.
126. H. Bernstein, 'Marxism and African history: Endre Sik and his critics', *Kenya Historical Review*, 5, 1977.
127. D. D. Kosambi, *An Introduction to the Study of Indian History*.
128. E. D. Genovese, *In Red and Black*, New York 1968.
129. J. Wenstein, 'Can a historian be a socialist revolutionary?', in B. W. Cook, A. K. Harris and R. Radosh (eds.), *The Past Imperfect*, II, New York 1973.
130. H. Bernstein, 'Underdevelopment and the law of value', *Review of African Political Economy*, 6, 1976.
131. For an example of history studied from the 'bottom up' see B. J. Bernstein (ed.), *Towards a New Past*, New York 1969.
132. E. E. Thorpe, *Negro Historians in the United States*, Baton Rouge 1958.
133. Engels, as quoted by G. Antalffy, *Basic Problems of State and Society*, Budapest 1974.
134. Cf. E. D. Genovese, *Roll, Jordan, Roll*, New York 1974, p. xvi.
135. E. D. Genovese, *In Red and Black*.
136. E. D. Genovese, *The Political Economy of Slavery*, London 1966. See also his very important work entitled *The World the Slaveholders Made*, New York 1969.
137. T. Nairn, 'The English working class', in R. Blackburn (ed.), *Ideology in Social Science*, London 1973.
138. Thornton, *The Imperial Idea and its Enemies*.
139. A substantial part of the following section is extracted from a paper by Bonaventure Swai entitled 'Precolonial states and European merchant capital in Eastern Africa' read at the Kenya Historical Association's Annual Conference, 1979.
140. S. Avineri (ed.), *Karl Marx on Colonialism and Modernization*, p. 11.
141. R. Robinson and J. Gallagher, *Africa and the Victorians*. L. Billet, 'Political order and economic development: reflections on Adam Smith's *Wealth of Nations*' *Political Studies*, XXIII, 1975. C. B. Macpherson,

The Political Theory of Possessive Individualism: Hobbes to Locke, London 1962; see also his The Real World of Democracy, Oxford 1966. P. M. Blau, Exchange and Power in Social Life, New York 1964.
142. Robinson and Gallagher, Africa and the Victorians, p. 2.
143. Ibid., p. 203.
144. Bonaventure Swai, 'The colonial Leviathan and Kenya', in A. J. Temu and Bonaventure Swai (eds.), Kenya under Colonial Rule.
145. Quoted by O. Onoge, 'The counter-revolutionary tradition in African studies: the case of applied anthropology', Nigerian Journal of Economic and Social Studies, 15, 1973, p. 329.
146. Robinson and Gallagher, Africa and the Victorians. P. M. Kennedy, 'The decline of nationalistic history in the West 1900-1970', Journal of Contemporary History, 8, 1973.
147. Bonaventure Swai, Antinomies of Local Initiative in African History, Dar es Salaam 1979. See also Swai, 'Local initiative in African history: a critique', Dar es Salaam 1977, mimeo.
148. Onoge, op. cit. See also his 'Towards a Marxist sociology of African literature', Dar es Salaam 1977, mimeo. J. Blaut, 'Are Puerto Ricans a national minority?', Monthly Review, 29, 1977.
149. F. Fanon, The Wretched of the Earth, Harmondsworth 1965.
150. A. Kuper, Anthropologists and Anthropology, Harmondsworth 1972. J. C. Miller, Kings and Kinsmen, Oxford 1976. B. Davidson, Lost Cities of Africa, Boston 1959; and The African Slave Trade, Boston 1961. R. Olive and G. Mathew (eds.), History of East Africa, I, Oxford 1963. I. N. Kimambo and A. J. Temu (eds.), A History of Tanzania, Nairobi 1969. A. D. Roberts (ed.), Tanzania Before 1800, Nairobi 1968. I. N. Kimambo, A Political History of the Pare, Nairobi 1969. J. S. Saul, 'Nationalism, socialism and Tanzanian history', L. Cliffe and J. S. Saul (eds.), Socialism in Tanzania, I, Nairobi 1972. R. Coupland, East Africa and its Invaders, Oxford 1974. P. Mitchell, African Afterthoughts, London 1954. A. M. H. Sheriff, 'Tanzanian societies at the time of the partition', Dar es Salaam 1974, mimeo.
151. Roberts (ed.), Tanzania Before 1800.
152. R. Menon, 'Zanzibar in the nineteenth century: aspects of urban development in an East African coastal town?' MA thesis, UCLA 1978. S. Lemelle, 'Class struggles in precolonial Africa', Maji Maji, 37, 1970.
153. J. Iliffe, A Modern History of Tanganyika, Cambridge 1979, pp. 1-2. G. and M. Wilson, The Analysis of Social Change, Cambridge 1968. Roberts (ed.), Tanzania Before 1800.
154. Iliffe, A Modern History of Tanganyika, pp. 52-3.
155. Ibid. See also Roberts (ed.), Tanzania Before 1800. Low, Lion Rampant. J. Depelchin, review of I. Wilks, Asante in the Nineteenth Century (Cambridge 1975), in Africa Development, II, 1977.
156. E. P. Thompson, The Poverty of Theory and other Essays, London 1978.
157. L. Seve, Man in Marxist Theory, Hassocks, Sussex, 1978.
158. E. Mandel, Marxist Economic Theory, London 1971.
159. K. Marx, Capital, I, Moscow 1971, p. 83.
160. W. Rodney, reviewing R. Gray and D. Birmingham (eds.), Precolonial African Trade (London 1970), in Transafrican Journal of History, I, 1971. E. A. Alpers, Ivory and Slaves in East Central Africa, London

1974; see also his *The East African Slave trade*, Nairobi 1967. J. E. G. Sutton, *Early Trade in Eastern Africa*, Nairobi 1973. A. C. Unomah, 'Vbandevba and political change in a Nyamwezi kingdom', Universities of East Africa Social Science Conference 1970, mimeo.

161. E. A. Alpers, *Ivory and Slaves in East Central Africa*. P. Curtin, S. Feierman, L. Thompson and J. Vensina, *African History*, London 1978. Bonaventure Swai, 'East India Company and the Moplah merchants of Tellicherry', *Social Scientist*, 7, 1979. D. Bryceson, 'Peasant food production and food supply in relation to the historical development of commodity production in precolonial and colonial Tanganyika', Dar es Salaam 1978, mimeo. R. E. Dumett, 'John Sarbah the elder and African mercantile entrepreneurship in the Gold Coast in the late nineteenth century', *Journal of African History*, 14, 1973.

162. K. Marx, *Capital*, III, Moscow 1974, p. 322. Quoted by I. Habib, 'Potentialities of capitalist development in the economy of Moghul India', *Journal of Economic History*, XXIX, 1969, p. 75.

163. Marx, *Capital*, I, p. 83.

164. See also R. Mukherjee, *The Rise and Fall of The East India Company*, Berlin 1957; B Davey, *The Economic Development of India*, Nottingham 1975; L. M. Hacker, *The Triumph of American Capitalism*, New York 1959; W. A. Williams, *The Contours of American History*, New York 1973; D. W. Nabudere, *The Political Economy of Imperialism*, London 1976. J. Overbeck, 'Mercantilism, physiocrasy and population', *South African Journal of Economics*, 41, 1973.

165. R. G. Fox, *Kin, Clan, Raja and Rule*, Berkeley 1971, pp. 8-9. See also R. E. Frykenberg, 'Traditional process of power in South India: an historical analysis of local influence', *Indian Economic and Social History Review*, I, 1963; and A. Southall, 'A critique of the typology of states and political systems', in M. Banton (ed.), *Political Systems and the Distribution of Power*, London 1968.

166. P. Anderson, *Lineages of the Absolutist State*, London 1974. H. Alavi, 'India and the colonial mode of production', *Socialist Register*, 1975. Bonaventure Swai, 'Notes on the colonial state with reference to 18th and 19th century Malabar', *Social Scientist*, 6, 1978.

167. See also C. Keyder, 'The dissolution of the Asiatic mode of production', *Economy and Society*, 5, 1976.

168. Iliffe, *A Modern History of Tanganyika*.

169. C. C. Wrigley, 'Historicism in Africa: slavery and state formation'. J. D. Fage, 'Slavery and the slave trade in the context of West African history'. J. Omer-Cooper, 'Kingdoms and villages: a possible new perspective in African history'. A. J. Hanna, *The Beginning of Nyasaland and North-Eastern Rhodesia*, Oxford 1956.

170. F. M. Mutibwa, *The Malagasy and the Europeans*, London 1974.

171. This section is based on Swai's 'On the international behaviour of precolonial states in the age of capital', Dar es Salaam 1977, mimeo.

172. R. K. Kent, 'How France acquired Madagascar', *Journal of African History*, X, 1968.

173. The term 'external arena' is borrowed from I. Wallerstein, *The Modern World-System*, New York, 1974.

174. Kent, 'How France acquired Madagascar'.

175. Mutibwa, *op. cit.* See also his 'Trade and economic development in nineteenth-century Madagascar', *Transafrican Journal of History*, II, 1972.
176. *Ibid.*
177. *Ibid.*
178. *Ibid.*
179. *Ibid.*
180. *Ibid.*
181. *Ibid.*
182. *Ibid.*
183. *Ibid.*
184. *Ibid.*
185. *Ibid.*
186. *Ibid.*
187. *Ibid.*
188. *Ibid.*
189. *Ibid.*
190. *Ibid.*
191. D. Arnold, 'External factors in the partition of East Africa', Dar es Salaam 1974, mimeo. H. A. C. Cairns, *Prelude to Imperialism*, London 1965. J. Gallagher and R. Robinson, 'The imperialism of free trade', in C. H. Nadel and P. Curtis (eds.), *Imperialism and Colonialism*, New York 1964. See also their 'The partition of Africa', in *The New Cambridge Modern History*, XI, Cambridge 1962. R. M. A. van Zwanenberg, 'Anti-slavery, the ideology of 19th century imperialism in East Africa', *Hadith*, 5, 1975. R. D. Wolff, 'British imperialism and the East African slave trade', *Science and Society*, 36, 1972. J. S. Galbraith, *Mackinnon and East Africa 1878-95*, Cambridge 1972. C. S. Nicholls, *The Swahili Coast*, London 1971. D. MacLean, 'Finance and informal empire before the First World War', *Economic History Review*, XXIX, 1976. A. H. M. Sheriff, 'The rise of the Zanzibar commercial empire', PhD thesis, London 1971.
192. Z. Marsh and G. W. Kingsnorth, *An Introduction to the History of East Africa*, Cambridge 1965. L. W. Hollingsworth, *Zanzibar Under the Foreign Office*, London 1953.
193. Menon, 'Zanzibar in the nineteenth century'.
194. *Ibid.*, p. 12.
195. I. G. Shivji, *Class Struggles in Tanzania*, London 1975.
196. *Ibid.* I. Shivji, *Class Struggles in Tanzania*, London 1975. A. M. H. Sheriff, 'The Zanzibar peasantry under imperialism 1873-1964', in E. Ferguson and A. M. H. Sheriff, *Zanzibar Under Colonial Rule*, London, forthcoming. Bonaventure Swai, 'The colonial state: a study of its establishment in Zanzibar'. J. E. Flint, 'Zanzibar 1890-1950', in V. Harlow and E. M. Chilver (eds.), *History of East Africa*, II, Oxford 1965. H. S. Newman, *Banani*, New York 1969. G. Kay, *Development and Underdevelopment*, London 1975. J. Gray, *History of Zanzibar from the Middle Ages to 1856*, London 1962.
197. Iliffe, *A Modern History of Tanganyika*.
198. K. Marx, *Grundrisse*, Harmondsworth 1972; quoted by W. Suchting, 'Marx on the dialectics of production and consumption', *Social Praxis*,

199. J. Depelchin, 'Political economy of Zanzibar 1870-1914', in Ferguson and Sheriff, *Zanzibar under Colonial Rule*.
200. Mangat, *Asians in East Africa*, Oxford 1969.
201. N. Bukharin, *Imperialism and World Economy*, New York 1973. R. Jenkins, *Exploitation*, London 1971. J. M. Rosenau, 'Pre-theories and theories of foreign policy', R. B. Farrell (ed.), *Approaches to Comparative and International Relations*, Evaston, Ill., 1966. H. Morgenthau, *Politics and Nations*, New York 1967. H. K. Girvetz, *The Evolution of Liberalism*, New York 1966.
202. T. O. Ranger, *The Recovery of African Initiative in African History*, Dar es Salaam 1969. See also his 'Connections between primary resistance movements and modern mass nationalism in East and Central Africa', *Journal of African History*, IX, 1968.
203. For an excellent and new way of discussing precolonial African kingdoms see J. J. Guy, 'Production and exchange in the Zulu kingdom', *Journal of Southern African Historical Studies*, II, 1978.
204. A. C. Unomah, 'Commerce and political centralization in Unyamwezi, Tanzania 1800-1890', Ibadan 1978, mimeo.
205. A. Shorter, *Nyungu-ya-Mawe*, Nairobi 1968.
206. R. G. Armstrong, 'The development of kingdoms in Negro Africa', *Journal of the Historical Association of Nigeria*, II, 1960.
207. For a detailed discussion of Ukimbu see A. Shorter, 'Ukimbu and the Kimbu chiefdoms of Southern Unyamwezi', D.Phil. thesis, Oxford 1968.
208. M. L. Chanock, 'Development and change in the history of Malawi'. For the broader intellectual context in which this debate has been taking place, see G. Haupt, 'Why the history of the working-class movement?' *Review*, II, 1978; E. Hobsbawm, 'Labour history and ideology', *Journal of Social History*, VII, 1974.
209. A. Shorter, 'Nyungu-ya-Mawe and the empire of the *ruga ruga*', *Journal of African History*, IX, 1968.
210. A. Shorter, 'Kimbu', Oxford 1967, mimeo.
211. Shorter, 'Nyungu-ya-Mawe and the empire of the *ruga ruga*'.
212. *Ibid.*
213. Cf. Habib, *op. cit.*
214. Shorter, 'Kimbu'.
215. *Ibid.*
216. Shorter, 'Ukimbu and the Kimbu chiefdoms of Southern Unyamwezi'. See also T. O. Ranger, 'Historical studies of rural development in Tanzania', East African Academy Symposium 1968.
217. *Ibid.*
218. Shorter, 'Kimbu'.
219. *Ibid.* See also Davey, *op. cit.*
220. F. Engels, *Ludwig Feuerbach and the End of Classical German Philosophy*, Peking 1979, p. 47. Quoted by S. Lemelle, 'Political and economic implications of trade in 19th century Bembalanda', Los Angeles 1977, mimeo.
221. D. Bryceson, 'Peasant food production and food supply . . .', p. 9. See also S. Lucas, *Utani Relationships in Tanzania*, Dar es Salaam, 1974.
222. Iliffe, *A Modern History of Tanganyika*.

223. J. M. Lonsdale, 'Origins of nationalism in East Africa', *Journal of African History*, Vol. X, 1968.
224. N. N. Luanda, 'The dilemma of the Third World worker', Dar es Salaam 1979, mimeo. P. Redmond, 'Songea Ngoni', *Tanzania Zamani*, 12, 1973.
225. G. Novack, *Empiricism and its Evolution*, New York 1971.
226. M. O. Ojiaku, 'Traditional African social thought and Western scholarship', *Presence africaine*, 90, 1974.
227. G. Connell-Smith and H. A. Lloyd, *The Relevance of History*, London 1972.
228. Fyfe, Introduction, *op. cit.*
229. Ranger, *Recovery of African Initiative.*
230. W. Rodney, *A History of the Upper Guinea Coast 1545-1800*, Oxford 1970, p. viii.
231. Kimambo, 'Historical research in Tanzania'. Iliffe, 'The recent historiography of 19th and 20th century Tanganyika'.
232. W. Rodney, *A History of the Upper Guinea Coast 1545-1800.*
233. Depelchin, 'African History', *op. cit.*
234. Kapteijns, *African Historiography, op. cit.*
235. Bernstein and Depelchin, 'The Object of African History', *op. cit.*
236. Fyfe, Introduction in *op. cit.*
237. Ranger, 'Towards a usable past', *op. cit.*
238. H. K. Wells, *Pragmatism*, New York 1957.
239. Kapteijns, *op. cit.*
240. T. Hodgkin, 'Where the paths began . See also Y.B. Usman, 'History, tradition and reaction: the perception of Nigerian history in the 19th and 20th centuries', Ahmadu Bello University public lecture, 27 April 1977. See also his 'Transformation of Katsina C. 1796-1903: The overthrow of the Sarauta system and the establishment and evolution of the Emirate', PhD thesis, Department of History, Ahmadu Bello University 1974. Also Tukur, M. M., 'The Imposition of British Colonial Domination on the Sokoto Caliphate, Borno and Neighbouring States: A Reinterpretation of the Colonial Sources', PhD thesis, Department of History, Ahmadu Bello University, 1979.

4. The Cult of Facts and Fetishism in Africanist History

When they severed or tried to cut ties with philosophy and literature, the better to 'reconstruct the past' and in that way to tell the story as it actually happened, practising historians wanted to reconstitute their craft as an independent field of study.[1] Yet it soon transpired that 'anyone who has tried to tell the story of historical events knows full well that, unless he analyses his information in detail so as to determine the significances in it, his story will be not history but chronicle, and he will be not an historian but an antiquary.' An historian has to 'penetrate the core of events' he seeks to describe; and in this venture, ideas are important.[2] This stance appears to be of importance not only to metropolitan historians, but also to imperial scholars, and even more so to postcolonial Africanist historians.[3]

But while historians have continued to grumble about the dearth of ideas in their craft - a situation which they have contrasted with that of the social sciences, like political science, which has been alleged to have a 'substantial corpus of literature' - they continue to use, produce, and reproduce such ideas.[4] To be sure, it has been asserted that, while historians use 'concepts and methods which both define their specific objects of knowledge and govern the ways in which they investigate them', 'these concepts are not produced within the discipline of history, or more precisely do not emanate from the enterprise of historical research (as the study of the "past").'[5] But it is also significant that the social sciences have no monopoly of ideas. Ideas are produced in actual social relations before they are refined and articulated by intellectuals, who are themselves social groupings dependent upon specific classes which are primary in that they are involved in actual production or its control.[6]

To say this is to emphasize that ideas are not 'natural'. 'The main danger for any scientists involved in the study of social phenomena,' it has been underlined, 'is that of taking anything for granted, of "problem-blindness".'[7] This is the foremost danger facing postcolonial Africanist historiography, which is as reductionist as it is nationalistic.[8] This observation applies to all the major topics dealt with in Africanist historiography and, as was illustrated in the latter sections of Chapter 3, to the state. In colonial historiography the idea of the state was considered 'un-African'. With the ascendancy of postcolonial historiography, the notion of the state was indigenized and in some cases nationalized with a view to glorifying the African past.[9] In both cases it was considered non-problematic. Its periodization within African history, as well as its nature, was considered unimportant. Thus description outstripped analysis, and reductionism, as partial as it was ideological, assumed a leading role.[10]

It is not the purpose of this chapter to discuss the origins of states in Africa or elsewhere. The materialist aspects of this process began to be studied in the last century by Marx and Engels, who had much to borrow from Morgan.[11] The effects of the penetration of European merchant capital on state formation in Africa, especially in East Africa, have already been discussed here, with the aim of showing the material basis of African political systems in the nineteenth century. This effort was undertaken with a view to showing the way out of the crisis within which postcolonial Africanist historiography is trapped. Postcolonial Africanist history seems to have been reduced to a lottery, a search for the lucky number, or a game of 'hunt the thimble'. This is the level to which the nihilist approach in Africanist history, in particular, is reducing the craft. In the course of doing so, however, even the kidnapping of slaves from Africa, which amounted to an endeavour to steal the whole means of production of the continent, is peddled as having been a normal business transaction. A method which claims to be objective but which produces such subjectivist conclusions needs to be examined. This chapter is intended to examine the historian's craft, or what has also been termed 'historical practice',[12] with a view to showing the superiority of the materialist method over the idealist one. We begin with a brief recapitulation of the ground already traversed.

The Enigma of Appearances

Normally called 'enlargement of scale' in postcolonial Africanist historiography, the notion of social change, *inter alia*, has served as a unifying theme in the professional study of African history since the end of the Second World War.[13] This theme, however, has of late been called historicist and nihilist.[14] Postcolonial Africanist historiography's fetishistic revival of a borrowed language, in the course of which traditions of the past are made to weigh 'like a nightmare on the brain of the living', is intended to glorify the prevailing post-independence order.[15] It is typical of historicism to reduce all thoughts and actions of the past to a genealogy of their components.[16] The ostensible objectivity of this approach has been attacked for being one-dimensional. Such criticism, however, has been conducted still within the empiricist problematic which constitutes the very terrain of postcolonial Africanist historiography.[17] Amid this contest has emerged the endeavour to use the development-of-underdevelopment theory in professional Africanist history. Even so, this postcolonial historiography is in a crisis;[18] it has been said that whatever stance is adopted by professional Africanist historians, pragmatism should be the lodestar of their response to this dilemma. Indeed, the deployment of underdevelopment theory in the professional study of African history has been perceived as a pointer in that direction,[19] but the effort has not been very successful.[20]

Uppermost in the minds of those professional Africanist historians who have called for a pragmatic response to the crisis in their craft is the conviction that success is measured in terms of survival, and that in the course of the struggle for existence crises are inevitable. Thus a discipline like African history should not be restricted to narrow themes. Rather it must adapt to unfolding crises by trying new approaches. Such a response, in this view, is indicative of the maturity of a discipline. But to respond to crises is one thing; to respond to them successfully, quite another. A successful response demands an investigation of the causes of the crises if an appropriate remedy is to be found and applied.

The main dispute in professional Africanist history has been over the interpretation of facts. Initially, it was maintained that the African past was not an integrated whole. This view was revised with the rise of the African petty bourgeoisies when the African past was historicized. Oral history became a fetish, and any study (as we have noted previously) which did not tap this source was considered incomplete. Failure to locate the 'African point of view' was blamed on the sources.[21] Such an attitude constitutes an empiricist reading of history, one in which its facticity and actuality are taken to be congruent.[22] Facts are considered natural and are therefore given an ontological status.[23] The fact that events arise and develop as part of a social whole is disregarded. The observation that 'no reading is innocent' and that 'plainly put, every interpretation involves its own theoretical and political presuppositions' is forgotten.[24]

Facts are 'themselves theoretical constructs'. They are neither the beginning nor the end of investigation. The 'starting point of thought is never the bare noting of prime datum.'[25] One has to go out to meet the facts, as it were. This action involves the projection of schemata with which to perceive them. But since such facts constitute part of an articulated social whole - rather than, as is normally believed, being circular - one has to go beyond the facts to come to grips with social reality.[26] Short of this, scholarship becomes a matter of describing a part of the whole and confusing it with the totality.[27] If another part of this totality happens to be discovered later, the first part is declared mythical so as to make room for the new finding. Truth becomes synonymous with an organic adaptation to new findings which in any case are static summations of a dynamic process,[28] as opposed to an absolute copy of reality. The definition of truth becomes its practical usefulness, its pragmatism, as well as being liable to the cognitive faculties of the observer.[29]

An empiricist reading of past events is synonymous with describing their appearance. This amounts to a portrayal of the world 'as a chaos of discrete facts possessing no comprehensible objective structure'.[30] In such efforts, however, scholars usually come across contradictory evidence. Thus, while professional Africanist historians have collected oral data to demonstrate the equation of 'change' with 'enlargement of scale' in the African past, it has also been shown by other scholars that the opposite of such trends occurred in that selfsame past.[31] There has also been a lively debate by professional historians on whether 'indirect rule' in colonial Africa was benevolent or, as has been maintained by African nationalists, violent and destructive. Evidence has been produced to support both points of view.[32] 'The sphere of exchange' (appearances), it has been observed, 'possesses the double presence of an optical illusion. Each side of it is true in a way, but only if the other side is blocked out of view; and the whole, as a real whole, is impossible.'[33] Trapped on the level of appearances, scholarship becomes a process of shuttling between opposite points of view. Nevertheless the contradictions within such scholarship reflect the basic contradiction of capitalism of which it comprises an articulated part. This is the contradiction between the legitimizing role of the system and its performance of the function of capital - a contradiction which is found in many of the constituent parts of the system.[34]

Thus it seems advisable to note that the constituent elements of the capitalist system will only be understood if the mechanisms of the system itself are clear in our minds. This is so because the system presents itself in a way that it is and it is not. So, too, do its articulated parts. Social relations appear as if they were relations between things held together by a hidden celestial hand.[35]

Such considerations have not been taken seriously in professional Africanist history. The discipline was brought into existence as an ideological intervention against colonial historiography, which in most cases was treated in reductionist terms.[36] Neither the method employed in the discipline nor the discipline itself was at issue. Its theoretical content was in most cases nebulous. The crisis of method was explained away as a crisis of data. Its solution, therefore, was simply held to depend on the quantity and quality of data. Historians were urged to be more positivistic, notwithstanding the injunction that, if people are consistently misinterpreting the data, they are doing more than misinterpreting.[37] Professional African history was thus turned into a game of 'hunt-the-thimble',[38] but 'the "inner truth" about Africa' remained elusive.[39] In the discussion that follows we shift the focus of analysis to its proper terrain: the production of social knowledge.[40] This attempt is undertaken with a view to showing the impossibility of attaining any objective historical knowledge of Africa by using the empirical method.

The point to be made immediately is that the production of knowledge is a social process to be understood in the context of society, which is historically determined.[41] Under capitalism, as well as its role in serving the purposes of capital, knowledge is intended to legitimize a particular historical course.[42] Thus in the case of African history, colonial historiography denied African societies their past so as to legitimize the process of 'colonial enlightenment'. Postcolonial Africanist historiography, on the other hand, sought to resurrect the precapitalist African past with a view, however, not to elucidating but obfuscating the real impact of that 'colonial enlightenment', as well as the ongoing imperialist context of postcolonial African social formations.[43] African postcolonial historiography did not go beyond exposing the chauvinistic content of colonial historiography.[44]

The Fallacy of Objectivism

Like world history the term, African history, has been used widely and at times wantonly. But what is African history? Perhaps the answer to such a question is too obvious to be considered seriously by the learned and erudite. The common view is that African history is the study of the African past or its remains as well as the results of such scholarly investigation. An historian of African history is therefore concerned with remains of the African past, from which he can collect facts to be ascertained in the course of reconstructing history, so as to show it as it really was. Facts are past events made by men in the form of such things as social, political and economic institutions. The duty of an historian is to get the facts right and to present them with strict and clinical objectivity.[45] This historical method of collecting and assessing facts is called objective empiricism.[46]

Rigorous use of the empirical method to study the past was established in the nineteenth century by such prominent professional scholars as Ranke. Nowadays Ranke is mostly remembered for having introduced into the professional study of history the 'cult of facts and documents'.[47] He saw the limits of writing history as determined by the availability of documents from which facts could be extracted, and the historian's detachment (objectivism),[48] which would guarantee that history is written objectively. 'The virtue of a thing, Plato tells us in the *Republic*, is that state or condition which enables it to perform its proper function well. The virtue of a knife is its sharpness, the virtue of a racehorse its fleetness of foot.'[49] So, too, the cardinal virtue of detachment is an excellence which enables an historian to fulfil his professional function properly and efficiently. Detachment, neutrality, impartiality, or objectivism is considered an important precondition in the historian's craft. Commitment, on the other hand, signifies delinquency, a failure of professional rigour, since it tends to invite a confusion between facts and values.[50] Detachment is acquired by suppressing one's subjectivity. Such a mental posture enables an historian to acquire an 'Olympian view' of historical events, considered crucial in the production of objective knowledge.[51]

But, as one revolutionary historian observed, 'Nobody has yet clearly explained what this impartiality consists of'. A contemporary writer on the French Revolution, Madelin, 'slandering in his drawing-room fashion the great revolution . . . asserts that "the historian ought to stand upon the wall of a threatened city and behold at the same time the besiegers and the besieged": only in this way, it seems, can he achieve a "conciliatory justice". However, the words of Madelin himself testify that, if he climbs out on the wall dividing the two camps, it is only in the character of a reconnoitre for the reaction.' Nevertheless, it is just as well that such an observer is 'concerned only with war camps of the past: in a time of revolution, standing on the wall involves greater danger. Moreover, in times of alarm, the priests of "conciliatory justice" are usually found sitting on the side of four walls to see which side will win.'[52] Reading-room debates can be conducted with 'impartiality' and detachment. Ideal lineages of inheritance and mutation can be discovered. Thus it can be argued that 'this was mediated by that, and that was assimilated into the other, and all this went on in a world of discourse as congenial as the reading rooms in which we consult old periodicals.' But events take place in situations of actual social confrontation: there is a 'river of fire' in the real world of historical events.[53]

Even so, there is a scholarly tradition which maintains that an historian is not supposed to pose as a judge of past personalities. Rather he is expected to narrate their point of view accurately, nothing more and nothing less. In such an effort it is supposed that the subject and object of historical research are separate entities, and that in the course of recording historical events the mind of the subject remains passive. Judgements are reserved to the historian as an individual; as a professional, he is supposed to be objective. Such an approach is based on the belief that, for modern societies, the past is dead and thus of no relevance to current trends and developments. This is supposedly so because modern societies are interested in changing the present and are thus forward-looking rather than conservative and backward-looking. The latter quality is felt to be a hallmark of 'pre-modern' societies, whose past is regarded as a living entity comprising a continuum with the present and with the future of such societies.[54] For the professional historian, however, the 'dead past' which is his stamping ground is more like a scientific curiosity, to be investigated critically for its own sake, rather than a source of ideological ammunition with which either to fight against or defend the prevailing order.[55] In 'modern' societies, in the empiricist view, the past and the present are as different from each other as night and day.

Two seminal points stand out about the empirical method as it applies to professional history: it believes that an historian is capable of becoming objective by suppressing the subjective element within him, and that his subject can also be treated objectively given the rise of the modern society.[56] It has been argued that the professionalization of history is inextricably linked with the rise of the 'modern society', whether this is understood as the industrial system or its political institutions. According to Toynbee, the subjugation of 'the ancient kingdom of thought' to scientific thought which is critical as well as positivistic, and its application to the physical world, constitute the industrial system. Scientific thought also found its way into the 'continent of human history', where it was applied. 'Historical thought', therefore, is among the 'foreign realms in which the prestige of the Industrial system has asserted itself; and herein a mental domain which has had a far longer history than our Western Society and which is concerned not with things but with people'.[57]

The application of the scientific method to the realm of historical thought seemed so impressive that:

> Some historical teachers of our day deliberately describe their 'seminars' as 'laboratories' and, perhaps less consciously but not less decidedly, restrict the term 'original work' to denote the discovery or verification of some fact or facts not previously established. At the furthest, the term is extended to cover the interim reports upon such work which are contributed to learned journals or to synthetic histories. There is a strong

tendency to depreciate works of historical literature which are created by single minds, and the depreciation becomes the more emphatic the nearer such works approximate to being 'Universal Histories'. For example, Mr H.G. Well's *The Outline of History* was received with unmistakable hostility by a number of historical specialists. They criticized severely the errors which they discovered at the points where the writer, in his long journey through Time and Space, happened to traverse their tiny allotments.[58]

The industrialization of historical thought seems to have advanced to such an extent that 'it has even reproduced the pathological exaggerations of the industrial spirit'.[59]

In modern society, as opposed to traditional societies, 'real history', 'the learned monograph or article resting upon original research', the collection and establishment of facts considered as 'the indestructible atoms of the past', is possible. Besides collecting the indestructible atoms of the past, an historian is supposed to add them one to another and so help construct a solid element of true history. The learned monographs and articles would, in turn, be added to each other and so enable the writing of 'a definitive, universal history in some remote future'. 'The gathering of materials bearing upon minute local events', 'the collection of MSS and the registry of their small variations, the patient drudgery in archives of state and municipalities, all the microscopic research that is carried on by armies of toiling students', all the monographs on various obscure subjects 'serve as chapters in a single historical work', universal history. This, however, cannot be fulfilled by one mind. Rather, it will be the result of the efforts of myriads of individuals.[60]

The founders of scientific historiography believed in the objective collection of facts.[61] *Prima facie*, such an attitude seemed a pointer to the tendency to collect facts in a mindless fashion. But behind every fact, it was also believed, was an idea. Expressed in historical events were thoughts considered even more important than their form. For the nineteenth-century English historian - Macaulay, for example - the Crystal Palace expressed the idea of progress embedded in the minds of people who lived in Victorian England. Thus it was necessary to take note of the thought behind an historical event.[62] Even so, Ranke advised the inexperienced historian to take care of the facts and leave the rest to the hidden hand of Providence. This was so because it seemed there was no way that, in studying history for its own sake, a professional could avoid contributing a sentence or so to the realization of universal history. As with the sovereignty of the market in a *laissez-faire* economy, Providence would play an appreciable role in ensuring a fair and objective recovery of the past unencumbered by personal opinions.[63]

Two points have to be borne in mind when discussing objectivity: the assumptions about the state of the subject and the object which, according to empiricist epistemology, are different entities. The first assumption concerns the state of the subject, especially its potential to comprehend an object objectively. This has been alluded to a number of times. The second assumption appears more complicated. This is that, while it is agreed that subject and object are different entities, to what extent is the former a condition for the existence of the latter? Is there a difference between things in themselves and things as perceived? For some observers, 'social reality past and present has a structure and meaning of its own that the scholar discovers in the same way an explorer discovers an ocean or a lake. The structure is there to begin with.' For others, on the other hand, the matter is more complex than this.[64]

Despite his empiricist reading of events, Immanuel Kant maintained there is a difference between things in themselves and things as perceived. The former are unknowable, and so a researcher has to be satisfied with what he perceives. This is a question of appearance and reality, phenomenon and essence. Compared with Kant, the German philosopher Hegel was more subtle. Hegel argued that, while the knowledge of an object originates from sense experience, the perception of it is restricted to the level of appearance. Since appearance is false, truth is arrived at by a rigorous criticism of sense experience. From this, however, Hegel concluded that only the results of such a process, ideas, are real.[65] For him, then, reality is the construction of thought. The mind governs the world. This is so because, if, according to Kant, things in themselves are unknowable 'we cannot know of them and we cannot know that they are. Hence we must conclude that reality is reality-as-we-apprehend-it.'[66]

It is within such an epistemological tradition that Ranke sought to write history as it really was. Despite all efforts to restrict his career to ascertaining the facts of history, Ranke found himself — perhaps due to the hidden hand of Providence — praising the Prussian state which Hegel also found to be real and rational.[67] Ranke wished to flee from the confused affairs of the prevailing order into the serenity of the past; but the gravitational pull of the present was too strong for him to attain an Olympian view with which to perceive the mundane events of previous epochs. Ranke's objectivity, it was subsequently observed by Droysen, was the objectivity of a eunuch.[68] Moreover, the Paris Commune, the First World War, and the October Revolution, coupled with the growing popularity of Marxism, spurred bourgeois scholars to begin doubting the supposed rationality of men. Men and their activities had been considered rational in the sense that they took into account the implications and consequences of their actions. By the end of the nineteenth century, however, social scientists like Freud and Weber began to contend that beneath the veneer of man's rationality was a deep-seated irrationality, which according to Social Darwinism was inherent.[69] Historians were slow to adopt such notions, but it was not long before Burckhardt and others began to argue that, just as it was hard for men to divest themselves of their own selves, so it was almost impossible for historians to suppress their subjectivity in order to attain the necessary objectivism for writing objective history.[70]

By the beginning of the twentieth century, and especially after the First World War, historians were openly admitting that what they were writing was not the absolute truth, but a selection of it. Much of the selection, too, was 'refracted' through their own minds. It was also realized that what was regarded as a passive and neutral mind was in actual fact very much influenced by the prevailing climate of opinion.[71] History, Herbert Butterfield declared in 1931, is not studied for its own sake but for the sake of the present.[72] History, asserted Oakeshott, is the historian's experience. For Theodor Lessing, history was nothing more than an 'irrational attempt to read subjective desires into a meaningless subject matter'.[73] 'Progressive historians' in America were equally pessimistic about the possibility of writing history as it really happened.[74] Ranke had advocated what amounted to a cult of facts. The founder of pragmatism, the American philosopher John Dewey, like Emerson who had anticipated him, believed: 'No facts to me are sacred; none are profane.'[75] Since then it has been admitted even by some professional historians that 'facts have crumbled along with the Newtonian system of the universe. Ranke would have been bewildered by a judgement essential to modern science: "The person of the experimenter is himself part of the experiment." Or, to put it in terms of the historian: "Impartiality gives a more dangerous bias than any other." '[76]

Nineteenth-century confidence in professional history has given way to pessimism; so much so that even facts are now doubted. The ideology of academia which was previously stated so confidently is no more. History now seems to be nothing more than what a professional chooses to tell his audience. Call it objectivity, subjectivity or what you will, historical facts as well as history itself are now regarded as a creation of the historian; they do not exist outside his own mind.[77]

Even metropolitan professional historians' treatment of the history of colonial and postcolonial societies has come under sharp criticism. For quite some time such history has remained too patriotic, it has been said. This patriotism was shown not only in the works of Ranke but also in those of many prominent English historians like Macaulay, Acton, Seeley and Ashley. The last-mentioned, for example, wrote of the British Empire as 'the mightiest of instruments of good' and the 'fairest hope of humanity'.[78] But it has been discovered subsequently that the British Empire was not like that.

To many of the new breed of historians, the empire was an instrument of plunder. Thus Luthy has written somewhat pessimistically that 'the seemingly inexhaustible treasury of philosophical propositions about the justice and injustice, the blessings and the crimes, of colonialism [are] propositions accumulated in a debate that has gone on in Europe ever since there have been European world empires; and [that] those advanced by the "realists" and the "idealists" are at bottom the same as those of three hundred or four hundred years ago.' Nothing has been added 'to what was said better and more pungently by Abbe Raynal and the men of the Enlightenment'. If the defenders of colonial empire have grown indignant over the debate and answered the charges by counter-accusations of 'Soviet imperialism', 'Arab imperialism' etc., 'then all that is left in the end is the disreputable proposal to reach a friendly agreement: why do we pluck out each other's eyes, we are all vultures?' That leaves us only one difference: 'the one that cannot be eliminated — the great disparity of vitality, voracity, and self-confidence among the vultures; and here no arguments help.'[79]

Even so, belief in the inevitability of progress is no more. Society no longer appears to be a branch of physics. Professional history is in a crisis.[80] Thus, as if history had been using a method peculiar to itself, professionals have now sought to avert the crisis by recommending the use of social science's methods of quantification and so on in their discipline. For example, Berkhofer has asserted that the notion of stimulus and response used in history is too mechanistic because it does not include the 'empirically unobservable' which intervenes between the subject and its object. For him the 'empirically unobservable' includes 'timeless' cultural values like 'possessive individualism', which influence the way an object responds to its stimuli.[81] Professional history, therefore, is turned into an instrument for imparting 'educational values' which are intended to 'suggest a range of potentially workable solutions for current social problems'.[82] So a good piece of professional history is the study which is 'studded with cultural and political curios'[83] supposed to be celestial. It has also been recommended by some American professional historians that the only way to overcome the crisis of professional history is to make it less 'tribalistic' and more internationalist, as was done by Spanish imperialists as early as the sixteenth century.[84] But the American Historical Association's endeavours in this direction, in the case of the history of the Philippines, have proved only a useful tool for perpetuating imperialist control.[85]

The Material Basis of Academia

Perhaps this 'radical' change in thinking about their craft by professional historians is symptomatic of the dynamism inherent in the writing of history. It could also be that, however weird, the various views and interpretations produced in the course of writing history belong, in the final analysis (it might be added), to the totality of human knowledge.[86] Such change might underline the reason for rewriting history every generation or so. But it seems to others, that change *per se* is not crucial; rather the quality of change is more important. It may be that topics of research are determined not by individual choice, but by the prevailing historical conditions under which the choice is made. To know the nature of such historical conditions is of paramount importance because they are not neutral. The problem of objectivity in history should be discussed within such a context.

For many professional Africanist historians, however, the empirical method was understood to be Talmudic. To start with, the empirical method was employed in the study of African history along with all the cultural and political curios of liberalism.[87] But soon it was declared that such curios, as well as the philosophy which constitutes their basis, were foreign to the African personality. So there followed the search for methods of conceptualization and doctrines supposed to be typically African. The fact that capitalism is an enemy of tradition did not worry scholars steeped in such investigation.[88]

There is a tendency to forget that the bourgeois revolution, although centred in Europe, has had a worldwide impact. The bourgeoisie 'compels all nations, on pain of extinction, to adopt the bourgeois mode of production; it compels them to introduce what it calls civilization into their midst, i.e. to become bourgeois themselves. In one word, it creates a world after its own image.'

> In place of the old local and national seclusion and self-sufficiency, we have intercourse in every direction, universal interdependence of nations. And as in material, so also in intellectual production. The intellectual creations of individual nations become common property. National one-sidedness and narrow-mindedness becomes more and more impossible, and from the numerous national and local literatures, there arises a world literature.[89]

This world literature emerged in the course of the bourgeoisie making its own anthropological view of the world dominant. Leading bourgeois ideas became the central ideas of world literature. This was done by denying colonized societies a culture of their own. Colonial societies were assumed to exist only in the present and so were declared raw materials for colonial enlightenment. With the enforced conclusion of the enlightenment, its processes were renamed 'modernization' and in that way nationalized, so as to become part of the national heritage of postcolonial societies. Postcolonial historiography served a useful purpose in this process of nationalization, a process which, it must be stressed, was reformist rather than revolutionary.

Yet the question still remains: why have historians insisted so vehemently on the importance of political and cultural curios in the writing of history? Is possessive individualism, for example, celestial? And what about the idea of progress? Is there such a thing as progress in general? The question need not detain us. For the nub of the matter is that professionals claim that such ideas are recovered from the neutral facts they analyse, not injected into them. This is the version of empiricism which 'rests the scientificity of a theory upon the immediate correspondence of theory and fact'. But 'facts are themselves theoretical constructs', and the real is not 'immediately present in the phenomena accessible to our observation'.[90]

All this implies that facts are not reality itself, but a part of it. The empiricist tendency to isolate one component of an articulated whole so as to render it supreme has in most cases resulted in empty metaphysics.[91] Even the attempt to assemble facts takes place within a given problematic. This problematic constitutes neither the intentions nor the specific propositions of the author, but the structure of problems to be solved and the way they are solved. The questions comprise the reference system which determines the answers given. This is what determines why a scholar attempts certain tasks and excludes others.[92] The persistent concern with the actions of the individual in African postcolonial historiography, when this had not been present in colonial historiography, for example, is not to be taken lightly. Notwithstanding the fashionable tendency by professional scholars to associate their work with Graeco-Roman civilization, Egyptian civilization, or other ancient cultures, the 'billiard-ball universe' dominant in their thinking is a product of the bourgeois revolution.[93] They too are part and parcel of this revolution which they have helped realize and maintain. Historians can continue to cite Thucydides or Herodotus as the father of their craft, and social scientists as a whole can keep on going back to Plato's works for reassurance; but it has also to be remembered that each epoch creates its own organic intellectuals whose role is to act as intermediaries between the dominant and exploited classes, and that the professional historian, in spite of his professional regalia, is a product of the modern world which he is also helping to sustain.[94] Capitalism, as a revolutionizer, is an enemy of tradition. It has created not only the proletariat but also the modern academic.[95] Social knowledge has become an important component of production. It is directed against the worker in the form of machines, industrial sociology and so on with a view to realizing a steady and if possible increased flow of surplus labour to augment the accumulation of dead labour.[96]

Perhaps in this, it may appear that history which is concerned with the 'dead past' has no role. Professionalism, therefore, may be possible in history in a way that would have proved impossible in, say, rural sociology - which has always maintained that its object of study, the peasant, has permanently remained a problem to reckon with since he has refused to be subjected to the rigours of capitalist penetration. But the concepts used in rural sociology and those of history are not different. This is so, for example, with the notions of social change and modernization rampant in discussions of both African history and rural sociology.

As opposed to other social scientists, historians 'are prone to a particular mystification in that the generic object and the name of their discipline are the same, i.e. History is the study of history.' Thus historians face a 'lamentable problem: their discipline has no object'. Social sciences like economics have problematics that define their concepts and objects. This may appear not to be the case with professional history. But this is so only at the level of the ideology of academia. In practice, historians use concepts which are borrowed from the other social sciences[97] — for instance, the idea of the 'billiard-ball universe' in which the world is posed as a congeries of self-contained entities guided by the notion of social contract.[98] In this manner history, like the other social sciences, helps to mystify the social relations of production by describing human relations as relations between things subject to the market. Society is seen as an aggregation of discrete things, a reified structure which masks the basic social conditions that transform the worker into a thing to be exchanged for wages.

The professional historian contributes to this process of fetishism by either upholding ideas appropriate for this or, in his actual process of writing, by taking facts as impenetrable atoms to be confirmed, rather than as historically determined cultural products to be studied as part of an articulated whole. The tendency to confuse facts with reality itself is associated with the rise of the bourgeois world-view called empiricism, whose method of conceptualization is called the empirical method. This method was understood as an alternative to medieval scholasticism. It constituted a component of the bourgeois revolt against the feudal order dominated by papal scholarship. The method was, in fact, an imitation of what was being done in the natural sciences whose results had proved so impressive. The early social scientists sought to make the study of society a branch of physics so as to discover the motions of the social universe.[99] In view of the hostility the natural scientists faced from the Church, they claimed neutrality for their study. Thus was born the central supposition of scientific ideology, which has been applied in the study of the social sciences with such rigour that nowadays 'countless pure scholars pass their lives accumulating a maximum of knowledge in a small, limited and partial field and believe themselves to be anthropologists, historians, linguists, philosophers and so forth.'[100]

It has to be stressed that this scientific ideology was born in a specific social context and was posed as a challenge to a specific social order.[101] If this is understood in Madelin's sense, as quoted earlier, the neutrality of this scientific ideology becomes suspicious. Objectivism, at the beginning of the bourgeois revolution, was a partisan goal. Why should it be otherwise today?[102] We have already made reference to the argument put forward by Plato, that 'the virtue of a thing . . . is that state or condition which enables it to perform its proper function well.' Thus, as we saw, 'the virtue of a knife is its sharpness, the virtue of a racehorse its fleetness of foot,' and the virtue of an historian his detachment, which enables him to write objective history.[103] But this is only true if we know the condition of that virtue, for it is not celestial. Suppose that the virtue is false? What becomes the function of a knife which is false since its condition of existence, its sharpness, happens to be non-existent? The same thing could be said about scientific ideology or objectivism, which is a condition, or the virtue, of academicism. Scientific ideology cannot be neutral if from its very birth it was partisan.

Facts, we have already said, have as it were to be met. They do not just sink into our heads. In the course of recording them we use theoretical constructs which also help us transcend those very facts with a view to comprehending their inner reality. Myths were used as theoretical constructs by various precapitalist societies as an aid to understanding events. In most cases they discovered the intervention of a god as an explanation for a myriad of occurrences.[104] With the bourgeois revolution, the motives of men as individuals replaced the hidden hand of Providence. The basis of such motives was disregarded, and thus a loophole was supplied through which bourgeois ideology, in such forms as the sovereignty of market relations, was smuggled.[105] This one-dimensional treatment of facts was considered natural and universal. This world-view was imposed on the exploited classes and the colonial societies with a vigour and violence comparable to that of the Vandals.[106]

Universities and Professionalism
It has been alleged that the work produced in universities, which constitutes an important base for the production of social knowledge, is based on choice,

and that such choice is guaranteed by the autonomy of the institutions from where social knowledge emanates. Such an allegation should not be dismissed lightly, but its basis must be established. The basis of academic ideology is the university, a powerful social milieu in its own right. It exerts tremendous influence on the work done on it, despite claims of neutrality and freedom of choice. Here too are preserved 'narrow professional prejudices and crass career constraints', upheld by their inheritors as the basis of freedom of choice.[107]

A major duty of a university is to produce professionals in what are considered important areas of study and to perpetuate professionalism, which is regarded as a mark of excellence:

> The professions now have considerable status and respect in society. Professional respectability fully emerged only with the development of codes of conduct and qualifying institutions in the last century. The respectability of professionalism has enhanced its desirability in the eyes of many, so that now the term 'professional' is in everyday usage to denote excellence of quality in almost any activity. When a task is done well, it is praise to be told that it is a professional job. Similarly, in the categorization of people as professionals or amateurs, the professional, though operating for money, is considered to be better trained and usually more dedicated than the amateur.[108]

A professional is supposed to be a specialist in some minute field of study, craft or trade. In history, for example, a professional is supposed to concentrate on the study of a small area to help him produce a monograph or an article.[109] The tendency is to avoid employing general concepts and ideas so that one can give the impression of knowing what one is talking about. The sort of criticism that such an approach yields is discreet, and can thus be ignored or absorbed. The greater the number of recondite conundrums used, the more professional the study becomes.[110]

Professionalism is also supposed to be largely cerebral, and is intended to offer 'advice'. Each profession is supposed to have some form of theoretical background, like historiography in history, 'which requires specific training and education, and which forms the core of the professional expertise'. Some kind of a representative institution, perhaps publishing a newsletter or preferably a journal, also makes the profession more respectable. With such an institution follows the establishment of a code of conduct that is supposed to make the profession altruistic. This altruism is intended to give the profession a core of moral qualities stressed by the professional code, such as impartiality, responsibility, competence and so on.[111]

Professionalism in history is acquired through a long apprenticeship of undergraduate and postgraduate work, followed by the publication of monographs and articles. It is said that the seminar method popularized by Ranke offers the best path in the process of initiation to professionalism. In the seminar system, it is alleged, the student is only guided to choose what he wants. Market relations, it seems, also prevail in the seminar room! But what does the student have to choose, if not the crass professional prejudices handed down from one generation to another since the age of Ranke himself? If one is courageous enough to challenge such prejudices, there is an examination of one kind or another at the end of one's apprenticeship. In most cases the results of such an examination are not available from one's professional guide (adviser) unless one has passed the examination. If one has failed, one is supposed to check the results with a bureaucratic organ which is as hard as rock, and impervious to all questions that might be asked about results of the examination. Indeed the police are at times called in, if it is felt that the manner in which the questions are asked constitutes a threat to law and order on the campus.

If one does eventually get through the long and frustrating postgraduate apprenticeship and find a job with a university, one enters the academic life of teaching and writing. Gone are the days when, as in the University of Guatemala in the sixteenth century, the selection of a candidate for a teaching post went as follows: 'A child inserted a knife at random between the pages of one of the books in the mediaeval curriculum ... the candidate opened the book at the page ... and defended one of the propositions on the page, in Latin, before a committee comprising the bishop, the rector, the dean of the cathedral, one of the professors and the senior doctor.'[112] University posts were also bought. Some professors were so ignorant that students never bothered to attend their lectures. But such professors consoled themselves with the belief that their students were preparing for examinations.[113]

Things have changed with the passage of time; but it seems that professional qualities are always sought after by those who make appointments in universities. Thus a senior Oxford proctor complained in 1936 that:

> The increasing traffic of senior members with what I may call the vulgar currency of party politics, their closer association with the more controversial aspects of undergraduate life, these are new and in my opinion disturbing phenomena. A reasonable detachment of outlook is the condition precedent of education. The maturing mind is more receptive than relevant, sentimental rather than sceptical, and it is the jealous care of a tutor to persuade his pupil that it is possible to be dispassionate without ceasing to be generous. This task is apt to be obscured by the dust of popular recrimination.[114]

Many prejudices like these have been imported to Africa along with the institutionalization of university education. There have been complaints about falling standards, and the search for alternatives to the liberal model of a university, but this is an aside to the central issue.[115]

As well as ensuring that the teacher maintains a moral code appropriate to his profession, the university has to see that he publishes in learned journals and the like, so as to be promoted through the various ranks of the academic hierarchy. In this the university bureaucracy through the head of department plays a prominent role in maintaining the professional ethic. Normally journals and publishing houses determine what is considered worth publishing. But for the sake of promotion, the university bureaucracy also has a say. Thus are established what are normally called 'impartial rules' for determining what is academically acceptable. Like a producer of commodities, the author of an article has no control over what he writes. Rather, once it leaves his desk, what has been written is subjected to rules and forces independent of him. The production is turned into a thing. If the author is, as it were, lucky, the article or book can become a fetish powerful enough to dominate even his own life. Otherwise the article finds some place on a dusty shelf, there to be critically examined by mice and ants.[116]

Thus writing for publication may be compared to other forms of production. Although there is no actual creation of surplus value in this form of production, but merely consumption of it through state intervention with the basic producer or, as in capitalist-run universities, the entrepreneur, writing for publication is subject to its own rules which intervene between the producer and the consumer of articles and books. Established by editors of journals, publishers of books, and universities, these rules are not immutable. Rather they are historically determined, notwithstanding the dense ideology of academia which places a mediatory role between the consumer and the author of scholarly studies.

Like other forms of production, writing is a dialectical process between production and consumption. The production and consumption of published studies are opposites: each implies the other. In the production of academic work, there is productive consumption of the dominant ideas and professional prejudices enforced by the university hierarchy as well as data to produce work that is intended to satisfy the needs of consumption. The production of academic work makes its consumption possible, but consumption also supplies the need for such production. Something becomes a product only in relation to consumption, that is, when it satisfies a particular need. 'Thus consumption is necessary for the bringing about of a *product*, not merely as a stimulus to the production, not merely to initiate the process of production, but as a condition for *constituting* the result of that process as a product. Consumption . . . gives "the finishing stroke" to production (and thus produces its opposite).'[117] In this manner, too, a writer becomes a producer in the real sense. Production also influences consumption since there is no consumption in general but only the specific consumption which production helps to create. 'That is, production helps to produce not only the product to satisfy a [pre-existing] need but the precise nature of the need and hence the precise character of the consumption.'[118]

If applied to professional history, this dialectic helps us to understand that the emergence of postcolonial Africanist history was a result not only of the discovery of the efficacy of oral data as a tool to reconstruct history, but also a response to a felt social need which occurred in the aftermath of colonial enlightenment. The specific way in which this need was satisfied, whether through the resurrection of the glory of kings, resistances or technology, was left to the professional historian. But institutions of higher learning in which such a glorification of the past was made possible were established. Bureaucracies were established and academics hired from abroad to ensure success in the glorification of the African past. Where academics went contrary to the demands of this type of consumption, the bugbear of the dangers of foreign ideology was raised. The necessity of locating only the African point of view was reasserted. The possibilities of establishing an 'ideological department' that would reinforce the policing of mental production were explored. Contracts were terminated and people sent to remote places for showing a tendency to act in a way antithetical to the predilections of the dominant classes. And this is still going on. Academics are hired with a view that they will act as spokesmen for the dominant classes.[119] If they fail, the 'paymaster', through the university administration, sees it as his right to call the tune. This is done by outright dismissal or disciplinary action. In this context accusations of drunkenness or violation of other professional codes of conduct merely provide the excuse.

It has been said that universities provide a fertile ground for academic freedom where the activities of mental choice - the act of choosing one idea from another which has its own fascination - are possible. This is so because the university is, presumably, an autonomous entity. Whether this is so or not, however, one would like to know its basis.

The autonomy of the university is guaranteed by a charter or an act of parliament. Autonomy in general, however, is a metaphysical notion - one which becomes transparent when it is remembered that, pretensions of autonomy apart, power within the university is concentrated in the hands of the local dominant classes through direct appointments by the state, the instrument which helps one class to sit on the neck of another. The possibilities of the academics uniting in any form are frustrated by organizing them into hierarchical structures maintained by their seniors who are anointed by the state through the university bureaucracy. Students are even worse off. Faced with a frustrated academic community and a high-handed university bureaucracy, they have been driven into all sorts of strikes and demonstrations. But this has proved time and again that it is impossible to contend with the academic structure 'without coming into conflict with the state apparatus and without calling the whole system in question'. The university might be an autonomous entity with a mandate to provide cadres for private and public enterprise, but it is embedded within a larger articulated whole.[120]

In most postcolonial societies, university autonomy is a fiction. The police are located right within the campus. In the metropolitan countries, however, the hegemonic influence of the culture of the dominant classes is more dense, and the violation of autonomy more subtle. In any case, with the Vietnam War, the meaning of detachment has been questioned more than ever before. This comes out clearly in a sharp exchange between a radical historian, Howard Zinn, and a professional historian of 'respectability', Professor J.K. Fairbank. Like many other radical historians of the New Left, Zinn argues that 'a scholar actively pursuing the answers to the tragic events of the past cannot cut himself into pieces and preserve the political unity of the one piece labelled "historian", while all the other pieces are being consumed by moral outrage against a terrible reality.' Such an endeavour will only result in schizophrenia.[121]

For those who love life, as Bloch said, history is not the preserve of antiquarians. It is written for the living, and commitment is part and parcel of historical enterprise.[122] For this reason, therefore, Zinn challenged the American Historical Association to commit itself on the Vietnam issue. The following is Professor Fairbank's reply.

> [The American Historical Association and other historians do not] believe that the Vietnam War has affected their rights, opportunities, and procedures as historians, and because of that opposes 'politicization' of our professional association, that is, getting AHA officially to take a position on a public policy issue of concern to us all as citizens but not of concern primarily to us as historians. The AHA exists for professional purposes only.
>
> This distinction lies at the heart of the pluralism that gives AHA its legal freedom from interference, intimidation, or coercion by the government or other political forces. 'Politicization' is no joke. It can cut both ways. If we today could use AHA to support a worthy non-professional cause, others tomorrow could manipulate it for an evil cause. In other words, academic freedom has an institutional basis that we should not act to destroy.
>
> All this amounts to saying that the only freedom we can count on is freedom under the law. This makes possible great demonstrations and many other forms of expressing dissent. It also requires that one recognizes parliamentary rules and the agreed upon limits to the usefulness of professional associations. Having got results in the public scene by using your legal rights, you of all people should recognize that our structure of legal distinctions is worth preserving.[123]

The basis of autonomy, detachment and so on becomes clear: in the case of the American Historical Association during the imperialist war in Vietnam, Fairbank argues that its autonomy could only survive if professional historians kept quiet about the way that Americans were killing Vietnamese. Otherwise, that autonomy would be no more. Now that the Vietnam War has come to an end, historians can study it in a cool and detached manner which avoids either censure or praise!

It has been found necessary to digress into a discussion of the material structure and ideological basis of academia, around which various academic activities revolve, because this is an area which has been taken for granted for too long. Received wisdom must be examined, if the critical edge of academicism is to remain sharp. That said, we can again return to the somewhat narrower terrain of the production of historical knowledge. It was noted previously that the empiricist reaching after facts is one-dimensional. If there is an attempt to re-examine the prevailing order of things, it is only undertaken with a view to reasserting the bourgeois world-view. The enterprise of producing knowledge becomes a cyclical movement in which the answer is known even before the investigation begins. This proceeds through the process of adapting to new data. Dominant in this procedure is the pragmatic belief in the usefulness of what works. Usefulness also serves as the basis for the definition of truth. An idea is true if it is useful and works. A new idea, if it proves more useful, takes the place of a former one.[124]

Truth as Usefulness

At stake here is the criterion of truth. Should truth be defined as we perceive it or as a thing-in-itself? The positions of Kant and Hegel have already been noted. The tendency has been to deny the objective existence of anything. Thus Berkeley also declared that, as a thing-in-itself, an object is unknowable. To think of the existence of objective or absolute truth seemed to him chimerical. Objects were but collections of ideas; the existence of objects depends on man's perception of them. Things exist, said Berkeley, only because they are perceived: 'Their *esse* is *percipi*.'[125] From this position it was easy to conclude that only that which perceives, the mind or subject, exists. Such a way of thinking denies the objective existence of reality, necessity, causation and knowledge. Thus on the frequently discussed notion of exploitation, it could be said that exploitation begins only the moment people become conscious of it. If, therefore, people are not conscious of the fact that they are being exploited, then the phenomenon does not exist. Similarly, it has been said that Africa was a dark continent until Europeans became conscious of it. Before the fifteenth century, this kind of logic would suggest, the African heart was hardly beating. Even then the actual motion had to await colonial enlightenment. The same thing could be said about the idea of African history, which is supposed to have begun in 1945. Before that year, it seems, there was no African history because professional historians were unconscious of it. Things exist because they are perceived.

But let us not forget that for a long time it was believed that the earth was flat; for a long time it was believed and defended heatedly in institutions of higher learning that the sun moved around the earth. Subsequently it was discovered that the earth is round and that it is not the centre of the universe. When then did the earth stop being the centre of the universe? 'All science would be superfluous', it has been said, 'if the appearance, the form and the nature of things were wholly identical.' Furthermore, 'It is ... a paradox that the earth moves round the sun, and that water consists of two highly inflammable gases. Scientific truth is always paradox, if judged by everyday experience, which catches only the delusive appearance of things.'[126] Behind appearance is reality, and it is the role of science to penetrate the former in order to arrive at the latter. Appearance and reality are not congruent. Rather they constitute a dialectical relationship. That is the first principle to be remembered if objects are to be understood in themselves rather than as a collection of ideas with an existence determined by the efficiency and speed with which they can be perceived by the mind or subject.[127]

If applied indiscriminately, however, this principle 'regresses to an essentialist reading of history. Social development is interpreted in a closed one-sided manner in an attempt to sanctify the practices and functions of capitalist organization, by discovering them in "immutable necessities" of the past of which the "here and now" is shown to be the perfected confirmation.' As opposed to natural history, human history is made by men, who are also a product of it. Such a consideration invites the element of historical specificity which helps eliminate attempts to construct primordial conditions upon which is built the essentialism of capitalist society. The notoriety of essentialism is, for example, shown with regard to the notion of the possessive individual who is supposed to exist in a situation of abstract freedom and who is apparently armed with the capacity for wanton choice.[128]

That said, the professional historian takes the bare facts as his starting point. They are his given, other things being equal. Furthermore, the process of ascertaining the facts is supposed to be passive. But it has also been observed that the historian chooses from facts of the past and decides which ones should be made historical.[129] It therefore seems that production and reproduction of hypotheses occurs in the process of looking for the underlying reality, by criticizing the immediate world of facts.[130] This immediate world is neither natural nor the ultimate truth. It is a product of man's creative potential. Facts merely constitute the phenomena whose essence is located in fundamental human relations. Man's creative potential is shown in the making of (among other things) institutions, as well as in the endeavour to transcend them. Efforts to transcend the immediate world of facts, institutions and the like are an indication that the world of experience is not eternal but manmade. To carry out this work to perfection, man has to work and rework what he has already made. In that way history is pushed forward. But history moves in a dialectical fashion. Man's past efforts cannot, therefore, be reduced to the institutions which he has created. The whole of his history cannot be deduced from such institutions either. The institutions have to be transcended in order to comprehend the objective reality of the situation. Not that the institutions are mythical; rather they comprise the level of appearance which is dialectically associated with the world of reality.[131]

If history moves in a dialectical fashion, and if its facts are dialectically linked with a deeper level of reality, only a dialectical method can comprehend it. The dialectical method views man's remains of the past, facts, and so on, as part of an articulated whole rather than as the whole truth itself. It refuses to concentrate solely on the immediate world of experience and so help to fetishize it. It constantly criticizes the immediate world of experience with a view to comprehending the inner reality of fundamental human relations which constitutes the spring of history. The dialectical method is neither theological nor spiritual nor idealist. As one of its practitioners has argued, 'the world exists outside my own self and without me, and it has no need of me in order to exist.' But the real is also dynamic. Thus our appropriation of the real is but a relative truth, since the world is in constant genesis. Relativity, however, should not be confused with relativism. Relativity presupposes a dialectical relationship between relative and absolute truth, since, while subsequent discovery will make understanding of the real more comprehensive, it is by no means an alternative to earlier discoveries but a confirmation of them.[132]

'The question whether objective truth can be attributed to human thinking is not a question of theory but is a practical question. In practice man must prove the truth . . . of his thinking.' The limits of theoretical practice are those of social practice: production and class struggle. Here epochal and historical questions become dominant.[133] In professional history, however, objectivism was considered a condition of objectivity until relativism took over. But it is doubtful whether history occurs in such a serene atmosphere. The empirical method is reductionist and deduces what is put forward as a whole from the world of immediate experience. Therein lies its poverty.[134]

It is impossible to arrive at the objective truth by following the empirical method. This is so because, as we have stressed, the empiricist reading of history is one-dimensional. At best it encourages the reductionist view of history by which its movement is reduced to the realization of an idea. In this way the idea is traced back to the dim past for, it has been alleged, 'in society as in nature, the structure is continuous.' There is 'no beginning because the dense web of the fortunes of man is woven without a void', and we can trace things back uninterruptedly 'until we dimly decry the Declaration of Independence in the forests of Germany. No end, because, on the same principle, history made and history making are scientifically inseparable and separately unmeaning.'[135] Where such a discovery is impossible, it becomes a moral triumph for the historian if he can refrain from judging by showing that 'much might be said on both sides, and leave the rest to Providence.'[136]

The movement of history, however, does not comprise the realization, or otherwise, of such progress. Indeed, both aspects of history can be reconstructed from the past. But that is the world of description, which is encouraged by the empirical method but which fails to transcend this world so as to come to the inner mechanisms which act as its anchorage.[137] The collection of facts from old documents, *griots* and so on is by no means a scientific enterprise intended to render objective truth. Facts comprise nothing more than the motives of those who left them behind. As for what such facts stand for, that is another matter. To transcend them is the terrain of scientific enterprise.[138] If, however, the facts are merely collected, ascertained and so on because they are found to be fascinating, this is an indulgence in the cult of facts.[139]

The Failures of the Empirical Method: An Example

We have already offered some illustrations of the problems associated with objectivity in African history. In this section we intend to give another example with the same purpose in mind. The example relates to entrepreneurship and its role in development in African history. It was formerly believed that change in African history commenced with the colonial encounter.[140] Since the triumph of postcolonial Africanist historiography it has become clear, however, that the causes of change could not have been a Western monopoly. The causes of change and development were manifold, and included geographical, political and economic factors, and especially a sudden rise in population which induced technological innovation to step up agricultural production that would help feed the increasing number of mouths.[141]

African development was thus indigenous in its mainspring. Indeed, it has been said that, up to the Iron Age, Africa was ahead of the rest of the world. But it seems to have stagnated there until the colonial encounter, a situation comparable to that of Sung China, which towards its end also faced a high-level technological trap.[142] Change, it has been alleged, is a mark of innovation or entrepreneurs, the act of 'simply ... doing ... new things or ... doing ... things that are already being done in a new way'.[143] But such entrepreneurship needs an institutional setting conducive to its realization.[144] Authoritarian institutions are known to be antithetical to entrepreneurship, 'the true spring of human action',[145] because they encourage a dependence complex.[146] The rapid development of the West, on the other hand, was based on a special 'secret': the 'releasing [of] private enterprise from the dead hands of the state'. This allowed 'social energy ... to flow from the happy play of free minds, free markets and Christian morality: from this liberty to think, speak and worship, to inquire and invest, to buy cheap and sell dear, to accumulate and venture capital, to practise thrift and self-help'. This was lacking in precapitalist societies.[147]

If therefore the stagnation of the precapitalist, colonial and postcolonial societies has been termed paradoxical, it is a paradox which has been resolved by noting that all these societies lacked entrepreneurs.[148] Or, if there were entrepreneurs, they were few; and they lacked some of the qualities of entrepreneurship.[149] Such a phenomenon is explained, in turn, in terms of the political system prevalent in these societies. The system was, as has already been mentioned, authoritarian. However, why the phenomenon of entrepreneurship should be problematic, and not the political system in which the entrepreneurs live, is the relevant question.

Even so, associated with entrepreneurship is the ability to accumulate, a phenomenon which has been posed as another precondition for development:

> Thus primitive accumulation plays in Political Economy about the same part as original sin in theology. Adam bit the apple, and thereupon sin fell on the human race. Its origin is supposed to be explained when it is told as an anecdote of the past. In times long gone by, there were two sorts of people: one, the diligent, intelligent, and above all, frugal elite; the other, lazy rascals, spending their substance, and more, in riotous living. The legend of theological original sin tells us certainly how man came to be condemned to eat his bread in the sweat of his brow; but the history of economic original sin reveals to us that there are people to whom this is by no means essential. Never mind! Thus it came to pass that the former sort accumulated wealth, and the latter sort had

> at last nothing to sell except their own skins. And from this original sin dates the poverty of the great majority that, despite all its labour, has up to now nothing to sell but itself, and the wealth of the few that increases constantly although they have long ceased to work. Such insipid childishness is every day preached to us in the defence of property.[150]

The various branches of the social sciences take this as their stand for explaining economic stagnation, and any endeavours to look for alternatives are met with hostility.[151]

This has been the case with the attempt to use radical and more realistic concepts in professional African history. In the effort to establish local initiative in African history, the real enemy was found to be not colonial historiography, but what has been termed radical pessimism. Thus it has been observed that the 'Africanist historian who . . . emphasizes African activity, African adaptation, African choice, African initiative will increasingly find his main adversaries not in the discredited colonial school but in the radical pessimists.'[152] The concept of class has also been considered an enemy to contend with in professional African history; many professional historians of Africa consider the concept to be alien to the African milieu.[153] African societies were communalistic, they argue; the concept of class was therefore unknown.[154] This has been believed fanatically notwithstanding the fact that reading some of the works which employ such concepts is like moving from 'a kind of vacuum to a kind of plenum'. Marxism, it has nevertheless been asserted emphatically, is alien to Africa. More, it is an ideology to be fought persistently. Marx was at the start met with silence. Now there is an all-out war.[155]

In the course of waging this war, it has been said, more by way of an assertion than as an invitation to set about proving something in a scholarly fashion, that:

> One influential school of African history writing [the one we authors of this book wish to make a case for] is very much influenced by a version of this defensive approach [that sets out to view African history from European terms of reference!]. It doesn't spend its time seeking for vanished literate city-builders but it does set out to prove that African history is *similar* to that of the rest of the world and to Europe in particular; to show that general laws of human development apply to Africa; and all this with the admirable intention of demonstrating that Africa is not inferior or incapable of progress along the general path. Now, although this school speaks in terms of general laws of human society, it is using *European* development as its yardstick. Most of the writers in this school are Marxists of various kinds and they are trying to apply to Africa the Marxist analysis of European society. Marx didn't say a great deal about non-European society and while many Marxists are now arguing that to be true to the spirit of their master they should apply

his techniques rather than this conclusions to Africa, much Marxist writing about Africa has in fact tried to make it fit into the same pattern which they use to explain European events. They use terminology first applied to Europe - like 'feudalism'; and they hold to a view of the primacy of material, technological and productive development which is not all that different from the view of the nineteenth-century European writers who first evaluated African society.[156]

One wonders whether Marx was as crude as that.[157] Moreover, it should be emphasized that the radical work which has been written about Africa has been more dense in concepts and more convincing than the crude, reductionist and idealist Whig interpretations of African history, whose crisis has been the concern of this book.[158]

Perhaps Marxism is alien to Africa; perhaps ideas like entrepreneurship are indigenous to Africa; but the latter ideas, though pretending to be factual, have done more to obfuscate the African reality under imperialism than has so far been realized. If change is the product of the heroic deeds of the 'elect',[159] then the stagnation of Africa can be blamed on Africans themselves. But, then, what about those who refused Africa the chance of having its own entrepreneurs? Development, too, becomes a function of capital. Thus African stagnation is explained in terms of lack of entrepreneurs and capital. Implied in this is the advice that, if Africa wants to develop, then it must invite more capital and entrepreneurs.[160] Thus is popularized the idea of 'development by invitation'.[161] Development becomes a matter of injecting foreign entrepreneurs, capital and technology into the economy. Such ideas are peddled throughout Africa, in lecture theatres, books and articles, with a view to subverting the minds of the young and reconditioning those of the old.[162]

To see entrepreneurship as the precondition for development, however, is to be mesmerized by the appearance of capitalism, whose reality lies elsewhere. Moreover, to argue that entrepreneurship is the cause of change or innovation is not to say much since in reality the three terms are synonymous. Change cannot be the cause of change! The phenomenon has to be penetrated and located in the sphere of social processes which act as its spring.[163] The same can also be said of the heroic deeds of technological change.[164] A discussion of African stagnation has to be situated within the imperialist trap to which the continent has been relegated since the commencement of colonial enlightenment. The process of colonial enlightenment was intended to facilitate the extraction of surplus labour, which proceeded side by side with the ruralization of the continent. All sorts of innovation were geared to exploiting the African peasantries. How the exploited could have, at the same time, become entrepreneurs and so acted as agents of capitalist exploitation is an insoluble and abstract metaphysical quandary. But the empirical method, which does nothing more than reproduce the paradoxes of the capitalist world, will never go beyond positing such conundrums:

Vulgar economy actually does no more than interpret, systematize and defend in doctrinaire fashion the conceptions of the agents of bourgeois production who are entrapped in bourgeois production relations. It should not astonish us, then, that vulgar economy feels particularly at home in the estranged outward appearances of economic relations in which these *prima facie* absurd and perfect contradictions appear, and that these relations seem the more self-evident the more their internal relationships are concealed from it, although they are understandable to the popular mind.[165]

But all science would be a mere technical activity if it meant solely recording and collating the ideological products of existing empirical practices.[166]

Critical Theory: The Only Historiographical Alternative

The discussion so far in this chapter could be illustrated further with the aid of an ancient Roman mythological figure, Cacus, who used to steal oxen 'by dragging them backwards into his den so that the footprints made it appear they had gone out from there'. Marx is known to have reacted to this story by exclaiming: 'An excellent picture, it fits the capitalist in general, who pretends that what he has taken from others and brought into his den emanates from him, and by causing it to go backwards, he gives it the semblance of having come from the den.' This story Marx compared to bourgeois ideology, which 'does not so much falsify the facts as misinterpret them so as to reverse what has taken place'. 'The footprints are there for all to see, but if we limit ourselves to what is immediately apparent [the subject matter of "empirical" social science] we will arrive at a conclusion that is the exact opposite of the truth.' However, by examining what led up to the event in question, as well as 'the surrounding circumstances – that is, its real history and the system of events in which it resides' – it is possible 'to understand what really happened and why'. We must let our mind wander away from the footprints left by Cacus's oxen if we are to come to grips with reality.[167] Such is what this chapter has attempted to advocate. This is also what has been termed the critical theory.[168]

If only for the sake of amplification,[169] crucial to the notion of critical theory is the view that the commonsense opinion of the world is not necessarily the true and realistic one. This is because the appearance and essence of reality do not necessarily coincide. Copernicus and Galileo had to use a method which was equally critical to prove both theoretically and experimentally that the world was round. But as Galileo is known to have complained: 'As I wished to show the satellites of Jupiter to the Professors of Florence, they would see neither them nor the telescope.' Rather they 'invoked the traditional authority of Aristotle', who had taught that the earth was 'fixed and perfect', 'and finally invoked the power of the Index and the Inquisition against Galileo to force him to recant his views'. Intellectual McCarthyism did not begin in the 1950s. Galileo's ideas, however, eventually won the day, and medieval scholasticism was subordinated to the bourgeois intellectual revolution. Now the latter is on the defensive.[170] Ideas, then, are part and parcel of society, and they are just as much of a threat to the vested interests in society as they are a boon to the revolutionary forces.[171]

The critical method is intended to apprehend reality. In this, the force of abstraction is crucial. Here we come into collision with not only empiricist historians, but also radical ones. To abstract is an anathema for empiricists. Those who indulge in abstraction, they remark snidely, move 'with rare freedom in empirical matter'.[172] Thus they advocate that empiricists be required to give a detailed factual account of the past rather than to theorize.[173] Such a thought seems to be an invitation to view historical phenomena 'separately from each other, by bits and pieces', rather than to comprehend the phenomena 'in their inner connection as an integrated totality'.[174]

The second type of opposition has come, as has already been indicated, from radical historians, especially the Marxist historian E.P. Thompson. Thompson's reaction has been prompted by the Althusserian school of Marxism, particularly Hindess and Hirst, who have declared that 'Marxism, as a theoretical and a political practice, gains nothing from its association with historical writing and historical research. The study of history is not only scientifically but also politically valueless.'[175] Thompson has declared that Althusserianism is based on limited academic learning and thus has no general validity. Althusser, Thompson argued, has 'no category, or way of handling experience'. He thus 'falsifies the dialogue with empirical evidence inherent in the production of knowledge or knowledge production'.[176] Thompson's reviewer, Gray, has urged that undue abstraction or theorization if uncontrolled by the 'empirical idiom' may, as was indicated in Chapter 1, produce 'a kind of creeping epistemological paralysis'.[177] The undue fear of theory harboured by empiricists, Thompson has urged, is devastating for historical practice. So, too, is an unwarranted treatment of 'empirical matter' as a bugbear. Thus Thompson finds Althusser, Popper and Raymond loitering in the same arena, that of frustration. Thus too, Thompson argues that one should not assume 'a guilt of some sort' with regard to history 'without scrupulous enquiry into its practice'.[178] For this reason, he advocates a dialectical interplay between theory and empirical matter:

> Historical practice is above all engaged in this kind of dialogue; with an argument between received, inadequate, or ideologically informed concepts or hypotheses on the one hand, and fresh or inconvenient evidence on the other; with the elaboration of new hypotheses; with the testing of these hypotheses against the evidence, which may involve interrogating evidence in new ways, or renewed research to confirm or disprove the new notions; with discarding those hypotheses which fail these tests, and refusing or revising those which do in the light of this engagement.[179]

Such seems to be the remedy for the so-called 'poverty of theory' which results when empirical matter is determinant.

Indeed, since the Cultural Revolution and the death of Mao Tse-tung,

Chinese historians too are advocating 'Faithfulness to Facts in Party History Research'.[180] The July issue of the monthly *Lishi Yanjiu (Historical Studies)* commented that 'while fidelity to facts isn't all there is to historical investigation, it is the basis for this work. Only by grasping the accurate facts can one have a basis for making a scientific analysis and bringing to light the inherent laws of history.' 'A correct conclusion,' it was reiterated, 'cannot be drawn if the historical facts themselves are wrong.'[181] But *Lishi Yanjiu* did not end there. Rather, on how to write the correct history of the Party, it said:

> It is wrong to evade the fact that bad persons, bad things, shortcomings and errors did occur within our Party. It is even worse to ascribe all achievements to those persons who are positively evaluated and all shortcomings and errors to those who are negatively evaluated. This is typical of the metaphysical approach which denies contradictions, denies struggles, denies that things develop and are mutable, and considers that what is bad is all bad.[182]

Here then we leave the arena of historical method as an interplay between theory and facts for the actual reality which we want to comprehend. Appearance is and is not. Facts are and are not. Here, too, it should be emphasized, whatever attitude Althusserians have about history, they are right on this score. 'The concrete is concrete because it is the concentration of many determinations, hence the unity of the diverse.'[183] Short of realizing this, we shall again return to the empiricist reading of history which is one-dimensional. To apprehend the concrete, as has been said by many detractors of historical materialism, does not imply movement 'with rare freedom in empirical matter'. Instead detailed appropriation of the empirical matter, coupled with the 'analytical division of the material into its constituent abstract elements', precedes the exploration of the 'decisive general connections between these elements', and the 'discovery of the decisive intermediate links which effect the mediation between the essence and the superficial appearance of the material'. This is followed by empirical verification of the analysis, and the discovery of more data, new connections and so on, 'in the infinite complexity of reality'.[184]

Establishing connections between elements of the totality with a view to apprehending the latter is an important stage in the logic of dialectics. Here, the materialist differs from the empiricist, who claims that the elements as embedded in the facts speak for themselves, and thus gets tantalized by their appearance which, to say the least, is but an aspect of the totality. Such is the danger of 'positivistic narrowness' or 'problem-blindness'. The same argument can be advanced in the case of professional history, which apparently survives on the discovery of new terrains of fact. Indeed, facts are determinant. Moreover, the enterprise of professional history, to some extent, comprises a dialogue between theory and facts.[185] Thus, too, Lenin maintained that, at each stage of an analysis, the dialectical method presupposes 'control either by facts, or by practice'.[186] But it is a control which also implies a totality of the historical process. Professional history seems to have overlooked this logic of dialectics, and in so doing it has failed to go beyond the level of counterfactualization.

Professional historians consider historical events unique and so tend to discuss particular clusters of them independently of others.[187] In this regard historical events are described in minute detail, and micro-history takes precedence over macro-history. But as R. Samuel has observed: 'No subject in history is intrinsically "micro" or "macro", mainstream or marginal, big or small. Everything depends on the way it is studied. The local study may be myopic, but then it is possible to hold eternity in a grain of sand.'[188] Thus too Lenin emphasized: 'the individual is the universal . . . . Consequently, the opposites [the individual as opposed to the universal] are identical: the individual exists only in the connection that leads to the universal. The universal exists only in the individual and through the individual. Every individual is [in one way or another] a universal. Every universal is [a fragment, or an aspect, or the essence of] an individual. Every universal only approximately embraces all the individual objects. Every individual enters incompletely into the universal, etc.'[189] Similarly, in the epoch of imperialism, no events in African history can be discussed outside the circuit of capitalist development. To do so is to indulge in abstract empiricism, which is ideological and bourgeois.[190] This argument will be illustrated with the aid of the 'Joseph Merinyo case'. We do so lest the empiricists go on with their accusation: 'You are too high up there: come down to earth.'

The Case of Joseph Merinyo and the KNPA in Tanganyika

In July 1930 Monckton, the manager of Messrs. Monckton and Co., agricultural produce exporters who specialized in, *inter alia*, buying coffee from the Kilimanjaro Native Planters Association (KNPA) and shipping it abroad, wrote to Molloy, his branch manager in Moshi, to inquire 'why from Y consignment onwards to E' of that year's coffee from Moshi, 'there is no surplus shown as formerly?' He also required Molloy 'to state how this surplus has been dealt with'.[191] Molloy wrote back to say that he did not understand what his superior exactly wanted.[192] Thus Monckton took time to explain in detail that 'it is universal experience that when small parcels of commodities are purchased and bulked, an excess results from the turn of the scale, conversely there is a loss when commodities are retailed.' Hence he again demanded: 'explain why surpluses have ceased.'[193]

Molloy got angry and attributed Monckton's attitude to 'ugly rumours circulated by narrow-minded, jealous, suspicious, uneducated and idiotic people of low breeding'.[194] Thereupon Monckton, who was still keeping his cool, referred the incident to the government of Tanganyika. The colonial government appointed an accountant, Griffith, to inquire into the matter.[195] In his report he observed that the 'coffee surpluses' had been misappropriated by Molloy. But he also added that 'such misappropriations could not have been conducted by Mr Molloy w/o the assistance of certain officials of the KNPA . . . . Books show that from March 1929 to March 1931 only Shs.

10,379/90 was collected from members for subscriptions, whereas with 13,000 members Shs. 26,000/- should have been received from the two years.'[196] Moreover, officials of the KNPA gave loans to one another freely. All this convinced Griffith that the Chagga were 'not competent to control such large interests as are involved, and ... that a reliable European Firm [should] be requested to take over this work, subject to the direction and supervision of the Administration and that the Books and Accounts be written up by the same Firm (subject to Audit) at an agreed rate of Commission on coffee sales and a definite fee for keeping the said books of Accounts.'[197] KNPA had been established in 1924 by a group of Chagga *kulaks* who had been encouraged to do so by Sir Charles Dundas and Sir Donald Cameron, both of whom saw it as an aspect of indirect rule in the economic sphere. With the departure of Cameron in 1931 it seems that the colonial government was no longer interested in indirect rule, at least where cooperatives were concerned.[198]

Further investigation led to the discovery of more skeletons in the KNPA cupboard. It was found that Merinyo, the Association's president, had embezzled £21 and that he had also obtained '£120/16/0 from the firm of Sharif Jiwa and Co., Moshi, by false pretence'.[199] Merinyo was prosecuted and imprisoned. A committee of the KNPA protested against the manner in which Merinyo's case had been handled, but in vain. The colonial government was determined to punish Merinyo.[200]

With Merinyo safely in prison, the Tanganyika Government pounced on KNPA itself. If the government had originally been of the opinion that KNPA was useful, it was no longer so after the Merinyo case.[201] A weekly journal, *East Africa*, which was a mouthpiece of the settler community, was of the same opinion. In its editorial of 16 July 1931 it announced:

> We have yet to meet any sound judgement of the position who believes [*sic*] the KNPA necessary to the development of the Native coffee growing industry; indeed, some of the most ardent advocates of that development hold that the Native growers are unfairly penalized by the present inefficient organization, to which they are compelled to contribute on the basis of a cess, and there is good reason to believe that the great majority of the Native growers object to the Association, the utility of which they fail to recognize, though they realize that it has been a lucrative source of income to some of their leaders and their hangers on.[202]

In 1932, KNPA was abolished, on the grounds that it had become a hive of *fitina* (intrigues). In its place was formed the Kilimanjaro Native Cooperative Union (KNCU) which, according to the colonial government, was intended to separate economic activities from politics, and so disabuse the cooperative movement of *fitina*.[203] Emphasis was now placed on efficiency in the collection of coffee from producers. KNCU was made the only legal body with the power to purchase 'native coffee' and sell it to exporters.[204] An economic adviser of Irish extraction, A.L.B. Bennett, was appointed KNCU's economic adviser. After performing some initiation ceremony, he was made a 'friend of the Chagga'. In the 1920s the Chagga had got a colonial grandfather by the name of Charles Dundas; now they had a *mbuya* imposed on them.[205]

The events which led to the demise of KNPA and the formation of KNCU have been interpreted variously. At one point they were regarded as the quintessence of 'native corruption'. Subsequently they have been seen as the embodiment of African initiative, and so on.[206] It is a good example of the problems of 'abstracted empiricism'. And it shows the necessity of viewing modern historical events in Africa within the broader context of an international problematic. Failure to do this results in various kinds of reductionism coupled with much intellectual dissatisfaction.[207] The formation of KNCU should be discussed within the wider context of the Great Depression.

The Depression was a worldwide phenomenon which affected the capitalist economy rather adversely. Of all the East African colonies, Tanganyika was hit most seriously. Railway traffic declined, and so too did government revenue.[208] Adverse weather and a locust invasion intensified the crisis. There was no solution to hand. The colonial government obtained most of its revenue from levies on exports of agricultural produce. It was logical, therefore, that it should embark on what came to be termed the 'grow more crops campaign'.[209] The British Imperial Government was also interested in seeing that the colonial economy revived quickly. The Colonial Development Fund was established with this aim in mind.[210]

As the 'grow more crops campaign' was stepped up, it was realized that markets for agricultural produce were equally important. This idea had been emphasized in the 1920s. In the 1930s it was reiterated more vigorously. It was thus considered appropriate to have greater control of cooperatives where they were already in existence, and to establish others where there were none. A number of ordinances were also promulgated with the intention of centralizing markets: the Trades Licensing Ordinance, the Itinerant Traders Ordinance. the Markets Ordinance, the Coffee Ordinance, and the Cooperative Societies Ordinance.[211]

These draconian measures disturbed even some colonial proconsuls. To clear their consciences, therefore, they looked for an excuse. In Tanganyika, one official observed:

> Recently the people of Great Britain have been driven by world economic conditions to abandon a long cherished tradition of free trade and to substitute tariffs and a multitude of other restrictions, and if we are to maintain our little place in the world economics, it seems to me perfectly clear that we also recognize that unregulated and inefficient trading will, in fact, simply put us out of the world's markets for the time being.

He also noted that the trend of events made it very unlikely that nineteenth-century economic theories about the 'unrestricted flow of trade and the right of any individual to buy and sell as and where he pleases . . . [will] be re-established'. Such was a confirmation of the era of interventionism.[212] Further restrictions were introduced during the Second World War, when the era of marketing boards in Tanganyika dawned. These were intensified after the War, when Britain had to be bailed out of the economic mess in which it was trapped. And so things have been ever since, although in a nationalized form.[213]

Three names, among others, have been mentioned in the course of this discussion with regard to the notions of colonial innovation and preservation, and even more so in connection with the origins of the cooperative movement in Tanganyika: Cameron, the second British Governor in the territory, who is reputed to have consolidated if not also laid the foundation for indirect rule in the area; Dundas, a District Commissioner in Kilimanjaro, who was later to become Cameron's Chief Secretary; Bennett, who became adviser to the KNCU when it succeeded the KNPA in 1932; a fourth name to be mentioned is that of Harrison, the Director of Agriculture in Tanganyika in the 1930s. Cameron, Dundas and Bennett wanted to see Africans developed in their own tribal lands. They wanted to preserve as much of what was 'tribal' as was permissible. Where this was not the case, especially in areas where commercial agriculture was not encouraged, the three British officials encouraged migrant labour. Harrison, however, regarded the 'native district' as an estate to be harnessed under capitalism. For him, or so it sounded, innovation was more important than the doctrine of preservation.

Cameron regarded the cooperative movement as a form of indirect rule in the economic arena. Here too, therefore, he appeared less of an innovator than Harrison. Cameron praised the establishment of the KNPA immensely. But in 1932 this Association was disbanded and replaced by a more pliable organization. This action was taken because of what was viewed as the rise of too much *fitina* in Kilimanjaro, coupled with the economic pressure put on the colonial government by the Great Depression. Here the goals of preservation and innovation seemed to be in conflict. But this was only so at face value. To concentrate too much on the appearance of contradictions in most cases leads to a blind alley.

The epoch of imperialism has been characterised as 'the era of the oppression of nations on a new historical basis'. It is also the era when capitalism 'becomes parasitic: imperialistic'.[214] Politically, the state becomes interventionist, the more so in the colonies, where the control of labour by capital is still formal. Such has also been termed formal subsumption of labour, whereby capital accepts the existing process as it finds it but directs it to achieve its needs. This should be contrasted with real subsumption, whereby capital transforms the labour process to satisfy its needs for more raw materials and so on. Under conditions of real subsumption, capitalist exploitation is mystified by forces of the market. Where formal subsumption is dominant, force mediated by paternalism is normally prevalent.[215]

The idea of paternalism was not intended to preserve the 'native and his institutions', as has been reiterated time and again by colonial administrators and social anthropologists of all kinds. This doctrine was intended to pamper capital, given the formal control of labour by capital. Labour, on the other hand, had to be coerced constantly to ensure that it was subjugated to the whims of capital. It has been said that colonial proconsuls believed in what they practised, and that their beliefs influenced their actions greatly. Certainly they believed in paternalism, but we must look for the social basis of such beliefs. This is important lest we get lost in one kind of mysticism or another.[216]

The cooperative movement was introduced into the British colonial empire in the latter half of the nineteenth century. Supposedly based on the Raiffeisen model, it was not long before the cooperatives degenerated into instruments of colonial parasitism camouflaged in paternalist verbiage about protecting rural life. Preservationism as a doctrine was whipped up vigorously in the latter half of the nineteenth century with the rise of monopoly capitalism and the doctrine of Social Darwinism. Social Darwinism, as a mark of imperialist chauvinism, was intended to conceal the new level of rapacity being attained by the endeavour to reproduce capital on a global scale. The cooperative movement was intended to fulfil this new trend. It formed the basis of colonial paternalism.[217]

The colonial state was paternalistic not to the natives, but to capital. If, in the case of Kilimanjaro, Dundas has been called a grandfather of the Chagga, that should be turned on its head and set the right way up. This is also true with regard to Bennett, the acclaimed friend of the Chagga. Both were in favour of capital penetration. Their doctrine of preservationism was intended to preserve capital, in line with the social relations of parasitism. Innovation was always made if this could lead to the process of preserving capital. If there was conflict between innovation and preservation, it was merely revolved around how best to perpetuate the conditions of parasitism.

Innovation and preservation, the notions used in the course of establishing colonial markets, as well as in other contexts, were two sides of the same coin. Their unity lay in the fact that they were both evoked in the interests of colonial parasitism. Their conflict supplied what seemed to be a natural way of justifying the social relations of colonial parasitism.[218]

The debate on innovation versus preservation has been alluded to because it also affected the fall of the KNPA and the rise of the KNCU. KNPA had been regarded as a good example of indirect rule in the economic sphere. But following the Joseph Merinyo case and the rumours which ensued, the KNPA was abolished and the KNCU established under tighter governmental control. So-called indirect rule in the economic sphere melted away. But this took place during the Great Depression, when the colonial government in Tanganyika was calling for stricter control of the 'colonial market' in order to allow a more efficient system of surplus labour extraction from the peasantry. Call it initiative or response, the Joseph Merinyo case gave the colonial government the occasion rather than the cause for intervention. The manner in which the intervention was carried out, though, was conditioned by the historical events *in situ*. Such is the manner in which local events which are supposedly unique interact with more general occurrences and so give way to others. The historical process which is a result of many determinations and mediations should not be forsaken for so-called unique events. Rather the two should be analysed simultaneously, and their dialectical relationship revealed.[219]

Conclusion

Professional Africanist history has been written within the prism of the dichotomy of appearances versus reality, legend versus facts, colonialism versus nationalism, and so on.[220] A similar dichotomy was used in colonial historiography. But while the latter used the imperial system as its focus of analysis, the former has taken recourse in the idea of the nation. Just as in European history, 'the spirit of Nationality has appealed to historians with special force, because it has offered them some prospect of reconciling the common human desire for unity of vision with the Division of Labour imposed upon them by the application of the Industrial system to their work'.[221] In the same way with African nationalism it has been said that 'there is no "African response" but a multitude of African responses; no "African initiative" but a multitude of initiatives; no single source which can document *the* African attitude but only sources which can document *an* African attitude.'[222] As voices of an aggregation of individuals, however, Africans contributed in various ways to the nationalist movement. Why this happened is of no concern to the professional historian. The crucial thing is that it happened and that the historian should find out how it happened.[223] Somehow, the motives of aggregates of individuals find a common course through the hidden hand of Providence.[224]

Crucial in the production of social knowledge is not only the product but the active element in the production of that knowledge. There are two such elements in knowledge which are normally dismissed as subjectivism: that element which confirms the prevailing order of things and also that which seeks to transcend it with a view to releasing the human potential for unlimited development. Colonial historiography was an affirmation of the process of colonial enlightenment, which allegedly was intended to release 'native potential' from the frustrating tribal cage which was assumed to be against modernity. Under colonialism, the introduction of modernity was supposed to confirm the triumph of the individual, a necessary condition for entrepreneurship and development. And now that 'African rationality' has been underlined in African postcolonial historiography, the active element emphasized in colonial historiography — modernity — has been confirmed as being typically African. In colonial historiography the active element was maintained under the aegis of paternalism. Now, however, the idea of 'rational choice' has taken over.

In view of this, professional Africanist historians have accepted the prevailing order as natural and have meticulously traced its development back into the dim past. In some cases this has been carried as far back as the Olduvai Gorge to ensure that the living are in close communion with *Zinjanthropus boisei*![225] The prevailing order is accordingly snapped from its mooring in the imperialist world so as to seek its glorification in the past.[226] What is essentially a product of the imperialist present is thus historicized and associated with the ancient past so as to confuse the causes of the forces which have made it such that some people today eat the fruits of others under the pretext that they suffered under colonialism. As for those who are now suffering with bitterness because their sweat is used to wash the feet of others - sorry, we all suffered!

This is the kind of situation which must be transcended by the other type of active element in knowledge. History is littered with the efforts of the poor and their organic intellectuals to transcend the given order, so as to take control of the process of development and deliberately plan for the future. It is also watered by the blood of those to whom fell the Promethean task of storming the heavens. The duty of an historian, professional or otherwise, is to report this objective siutation as well as the material forces which brought it about.[227]

So far, however, postcolonial Africanist historiography has distorted this reality. Many Africanist historians have claimed that their studies are objective, but theirs has been 'the objectivity of a eunuch'. The empirical method which is dominant in professional African history claims non-partisanship as the precondition for producing objective knowledge. Partisanship is treated as a mark of delinquency, a denial of rigour, and an impediment to the possibility of discovering truth. But as we have already noted more than once, the empirical method is also partisan.[228] How, then, it can also be instrumental in producing an objective history of Africa is a mystery which not even its ardent supporters have been able to resolve. Perhaps all that one has to do is to believe. But, to substitute intuition and introspection for serious investigation and experimentation is indicative of decadence. If that is not the case with the bourgeois world, it certainly was so with Scholasticism and Confucianism in the past.[229] The empirical method is bankrupt; its nihilist tendency attests to this.[230] The manner in which it has been introduced to the study of African history and its subsequent failure to produce an objective history of the continent has shown the barrenness of the method. This aridity, though, is not to be attributed to 'the thing called history' but to the class it is supposed to legitimize. Was it not Fanon who said that the African petty bourgeoisies are a bankrupt lot who are committed to turning Africa, its culture, and its wealth into a desert where nothing will grow?

References

1. F. Stern (ed.), *The Varieties of History*, New York 1956, p. 16.
2. D. A. Low, 'The anatomy of administrative origins: Uganda 1890-1902', Makerere 1958, mimeo.
3. H. S. Hughes, *Consciousness and Society*, St Albans, Herts., 1974.
4. D. A. Low, 'Lion Rampant', *Journal of Commonwealth Political Studies*,

II, 1964. See also his *Lion Rampant*, London 1974.
5. H. Berstein and J. Depelchin, 'The object of African history: a materialist perspective', Dar es Salaam 1977, mimeo. L. Althusser and E. Balibar, *Reading Capital*, London 1970. H. Bernstein, 'Marxism and African history: Endre Sik and his critics', *Kenyan Historical Review*, IV, 1978. J. Depelchin, 'Towards a problematic history of Africa', *Tanzania Zamani*, 18, 1976. See also his 'Towards the production of materialist epistemology', Dar es Salaam 1977, mimeo. B. Hindess and P. Q. Hirst, *Precapitalist Modes of Production*, London 1975.
6. Q. Hoare and G. N. Smith (eds.), *Selections from the Prison Notebooks of Antonio Gramsci*, London 1971. P. Anderson, 'Antinomies of Antonio Gramsci', *New Left Review*, 100, 1977. E. P. Thompson, *The Poverty of Theory and Other Essays*, London 1978. Mao Tse-tung, *Four Essays on Philosophy*, Peking 1966. J. O'Brien and P. Newcomer, 'Where do good ideas come from?' NE Anthropological Association Meetings, 1974.
7. See E. Mandel's introduction in K. Marx, *Capital*, I, Harmondsworth 1976. See also the introduction, Mandel, *Late Capitalism*, London 1975.
8. Bonaventure Swai, 'The contradictory past: historians and African history', Southern African Universities Social Science Conference, 1979.
9. J. Depelchin, 'African history and the ideological reproduction of exploitative relations of production', *Africa Development*, I, 1976.
10. A. Mafeje, 'The octopus and the clock: problems of reification in the social sciences', The Hague 1968, mimeo.
11. However, see also M. Bloch (ed.), *Marxism and Social Anthropology*, London 1975.
12. Thompson, *The Poverty of Theory and Other Essays*.
13. See the introduction in D. A. Low (ed.), *Soundings in Modern South Asian History*, London 1968, p. 18. See also his 'Buganda in Modern History', London 1971. The 1968 Universities of East Africa Social Science Conference devoted a lot of time to discussing this theme.
14. R. H. Palmer, 'Johnston and Jameson: a comparative study in the imposition of colonial rule', in B. Pachai (ed.), *The Early History of Malawi*, London 1972.
15. A better discussion of this is available in K. Marx, *The Eighteenth Brumaire of Louis Bonaparte*, Moscow 1967, pp. 10-12.
16. B. Brown, *Marx, Freud and the Critique of Everyday Life*, New York 1973, p. 31.
17. J. Depelchin, 'African history and the ideological reproduction of exploitative relations of production', *Africa Development*, II, 1977.
18. C. Fyfe (ed.), *African Studies Since 1945*, London 1976.
19. T. O. Ranger, 'Towards a usable past', in Fyfe (ed.), *op. cit.*
20. H. Bernstein, 'Sociology of underdevelopment vs sociology of development', in H. Bernstein, D. Cruise O'Brien and W. Nafziger, *Development Theory: Three Critical Essays*, London 1978.
21. W. Rodney, 'The year 1895 in Southern Mozambique: African resistance to the imposition of European colonial rule', *Journal of the Historical Society of Nigeria*, V, 1971.
22. A. MacIntyre, *Marcuse*, London 1970. See also H. Marcuse, *An Essay on Liberation*, Harmondsworth 1973, and *One Dimensional Man*, London 1973.

23. Brown, *Marx, Freud and the Critique of Everyday Life*.
24. A. Callinicos, *Althusser's Marxism*, London 1976, pp. 9-19.
25. *Ibid.*
26. R. Garaudy, *Marxism in The Twentieth Century*, London 1970, pp. 42-3.
27. P. Anderson, 'Components of the national culture', A. Cockburn and R. Blackburn (eds.), *Student Power*, Harmondsworth 1969, pp. 221-2.
28. Garaudy, *op. cit.*
29. L. Kolakowski, *Marxism and Beyond*, London 1969.
30. Callinicos, *Althusser's Marxism*, p. 19.
31. L. Kapteijns, *African Historiography written by Africans 1955-1973*, Leiden 1977.
32. M. Crowder and O. Ikime (eds.), *West African Chiefs*, New York 1970.
33. M. Nicolaus's foreword in K. Marx, *Grundrisse*, Harmondsworth 1973, p. 18.
34. Callinicos, *op. cit.*
35. A. Bose, *Marxian and Post-Marxian Political Economy*, Harmondsworth 1975, pp. 45-7.
36. H. Bernstein, 'Underdevelopment and the law of value', *Review of African Political Economy*, 6, 1976.
37. A. Mafeje, 'The problem of anthropology in historical perspective: an inquiry into the growth of the social sciences', *Canadian Journal of African Studies*, 10, 1976.
38. J. Ranciere, 'The concept of "critique" and the critique of political economy', *Economy and Society*, 5, 1976.
39. B. Davidson, *In the Eye of the Storm*, London 1972, p. 47.
40. H. Bernstein and J. Depelchin, 'The object of African history: a materialist perspective', *History in Africa*, 5, 1978.
41. H. Zinn, *The Politics of History*, Boston 1971.
42. J. Habermas, *Towards a Rational Society*, Boston 1970.
43. J. S. Saul, 'Nationalism, socialism and Tanzanian history', L. Cliffe and J. S. Saul (eds.), *Socialism in Tanzania*, I, Nairobi 1972.
44. Cf. K. Marx and F. Engels, *On Ireland*, London 1971.
45. D. Goel, *Philosophy of History*, Delhi 1967.
46. See A. Marwick, *The Nature of History*, London 1970. A. J. P. Taylor, *Englishmen and Others*, London 1956.
47. See E. H. Carr, *What is History?*, London 1962.
48. V. Kelle and M. Kovalson, *Historical Materialism*, Moscow 1973.
49. R. P. Wolff, 'Beyond tolerance', R. P. Wolff, B. Moore and H. Marcuse, *A Critique of Pure Tolerance*, Boston 1969, p. 3.
50. MacIntyre, *Marcuse*.
51. See Lord Acton's inaugural lecture on the study of history in his *Lectures on Modern History*, London 1964. A. Montefiore (ed.), *Neutrality and Impartiality*, Cambridge 1975.
52. L. Trotsky, *The History of the Russian Revolution*, I, New York 1932, p. xxi.
53. E. P. Thompson, 'Romanticism, utopianism and moralism: the case of William Morris', *New Left Review*, 99, 1976, pp. 88-9.
54. G. Muriuki, 'Background to politics and nationalism in central Kenya: the traditional social and political systems of Kenya peoples', B. A. Ogot (ed.), *Politics and Nationalism in Colonial Kenya*, Nairobi 1972.

55. J. H. Plumb, *The Death of the Past*, Harmondsworth 1973, pp. 11-16.
56. *Ibid.*
57. A. J. Toynbee, *A Study of History*, I, London 1956, pp. 2-3.
58. *Ibid.*, p. 4.
59. *Ibid.*, p. 5.
60. G. Connell-Smith and H. A. Lloyd, *The Relevance of History*, London 1972, pp. 37-40.
61. P. Gay, 'The history of history', *Dialogue*, 3, 1970.
62. J. H. Plumb, 'The historian's dilemma', in J. H. Plumb (ed.), *Crisis in the Humanities*, Harmondsworth 1964, p. 25.
63. Carr, *What is History?*, p. 14.
64. B. Moore, 'Tolerance and the scientific outlook', Wolff, Moore and Marcuse, *A Critique of Pure Tolerance*.
65. See M. Nicolaus's foreword in K. Marx, *Grundrisse*.
66. MacIntyre, *Marcuse*, pp. 23-4.
67. Taylor, *Englishmen and Others*, p. 16.
68. G. Igger, 'The new historiography in historical perspective', *Australian Journal of Politics and History*, XVII, 1971.
69. H. S. Hughes, *Consciousness and Society*.
70. Plumb, 'The historian's dilemma'.
71. Carr, *What is History?*
72. H. Butterfield, *The Whig Interpretation of History*, Harmondsworth 1973, pp. 8-9.
73. Igger, 'The new historiography in historical perspective'.
74. J. H. Robinson, *The New History*, New York 1962.
75. G. Novack, *Pragmatism versus Marxism*, New York 1975, p. 17.
76. Taylor, *op. cit.*, p. 14.
77. Igger, *op. cit.*
78. Quoted by P. M. Kennedy, 'The decline of nationalistic history in the West 1900-1970', *Journal of Contemporary History*, 8, 1973, p. 82.
79. H. Luthy, 'The passing of the European order: colonialism and the cargo cult', *Encounter*, IX, 1957, p.3.
80. R. L. Heilbroner, *The Future as History*, New York 1961, pp. 30-35. This crisis is also found in other disciplines within the field of social science. See for example W. E. Connolly (ed.), *The Bias of Pluralism*, New York 1969. M. Surkin and A. Wolfe (eds.), *The End of Political Science*, New York 1970.
81. R. F. Berkhofer, *A Behavioural Approach to Historical Analysis*, New York 1969, pp. 47-9. See also H. S. Hughes, 'The historian and the social scientist', A. V. Riasanovsky and B. Riznik (ed.), *Generalizations in Historical Writing*, Philadelphia 1963.
82. T. C. Cochran, 'History and cultural crisis', *American Historical Review*, 78, 1973, p. 10.
83. G. Wright, 'History as moral science', *American Historical Review*, 81, 1976.
84. L. Hanke, 'American historians and the world today: responsibilities and opportunities', *American Historical Review*, 81, 1975.
85. J. Fast and L. Franscisco, 'Philippine historiography and the demystification of imperialism: a review essay', *Journal of Contemporary Asia*, 4, 1974. See also E. Utrecht, 'American sociologists on Indonesia', *Journal*

of *Contemporary Asia*, 3, 1973.
86. This seems to be Raymond Aron's view which is quoted by H. Lefebvre, 'What is the historical past?', *New Left Review*, 90, 1975.
87. I. Jennings, *Democracy in Africa*, Cambridge 1963. J. F. Mbwiliza, 'The struggle for ideological hegemony and the politics of the transition to socialism', Dar es Salaam 1978, mimeo.
88. M. Shaw, *Marxism and Social Science*, London 1975.
89. K. Marx and F. Engels, *Manifesto of the Communist Party*, Moscow 1973, pp. 46-8.
90. Callinicos, *Althusser's Marxism*.
91. C. Boggs, *Gramsci's Marxism*, London 1976, p. 17.
92. Callinicos, *op. cit.*
93. See J. L. Blau's introduction in W. James, *Pragmatism*, New York 1967, p. vii.
94. Shaw, *Marxism and Social Science*.
95. L. A. Coser, *Man of Ideas*, New York 1970.
96. Habermas, *Towards a Rational Society*.
97. H. Bernstein and J. Depelchin, 'The object of African history: a materialist perspective'. See also J. Depelchin, 'Towards a problematic history of Africa'.
98. H. Laski, *The Rise of European Liberalism*, London 1962.
99. Heilbroner, *The Future as History*, pp. 22-7.
100. L. Goldmann, *The Human Sciences and Philosophy*, London 1973.
101. G. Novack, *Empiricism and its Evolution*, New York 1971.
102. H. Marcuse, 'Repressive tolerance', in Wolff, Moore and Marcuse, *op. cit.*, p. 81.
103. *Ibid.*
104. Garaudy, *Marxism in the Twentieth Century*.
105. Novack, *op. cit.* M. Nicolaus, 'The unknown Marx', in R. Blackburn (ed.), *Ideology in Social Science*, London 1972. G. Wall, 'The concept of interest in politics', *Politics and Society*, 5, 1975. H. K. Girvetz, *The Evolution of Liberalism*, New York 1966.
106. O. Onoge, 'Towards a Marxist sociology of African literature', University of Dar es Salaam 1977, mimeo.
107. Shaw, *op. cit.*
108. A. Chetwynd, 'Professionalism and the public interest', *Report of Proceedings of Town and Country Summer School*, University of St Andrews 1972, p. 71.
109. Toynbee, *A Study of History*.
110. Anderson, 'Components of national culture'.
111. Chetwynd, 'Professionalism and the public interest'.
112. L. Berry, *The University in Africa and in Tanzania*, Dar es Salaam 1970, p. 20.
113. Connell-Smith and Lloyd, *The Relevance of History*.
114. Berry, *op. cit.*
115. *Ibid.* A. J. Temu, 'Problems of creating the African university: the case of the University of Dar es Salaam', *Social Praxis*, I, 1974.
116. Shaw, *op. cit.*
117. W. Suchting, 'Marx on the dialectics of production and consumption in the introduction to the *Grundrisse*', *Social Praxis*, 3, 1975, p. 296.

118. *Ibid.*, pp. 298-9.
119. Boggs, *Gramsci's Marxism*.
120. See the introduction in B. W. Cook, A. K. Harris and R. Radosh (eds.), *The Past Imperfect*, II, New York 1973, p. 3.
121. *Ibid.*
122. *Ibid.*
123. J. K. Fairbank to H. Zinn, n.d. *Ibid.*, p. 342.
124. Novack, *Pragmatism versus Marxism*. H. K. Wells, *Pragmatism*, New York 1957.
125. Quoted by V. I. Lenin, *Materialism and Empirico-Criticism*, Moscow 1970, p. 12.
126. *Ibid.*, pp. 22-3, 40-1, 108-9.
127. J. Allett, 'The first principle of science: the penetration of false appearance', *Social Praxis*, 3, 1975. This principle is stated most clearly in Marx's notion of fetishism in *Capital*, I, Moscow 1975.
128. K. Korsch, *Marxism and Philosophy*, London 1970.
129. Carr, *What is History?*
130. Garaudy, *Marxism and the Twentieth Century*, p. 42.
131. *Ibid.*
132. *Ibid.*
133. Mao Tse-tung, *Four Essays on Philosophy*.
134. G. S. Jones, 'History: the poverty of empiricism'.
135. Acton, *op. cit.*, p. 17.
136. *Ibid.*, p. 33.
137. Callinicos, *Althusser's Marxism*.
138. See also Shaw, *op. cit.*, p. 42. For more on objective truth see M. Rutkevich, 'The theory of reflection and the ideological struggle', *Social Science*, I, 1970.
139. J. Horton, 'Combating empiricism', *The Insurgent Sociologist*, III, 1972. P. Hamilton, *Knowledge and Social Structure*, London 1974.
140. P. Mitchell, *African Afterthoughts*, London 1954.
141. B. A. Datoo, 'Towards a reformulation of Boserup's theory of agricultural change', University of Dar es Salaam 1976, mimeo.
142. M. Elkin, *The Pattern of the Chinese Past*, London 1973. J. T. C. Liu and P. J. Golas (eds.), *Change in Sung China*, Lexington, Mass, 1969.
143. Schumpeter quoted by I. Inkster, 'A smattering of history: marginal men and the cultural context of the English industrial revolution', University of New South Wales 1975, mimeo, p. 5.
144. L. Billet, 'Political order and economic development: reflections on Adam Smith's *Wealth of Nations*', *Political Studies*, XXIII, 1975.
145. Z. S. A. Gurynski, 'Entrepreneurship - the true spring of human action', *South African Journal of Economics*, 44, 1976.
146. E. E. Hagen, *On the Theory of Social Change*, III, Homewood 1962.
147. R. Robinson and J. Gallagher, *Africa and the Victorians*, New York 1961.
148. J. Iliffe (ed.), *Modern Tanzanians*, Nairobi 1973.
149. J. Iliffe, *Agricultural Change in Modern Tanganyika*, Nairobi 1971, p. 21.
150. Marx, *Capital*, p. 667.
151. M. Kidron, *Capitalism and Theory*, London 1974, pp. 12-15.
152. See the introduction in T. O. Ranger (ed.), *Emerging Themes of African*

History, Nairobi 1968, p. xxi. See also Ranger (ed.), *Aspects of Central African History*, London 1968, and *The Recovery of African Initiative in Tanzanian History*, Dar es Salaam 1969. R. H. Davis, 'Interpreting the colonial period in African history', *African Affairs*, 72, 1973. C. C. Wrigley, 'Historicism in Africa', *African Affairs*, 70, 1971.
153. K. Botchwey, 'Marxism and the analysis of the African reality', *Africa Development*, II, 1977. K. Grundy, 'The "class struggle" in Africa', *Journal of Modern African Studies*, 2, 1964. I. Shivji, *Class Struggles in Tanzania*, Dar es Salaam 1975. W. Rodney, 'Class contradictions in Tanzania', *The Pan-Africanist*, 6, 1966. S. Amin, 'The class struggle in Africa', *Revolution*, I, 1964.
154. P. E. H. Hair, review of W. Rodney, *A History of the Upper Guinea Coast 1545-1800* (Oxford 1970)' in *Bulletin of the School of Oriental and African Studies*, XXXIV 1971, p. 444.
155. E. Gellner, 'The Soviet and the savage', *Current Anthropology*, 16, 1975. I. Wallerstein, 'Class and conflict in Africa', *Monthly Review*, 26, 1975.
156. T. O. Ranger, 'How should we approach and assess African history', African history teachers seminar 1965 mimeo. H. Bernstein, 'Marxism and African history: Endre Sik and his critics', *Kenya Historical Review*, 5, 1977. H. Odera-Oruku, 'Marxism and African history', *Ibid.*, II, 1973.
157. K. Marx and F. Engels, *On Colonialism*, Moscow 1974.
158. C. Fyfe (ed.), *African Studies since 1945*, London 1974.
159. P. Mathias, 'Science and technology in processes of industrialization 1700-1914'; and R. Cameron, 'The international diffusion of technology and economic development in the modern economic epoch', *Five Themes*, Sixth International Congress on Economic History, Copenhagen 1974.
160. T. Szentes, *Underdevelopment and Socialism*, Dar es Salaam 1970.
161. N. Girvan, 'The development of dependency: economics in the Caribbean and Latin America: review and comparison', *Social and Economic Studies*, 22, 1973, pp. 2-4.
162. Mbwiliza, *op. cit.*
163. P. M. Sweezy, *The Present as History*, New York 1962, p. 275. See also J. Stein, 'Of Mr. Booker T. Washington and others: the political economy of racism in the United States', *Science and Society*, XXXVIII, 1974-5.
164. N. Rosenberg, 'Marx as a student of technology', *Monthly Review*, 28, 1976.
165. Marx, quoted by Callinicos, *Althusser's Marxism*.
166. P. D. Chakrabarti, 'Behaviouralism: a challenge to Marxism', *Social Scientist*, 4, 1976, p. 57.
167. B. Ollman, 'Marxism', *Monthly Review*, 30, 1978, pp. 36-7.
168. T. Schroyer, *The Critique of Domination: The Origins and Development of Critical Theory*, Boston 1975.
169. The following section is based on Bonaventure Swai, 'Trade and politics in eighteenth-century Malabar', Dar es Salaam 1979, Ch. 5; and on sections of 'The Merinyo case and the demise of KNPA: the political economy of the events in colonial Tanganyika', *Taamuli*, 9, 1979; 'The contradictory past: historians and Africanist history', Southern African

Universities Social Science Conference, 1979; 'Imperial proconsuls and the marketing of colonial produce: the origins of cooperatives in Tanganyika', Dar es Salaam 1979.
170. G. Novack, *An Introduction to the Logic of Marxism*.
171. Mao Tse-tung, *Four Essays on Philosophy*. J. O'Brie and Peter Newcomer, 'Where do good ideas come from?' NE Anthropological Association Meetings, 1974.
172. E. Mandel, *Late Capitalism*.
173. A. Mafeje, 'What is historical explanation?', Dar es Salaam 1971, mimeo, p. 2.
174. E. Mandel's introduction in K. Marx, *Capital*, I, Harmondsworth 1976, p. 18.
175. B. Hindess and P. Q. Hirst, *Precapitalist Modes of Production*, London 1975. J. Depelchin, 'Towards the production of materialist epistemology', *Utafiti*, II, 1977.
176. Thompson, *The Poverty of Theory and Other Essays*.
177. R. Gray, 'E. P. Thompson, history and Communist politics', *Marxism Today*, 23, 1979.
178. Thompson, *op. cit.*, p. 212.
179. *Ibid.*, p. 235.
180. *Peking Review*, 34, 1979, p. 5.
181. *Ibid.*
182. *Ibid.*
183. Mandel, *Late Capitalism*, p. 23.
184. *Ibid.*, pp. 16-17.
185. Thompson, *op. cit.*
186. V. I. Lenin, *Collected Works*, Vol. 38, Moscow 1961, p. 320. A. Mafeje, 'The octopus and the clock: problems of reification in the social sciences', The Hague 1968, mimeo. A. Kozharov, *Monism and Pluralism in Ideology and Politics*, Sofia, n.d.
187. G. R. Elton, *The Practice of History*.
188. R. Samuel (ed.), *Village Life and Labour*, London 1975, p. xix.
189. Lenin, *Collected Works*, Vol. 38, p. 361.
190. C. Wright Mills, *The Sociological Imagination*, Harmondsworth 1970.
191. Monckton to Molloy, 23 July 1930, Tanzania National Archives, TNA 26034.
192. Molloy to Monckton, 25 July 1930, *ibid*.
193. *Ibid.*
194. Molloy to Monckton, 18 August 1930, TNA 26034.
195. P. C. (Arusha) to Chief Secretary, 20 June 1931, TNA 26038.
196. Report on prosecution against J. P. Molloy (ex-manager of) Monckton & Co.'s branch at Moshi and J. Merinyo (ex-president of KNPA), TNA 26034.
197. Griffith to P.C., 11 June 1931, TNA 26034.
198. P. Gifford, 'Indirect rule: touchstone or tombstone for colonial policy', Gifford and Louis, New Haven, 1967.
199. Report on prosecution against . . . *op. cit.*
200. 'The KNPA meeting', 30 June 1931, TNA 26038.
201. See also Swai, 'The Merinyo case and the demise of KNPA: the economic context of two events in the history of Tanganyika'.

202. *East Africa* (weekly journal), TNA 26038.
203. P. C. (Arusha) to chief secretary, 25 August 1931, and chief secretary to P. C. (Arusha), 30 November 1931, TNA 26038.
204. Annual report, Northern province, 1934, TNA 11681.
205. A. C. Ofunguo, 'History of Kilimanjaro Chagga Citizens Union 1946-64', BA dissertation, University of Dar es Salaam, 1974.
206. *Ibid.*
207. Bonaventure Swai, 'The contradictory past: historians and African history'. Shih Chun, *On Studying some World History*, Peking 1973. G. Haupt, 'Why the history of the working class movement?'.
208. Chief secretary to all provincial commissioners, 14 October 1931, TNA 13044.
209. *Ibid.* See also 'Secretariat circular no. 36 of 1931, from senior agricultural officer: 'Improvement of quality of native crops'.
210. E. A. Brett, *Colonialism and Underdevelopment in East Africa*, London 1973.
211. TNA 10138.
212. *Ibid.*, p. 97.
213. H. Bernstein, 'Capital and the peasantry in the epoch of imperialism', Dar es Salaam 1976, mimeo.
214. J. Blaut, 'Are Puerto Ricans a national minority?', *Monthly Review*, 29, 1977.
215. E. Mandel, *Marxist Economic Theory*, London 1971.
216. A. J. Green, 'A socio-economic history of Moshi Town', MA Dar es Salaam 1979.
217. *Ibid.*
218. B. Davey, *Economic Development of India*, Nottingham 1975. A. Wolfe, 'New directions in the Marxist theory of politics', *Politics and Society*, 4, 1974.
219. A. 'Agh, 'Labyrinth in the mode of production controversy', Southern African Universities Social Science Conference 1979.
220. Cf. N. Harris, *Beliefs in Society*, Harmondsworth 1968, p. 25.
221. Toynbee, *A Study of History*, p. 10.
222. Ranger, *The Recovery of African Initiative in Tanzanian History*, p. 12.
223. T. O. Ranger, 'Connections between "primary resistance" movements and modern mass nationalism in East and Central Africa', *Journal of African History*, IX, 1968.
224. R. Albritton, 'The game analogy and bourgeois ideology', *Social Praxis*, 3, 1975.
225. I. N. Kimambo and A. J. Temu (eds.), *A History of Tanzania*, Nairobi 1969.
226. Saul, 'Nationalism, socialism, and Tanzanian history'.
227. Garaudy, *Marxism in the Twentieth Century*.
228. Marcuse, 'Repressive tolerance'.
229. Novack, *Pragmatism versus Marxism*.
230. Kozharov, *Monism and Pluralism in Ideology and in Politics*.

5. Towards an International Problematic for Africanist Studies

A Summing Up

For subscribers to colonial studies, as has been shown in Chapters 2 and 3, Africa comprised a collection of static tribes.¹ While the tribes contained people, they were nonetheless considered faceless and unpredictable.² In communities of this kind, communalism prevailed. Similarly there was unity of the living, the dead, and the unborn: a situation which made indigenous change hard to realize. If there was change, it was induced from without. Here, then, history could not be made from within. This was considered so because the making of history was a product of individual initiative, and there was nothing of the sort in precolonial Africa.³

Given this attitude, colonial proconsuls and defenders of imperialism believed that they were dealing with a *tabula rasa*. Thus, following the doctrine of 'the Dual Mandate',⁴ in Africa, Lord Leverhulme of Lever Brothers said in 1924, with regard to West African colonial social formations, that like 'children when they are immature and underdeveloped', the peoples of this area comprised excellent but unorganized 'materials for labour' to be organized by the 'white man'. The 'organizing ability is the particular trait characteristic of the white man' which would make the 'African native . . . happier, produce the best, and live under the larger conditions of prosperity when his labour is directed and organized by his white brother who has all these million years' start ahead of him.'⁵ Notwithstanding the myth of laziness, the duty of the African in this context was, as the saying goes, to 'work like a nigger'.⁶

The doctrine of mutuality has not changed, but the components of its equation have altered. The idea of the Dual Mandate was forged in the high noon of the Partition of Africa, during which, faced with stagnation, capital sought a 'leak . . . to slow the rise of the overall organic composition and the fall in the rate of profit'⁷ in an area hitherto considered an external arena fit for plunder.⁸ The supposed Dual Mandate and its concomitant, paternalism, typical of capitalism which presents itself as something it is not, was intended to pamper capital rather than the 'natives'.⁹ Hence, with the aid of the interventionist colonial state, the extraction of super-profits was made possible.¹⁰

But since the 1920s a new 'leak' for the capitalist system, the arms

153

economy, has come to the fore. This, coupled with the development of classes deposited with all their contradictions by capital in colonial social formations, changed the position in such formations from one of enlightenment to that of management.[11] The realization of management varied from one social formation to another depending on how they were articulated with the capitalist mode of production. The transition, however, made it possible for the 'African personality' to be asserted in its various manifestations.[12] This, it has been alleged, constitutes the assertion of the African reality which colonial proconsuls and theorists had attempted to deny.[13]

Assertions of this kind continue to be made, despite the crisis in postcolonial Africanist historiography. The intent of such assertions, as was declared in the preamble of the Workshop on the Teaching of History in African Universities, held at the University of Lagos in September 1977, remains 'to inculcate into Africans a sense of pride in their own past'.[14] Such an endeavour has entailed turning colonial assumptions on their head, but unfortunately not the right way up. Thus terms like 'tribe' have been displaced by more fashionable designations like 'ethnic community'. Thus, too, as has already been shown, the assertion that the unity of the past, present and future in African societies was indicative of stagnation has been turned on its head and used as evidence to show that African societies were conscious of history after all.[15] As for the assumption that Africans were not conscious of themselves as individuals, it has been asserted that *Homo psychologicus*, the abstract individual, was also a natural feature of Africa.[16] For positivists, the abstract individual is perfectly comprehensible outside society. His activities are considered external manifestations of his essential subjectivity, but the subjectivity is regarded as natural and thus beyond the terrain of scientific rigour.[17]

This is the kind of individualism which was injected into the study of Africanist history in conjunction with conventional historiography. But if such were the assertions deployed in the study of the African past, what emerged was not the history of individuals, but what has been termed nationalist history. Here, however, Africanist history is not unique; for in the search for the spirit of European history, to mention but one branch of professional history, historians have exhibited similar patriotic prejudices. The main snag about professional history is that, while there has been a decline in nationalist history in Europe, especially after the First World War, and even more so since the Second, this has not been the case with postcolonial social formations.[18] But is it true that nationalism has declined in capitalist Europe — or is it that assertions of this kind are now seen for what they are - mere forms of chauvinist obscurantism? To answer this it is necessary to understand the nature and meaning of imperialism.

The Essential Context for Understanding: The Era of Imperialism

Lenin, as was shown in Chapter 4, saw imperialism as 'the era of oppression

Towards An International Problematic for Africanist Studies

of nations on a new historical basis'; 'the division of nations into oppressor and oppressed'. This era constitutes the epoch of monopoly capitalism. In this regard, Lenin noted that capitalism does not really mature. Rather it becomes parasitic and imperialistic. During the period of monopoly capitalism, each capitalist country seeks to solve its deepening crisis by expanding its empire of colonies and semi-colonies in order to amass super-profits. It is a period which witnesses the intensification of exploitation and political oppression. From this there emerge two distinct political processes: 'among the oppressors, a cannibalistic form of warfare; among the oppressed, a struggle for national liberation'. Imperialist chauvinism, which found academic expression in Social Darwinism, takes the form of training 'the Negro to habits of industry' because 'you cannot manage without coercion'. The assumption, therefore, is that imperialism starts from a clean slate locally - an idea which is expressed in all kinds of cultural vandalism, in the form either of colonial assimilation or preservationism.[19] For this reason it has rightly been observed: 'In the colony, the imperialists impose the fiercest forms of cultural aggression, the purpose of which is not to assimilate the colonial people to the colonizer's nationality, but to pacify them by wresting from their culture all possible sources of resistance - including, if possible their language.'[20]

It is against this kind of vandalism, oppression and exploitation that Africans reacted. This reaction, as well as its variants, constitutes the stimulus which has induced professional historians to accumulate a good deal of information for the purpose of analysis. In most cases the effort has been geared to locating 'the African spirit', which presumably must be something totally different from anything European. But nothing has been so anti-colonial or anti-European, at least in terms of verbal ferocity, as nationalism. Much history, therefore, has been reduced to this nationalistic form, or variants of it.

But to indulge in this type of discourse without showing its material underpinnings is to be enamoured of fetishism.[21] Colonial nationalism is a product of the anti-imperialist struggle waged by all classes and particularly the working masses. Unlike nationalism in the epoch of the rising bourgeoisie, whose destination was mature capitalism, colonial nationalism constitutes the national liberation struggle whose ultimate destination is socialism. This struggle must be analysed in relation to imperialism whose ideology today is becoming more aggressive and chauvinistic.[22] Moreover - and to recapitulate - the destination of national liberation is not the demise of colonialism alone, but the emancipation of 'oppressed peoples, colonies, and semi-colonies, from imperialism'.[23] The former is but an interim measure.

Short of considerations of this kind, postcolonial Africanist historiography will continue to be trapped in the ideological impasse to which it has been relegated. This is what the previous chapters have shown. Many of the assertions in postcolonial Africanist historiography lack theoretical content. Much as they have shown some semblance of movement, they have presented these processes as if they were cyclical. Thus some Africanist historians have now come round to thinking that Trevor-Roper was not wrong in what he said about African history. For such historians, Trevor-Roper's assertions about the African past are no longer a subject of derision. His observations might have been absurd, but they were honest. Indeed Africa did have emperors, but to many outside observers they looked hungry and naked.[24] The problem with the African past was its 'undercivilization' as evidenced by rampant stagnation, especially in the realm of technology. Africans might take pride in the ruins of Zimbabwe, and other glories of antiquity, but they did not discover the plough. Ever since the technological advances of the African Iron Age,[25] the hoe has remained predominant — even right into the twentieth century,[26] the era of the space age.

The impasse in African postcolonial historiography has been not only in the fields of political, economic or social history but also in the craze which has of late surfaced about African technology. The Macaulayan ambition shown by many professional Africanist historians to turn the most obscure 'historical sources', especially the epics told by *griots*, into a celebrated study that would 'replace the latest novel on the lady's dressing-table' has died hard.[27] In short, professional Africanist history, generally, has no theoretical coherence of its own.

Western experience has usually been considered the model to be emulated by colonial and postcolonial societies. As with 'political and economic development', in the realm of technology the question has repeatedly been asked: 'Why has Africa remained backward in relation to the achievements of the West?' Formerly, the answer was simple. The backwardness of colonial and postcolonial societies was explained by the laws of Social Darwinism. Since 1945, however, prejudice has changed its scientific language.[28] Moreover, the rise of nationalism called for the glorification of the hitherto colonized societies. Technological progress was not a monopoly of the West, as the achievements of ancient China, India and Peru reveal.[29] Africa too, it has been argued, contributed tremendously to man's technological advance.[30] Such advance could also be indicative of the anomaly whereby most ancient societies were either technical without being scientific or scientific without being technical, but that is beside the point.[31] The heroic deeds of the few in such societies cannot be discounted.

Yet it has been argued further that Africa was technologically undercivilized, especially in the precolonial era. It follows that the continuation of such a phenomenon into the colonial period cannot be attributed to imperialist exploitation.[32] This has been explained in terms of the lack of a challenging environment which, whether adverse or bounteous, remained overwhelming to those who lived in it.[33] But to attribute progress solely to the environment is to be too fatalistic. Catherine Coquery-Vidrovitch has sought to analyse the peculiarities of African social formations in order to explain the persistence of technological backwardness.[34] She argues that, unlike Asian and European civilizations, Africa was neither bureaucratic nor aristocratic.[35] African social formations were too segmentary, and by implication lacked the necessary strata of people, to introduce technological innovation whether in the form of the plough or the wheel. Long-distance trade, too, failed to penetrate the autonomy of the subsistence village. A dualistic structure comprising the coexistence of the subsistence village and long-distance trade persisted. Coquery-Vidrovitch writes:

> No African regime, no matter how despotic, felt the need to eliminate communal village structures within its borders, before the village scarcely interfered with the process of exploitation. As long as the village transmitted its tribute to the chief of the district or of the province, it ran the life of the collectivity as it pleased. The leaders assured the worship of the clan's ancestors; the chief of the land allotted arable land to each family and to each generation; the women's group set the rules for transactions on the local food markets. There was no need to supply the ruler with a contingent of plantation labourers or caravan porters, jobs generally performed by royal slaves seized in foreign countries. The most frequent obligations were limited to military service in the time of war or, as in Dahomey, to the selection of some girls for the harem or the 'Amazon' corps, the elite female warriors of the king.[36]

African kings largely depended on plunder extracted from neighbouring societies. They did not, therefore, exploit their own subjects unduly.

But, in direct contrast to this picture, we have already shown in the case of the Kimbu that long-distance trade did entail the establishment of large concentrations of population domestically to facilitate the extraction of surplus labour in order to pay for imported luxuries which were reserved for the consumption of the dominant classes. Village economies and long-distance trade did not coexist as dualistic structures. Furthermore, it is not satisfactory to explain African technological backwardness in terms of the absence of bureaucratic and aristocratic systems comparable to those of Asia and Europe. For how could the kidnapping of slaves for the Atlantic and Indian Ocean slave trades, and elephant hunting for ivory, have induced the invention of the plough in Africa? What is more, technological stagnation did not end with the onslaught of colonialism. The African peasantry still depends on the hoe.

'Only in a context which sees the isolated facts of social life as aspects of the historical process and integrates them in a totality,' says Lukacs, 'can knowledge of the facts hope to become knowledge of reality.'[37] So, too, is it with facts about the backwardness of technology in Africa. Technology is not an entity independent of the society in which it is found. As an embodiment of the forces of production it is governed by the relations of production. In the epoch of imperialism it is defined in relations to capital, of which it is also a product.[38] Technology has existed in different societies and in various epochs. Today, in postcolonial societies, its special characteristics should be explained not in terms of the persistence of tradition but as a condition of capitalist relations of production which are anomalous.[39]

The question is this: why, notwithstanding the imposition of the capitalist mode of production on the so-called Third World, has economic development there not resulted in the production of machines by means of machines? Why, in other words, has petty commodity production persisted in the epoch of imperialism? This question cannot be answered solely in terms of backward technology. In India nuclear technology and the bullock cart have continued to exist side by side. In Africa capital-intensive and labour-intensive methods of production similarly coexist. The answer would seem to lie more in the nature of the relations of production deposited by capital, rather than in technology *per se*.[40]

Whenever the normal methods of capitalist accumulation have failed to thwart stagnation, capital has sought for loopholes to ward off the threat. In most cases this has necessitated the extraction of super-profits under conditions of formal subsumption of labour by capital. Under colonialism this entailed the extraction of absolute surplus labour mediated by the colonial state. Neither the labour process nor the production process was entirely dominated by capital under these conditions,[41] so petty commodity production under the command of capital was allowed to exist.[42] Petty producers still maintain some independence, since there is no real subsumption of labour by capital. Here then 'the capitalist regime everywhere comes into collision with the resistance of the producer, who, as owner of his own conditions of labour, employs that labour to enrich himself, instead of the capitalist.'[43] Such an attitude might be regarded as symptomatic of the idea of 'sons of the soil' comparable to that of 'freeborn Englishmen', but the conditions in which this was embedded should not be overlooked.[44] Reluctance to work for the capitalist regime caused the problem of scarcity of labour for mining and plantation concerns. But there was also a 'beggar problem' in the towns.[45] With increased capitalist penetration the chances for proletarianization seemed bright; but so too was the colonial concern to keep plantation and mining labour migrant.[46] The 'symptomology' of the colonial dilemma of peasantization versus proletarianization, the idea of the 'sons of the soil' versus the 'beggar problem', is indicative of the specific contradictions between labour and capital embedded in colonial social formations themselves.

The task of the human sciences is to study such contradictions in their historical specificity. But this entails that the various disciplines should break away from the dominant ideologies of ruling classes in which they are engulfed.[47] This is so because development of the human sciences is dependent on the nature and alignment of classes. In the feudal era scholasticism, which sought to perpetuate the medieval social order, prevailed. Its dominance was enforced to such a degree that papal scholarship continued to maintain that the world was flat even after it had been proved to be round. Bourgeois scholarship went beyond scholasticism, but then asserted the dominance of the empirical world at the expense of that of social reality. Now that bourgeois scholarship is being challenged by a method which seeks to go beyond the level of empiricism, it has become more and more opportunistic.[48]

A similar picture has been shown in professional Africanist history. In West Africa professional history seems to have stagnated at the juncture of the so-called African historiographical revolution; in East and Central Africa there is a quest to go beyond the level of both nationalist euphoria and nihilism. In South Africa, save for the work of radicals mainly in exile, professional history appears to have persevered with the propagation of the platitudes of colonial historiography.[49] These variations are all indicative of the differing alignment of classes in each of the areas mentioned. History, after all, is written not for the dead but for the living. It is influenced by, and also influences, the social conditions under which it is written. It may be, as the historian Adolf Stone has said, that history is precisely the historian's story, and nothing more.[50] The story may simply be the idiosyncrasy of the historian. Thus the endeavour to recover local initiative in African history has been said to be idiosyncratic.[51] But it has also to be noted (as observed in Chapter 4) that like a producer who produces in society, the historian thinks and writes in a specific society and is conditioned by its laws of motion which he, too, helps either to confirm or transcend.[52]

These issues, however, are avoided by professional Africanist historians in their quest to write learned monographs and journals using the figleaf of objectivism. 'The virtue of a thing,' to quote Plato once again, 'is the state or condition which enables it to perform its proper function well.'[53] The virtue of an historian is his objectivism. But what if, as we have already seen, the virtue is false? Plato had an answer to that too: it would be believed as a virtue as long as it worked. To maintain the city state, which was divided between the rulers and the ruled, and divided amongst the rulers, Plato observed:

> We will have to devise one of those useful lies of which we spoke, and if possible get the rulers themselves to believe it and in any case have it accepted by the rest of the citizens.' 'What kind of story would that be?' asked Glaucon. 'Oh, nothing very new,' I said: 'just a Phoenician story told by the poets, and located in many places. It has not happened in our time, and I am not sure that it could. It will certainly take a considerable amount of persuasion to put it over.' 'You seem reluctant to tell your story,' said Glaucon. 'Can you not just go ahead with it?' 'Very well, then,' I said: 'Here goes!'
>
> 'I will inform the rulers and their assistants, and then the rest of the citizens, that the training and instruction they had seemed to get had all been a dream: that in reality they had been fashioned and nurtured in the depths of the earth, and on being completed had been sent up to the light of day by their Earth Mother. For that reason they must protect the land which had been nurse and mother to them from its enemies, and regard the other citizens as earth brothers. "All of you who dwell in the City," we will tell them, "are brothers, but the god who made you mixed gold in the composition of those among you who are fit to rule. Silver entered into the composition of their assistants, and brass and iron went to the making of the farmers and other craftsmen. Your children will usually be like yourselves, but since you are all akin it is possible that a silver child may sometimes be born to a gold parent, and the other way about. Similarly the rest of you. The first and most imperative charge laid by God on the City's rulers is that they keep close watch on the children born among you and discern the metals

that have gone to their making. If one of their own progeny has iron or brass in its composition, they must have no scruple about putting the child among the farmers and workers whose nature it shares.[54]

Such is the invisible cage which helps to keep the order of the city state intact.

Just as every artefact and living creature has its virtue, 'so too we may say that each form of political society has an ideal condition in which its guiding principle is fully realized.' For Plato such a society is 'an aristocracy of merit in which the wise and good rule those who are inferior in talents and accomplishment.' The virtue in such an aristocracy is loyalty,[55] whose basis is the 'lie' we have quoted. This is how myths are used in society. Myths of this kind are not natural! They are made by man.[56] Likewise with the idea of objectivism. Its comprehension lies not in its wanton assertion, but in the endeavour to investigate its basis in the capitalist system. The same is true with objectivity in history. It will be hard to resolve the riddle of objectivity in history unless the system in which it operates is investigated.[57] In any case, as we showed in the last chapter, the debate has to be shifted to its proper locale — that is, the terrain of production of social knowledge.[58]

We have been arguing that an objective history of Africa must be written within an international problematic which takes cognizance of imperialism and the changing nature of capital.[59] This, however, should apply to other disciplines which are concerned with the recovery of African social reality. We will amplify this observation in the following section.

An Application of the Theoretical Problematic Being Proposed

The Political Economy of Tanzanian Educational History[60]

The emergence of African postcolonial societies in the aftermath of the Second World War engendered a re-examination of much of the erstwhile colonial mystagogy. This was undertaken with the intent to formulate policies considered more relevant to postcolonial societies. Education figured prominently in this kind of reconsideration of what was considered colonial. The endeavour was informed by the awareness that, like other aspects of social life, education is a function of the society in which it exists, and that systems of education differ from one society to another because of this. Colonial education had been intended to serve colonial social formations, and hence was irrelevant to postcolonial societies. Reform was, therefore, considered very pertinent. The matter seemed particularly urgent in view of the dysfunctional role being played by education in Africa. Education, it was argued, was intended to prepare people for their appropriate roles in society. Since African postcolonial societies were predominantly agricultural, it was felt that education should have a rural bias. This, however, education did not have, especially in the immediate aftermath of independence. But within a few years, the problem arose of school leavers who felt that their place was not in the countryside. Many of them, especially those who had completed primary education, drifted to the urban areas. In the towns it was feared that they could become a social menace. The drift was also disadvantageous to the countryside because it robbed the rural areas of their population, particularly of those young people potentially most productive. This was particularly unfortunate with the primary school leavers because, given their education, they could act as the yeast to leaven the rural dough.[61]

Education reform was thus considered necessary, and Tanzania was at the forefront of such efforts. An important pamphlet, *Education for Self-Reliance*, was published in the aftermath of the Arusha Declaration of 1967, which has been hailed by radicals, liberals and conservatives alike as a monumental experiment in educational reform. Experiment is the word; in this age of monopoly capital when society has been considered similar to an engine whose parts can be replaced and renewed at will so as to make the machine function more efficiently, the notion of social engineering, and by implication reform, is very much in the limelight. The talk of revolution, on the other hand, save with a view to smothering its content, has subsided.[62]

Tanzania could undertake this 'monumental experiment' because of the relative backwardness of its petty-bourgeois class. Resistance there was, but this was quickly squelched.[63] The reform was intended to 'reintroduce' agricultural education in schools, both primary and secondary. At tertiary level, at the University of Dar es Salaam, the idea was tinkered with, but was eventually reduced to asking students to make their beds and clear their rooms. Emphasis generally was placed on manual work. The aim of this was to combat elitism, which allegedly had been one of the crimes of colonial education. School gardens were introduced as a mark of self-reliance; though whether students have been able to feed themselves completely out of them is another matter. What is clear is that a lot of labour went into establishing school gardens. But the failure of this 'monumental experiment' has also been conspicuous.[64] So has resistance by students, as evidenced by the brutality of teachers in enforcing the big experiment.[65]

What went wrong? Reasons which have been adduced range from mismanagement and misunderstanding to student hostility.[66] But mismanagement and the like have been blamed for many other things. If it is to be used as an 'explanatory factor' in this instance, it is necessary to know why there is so much mismanagement, as has been alleged, in postcolonial societies. Education has been regarded as a new 'frontier' to help develop Africa. Why then has it failed? Like other frontiers, this one was evoked at a period when 'the time was out of joint'. It was intended to be 'the great escape', but turned out to be the escape that never was.[67] Idealists have argued that education reform, like other types of ideas, can bring about a revolution. But we have emphasized time and again that 'we do not set out from what men say they believe', but rather 'from their real, active life, and on this basis their real life-processes'.[68] It is important to locate the real basis of reforms in education. This seems to be a more satisfactory approach than simply taking educational reformers at their own word.

Within bourgeois societies, education reforms have been implemented at the instigation of capital, both in metropolitan, colonial and postcolonial societies.[69] The form of such reforms may differ, but the content is the same. Education reforms reflect the dynamics of the larger society in which they are introduced. They are not intended to bring about revolution, but to confirm a given social system by legitimizing specific social relations, imparting particular skills considered pertinent to a given social formation, and diffusing specific social maladies.[70] The argument that follows seeks to show that the education reforms introduced in Tanzania in the aftermath of the Arusha Declaration were intended to solve a specific economic crisis.

The emphasis placed on agriculture in schools was not a new phenomenon in Africa. The Phelps-Stokes Commission of 1924, which had been influenced to a very large degree by Booker T. Washington's experiment in industrial education in America, had emphasized the importance of education in agriculture in schools. The Advisory Committee on African Education in London had been equally assertive. That agriculture came to loom large in African schools, however, can be explained in terms neither of Washington's experiment nor of its discovery by colonial officials alone. Industrial education in America was intended to confirm a way of life peculiar to the Southern states.[71] In colonial Africa, agricultural education was also meant to serve a particular way of life which had been created following the articulation of precolonial African social formations with capitalism.

The initial research into the 'great experiment' - the subject of our present analysis - was carried out in the middle of 1969. It has been supplemented with further research recently.[72] The latter was stimulated by the failure of the 'great experiment' in education for self-reliance. This section is, therefore, primarily intended to explain that failure.

Attitudes versus Conditions as an Explanation of Primary School Leavers' Behaviour

The research on the plight of school leavers, as just mentioned, was conducted in two parts. The first part was undertaken in May and June 1969. The aim was to ascertain attitudes of primary school pupils towards white- and blue-collar work. This was followed by finding out how much these attitudes were adhered to, the criterion being the extent to which school leavers remained in rural areas once they had graduated from primary education after seven years of school. The research was done by using questionnaires (for class seven pupils) and interviews (for school leavers still in the countryside). The research was conducted in Mkuu, Rombo district, in Northeastern Kilimanjaro, Tanzania.

The second part of the research was conducted in January 1979. It was stimulated by the efforts of the Tanzanian Government to clear urban areas of what are termed 'loiterers', the unemployed people in towns who have also been dubbed 'exploiters'![73] While the research was done in Dar es Salaam, efforts were made to ensure that those interviewed were primary school leavers who had come from Mkuu, Rombo district. In most instances an endeavour was made to locate those respondents who had been originally interviewed in May and June 1969.[74]

The findings of the initial research can only be presented in summary form here. It was found that there were just as many pupils ready to do manual work in the countryside as there were aspiring to be clerks, doctors, teachers and so on. The idea that many primary school pupils want white-collar jobs, an attitude which goads them to drift to towns the moment they complete primary school education, is therefore, on this score, false.[75] The anomaly, however, is that, despite this apparently positive attitude, there were not many school leavers to be seen in Mkuu. Many, it was observed, do indeed leave for towns soon after completing their primary education.[76] As for the children of rich peasants, the majority find their way to private secondary schools, since their parents can afford to pay for this kind of education.

Like other areas of Kilimanjaro region in Northern Tanzania, Mkuu is a densely populated area. The possibility of school leavers creating their own households soon after graduating is minimal. Many of the roles which people of their age formerly played, notably herding cattle, have disappeared. Grazing areas have been turned over to cultivation, and cattle in Mkuu, as well as in most of Kilimanjaro, can only be stall-fed, largely by women. Moreover, the number of cattle has been reduced drastically. Whereas it was hard to find a household in Mkuu which owned no cattle in the 1950s, the opposite seems to be the case nowadays.[77]

The conclusion which was drawn from the attitudes of these school leavers, as well as from their conditions, was that 'we should not blame the youth that they are irresponsible, because they are victims of circumstances and forces they cannot control.'[78] Indeed, one of the circumstances which worried the youth most was the fact that, if they stayed with their parents until they were eighteen, they had to pay poll tax whether they possessed their own household or not. Poll tax had originally been a tactic used by the colonial administration to force Africans to become migrant labourers or to grow cash crops. Its effect could still be noticed in the 1960s. A lot of harassment accompanied the collection of poll tax.[79] Those who could not pay ran away to the bush until the wave passed, or fled to the towns where the system of administrative control was not as tight as in the countryside. The exodus to the towns started immediately after each Christmas to avoid the harassment meted out by chiefs, headmen and other colonial lackeys which began on the morrow of every New Year.[80]

Tanzanian peasants no longer pay poll tax but the exodus to urban areas is on the increase. The 1978 census results showed a marked increase in the Tanzanian urban population, much of which has been attributed to migration rather than to natural birth. In this regard, the further research conducted at the beginning of 1979 proved useful. Many of those who were interviewed showed that they had been forced to come to Dar es Salaam to find work which would enable them to buy clothes, shoes and so forth, articles which their parents could not afford to buy for them. Moreover, they felt that by working in Dar es Salaam they would be better able to help their parents as well as satisfy their needs more adequately. One respondent said that, however much he worked for his parents, they could not afford to buy him clothes for Christmas, articles considered essential in Christian Kilimanjaro. The migration to towns, he argued, is not induced by fear of manual work but by the failure to satisfy one's basic needs. Furthermore, he went on, many of those who migrated were not employed in white-collar jobs; nor were primary school leavers the only people who migrated to towns.

This seems to be a point which needs emphasis. Much as school leavers may be blamed for migrating to towns, they are not the only ones who are doing so.[81] Perhaps they should be considered irresponsible because, despite the education they have, they do not want to pay back what they owe to society by staying in the countryside.[82] But why so much should be expected from primary school leavers is the question. At most it shows the rather unrealistic idealism which has informed educational reform in Africa, and specifically Tanzania. Surveys of one kind or another have often been used to ascertain people's feelings on issues. Yet it must be emphasized that the conditions people endure are more important than attitudinal circumstances in determining their feelings. To ascertain the 'exact and positive knowledge of the conditions' into which primary school leavers are relegated is the concern of the rest of this essay.[83]

The Basis of Education in Colonial and Postcolonial Societies
Tanzania was first colonized by the Germans, who were superseded by the British following their defeat in the First World War. The Germans introduced formal education to Tanzania with a view to producing clerks to work in subordinate positions of the colonial administration. Such education was also given to chiefs in the belief that it would save them from the menace of 'rampant' corruption. The British followed suit. Missionaries, too, were involved in providing education to the African populace with the intent to produce catechists. In both cases only a few were chosen. The rest, therefore, had to be absorbed back into the rural economy. In both cases the education was markedly elitist; only very few were chosen from the many.[84] There is nothing which the ruling class fears more than a concentration of unemployed people, especially if there are some educated persons amongst them, and the colonial state feared this the more so since it itself was an imposition from without. The necessity to reproduce what has been termed traditional society with a view to ensuring the reconstitution and reproduction of the colonial labour force, therefore, became an important aspect of colonial policy. But such maintenance was only partial since precolonial African economies had to be articulated under imperialist hegemony to promote what amounted to plunder. This process engendered the disarticulation of African economies by separating agriculture from manufacture with the intention of destroying the latter. The African economies were deliberately ruralized and made complementary to the metropolitan ones. Here violence and market forces worked hand in hand. In this way, too, the export of labour and cash crops from the truncated economies became possible.[85]

The ruralization of precolonial economies through the destruction of manufacturing activities was intended to create a base for the production of raw materials and a market for imported manufactured goods. Where no raw materials were produced in the immediate vicinity, reserves to supply labour to those areas that were dominated by plantation or peasant agriculture were created. Initially there was peasant resistance to colonial innovation, as well as complaints by plantation owners of scarcity of labour. In both cases the 'native' was dubbed lazy, a phenomenon which was a pointer to the way in which labour was controlled by capital at that stage — i.e. formal control only.[86] The failure of migrants to satiate the plantation and mining economy's thirst for labour was explained in terms of the reputedly prevalent notion of 'sons of the soil'.[87] In the initial stages of the rise of capitalism in Britain, there was also a scarcity of labour for factories, which was in that case explained by the alleged prevalence of the idea of possessive individualism propagated by the 'freeborn Englishman'.[88] Yet, as in England, there was also the 'beggar problem' in Tanzania following the emergence of the so-called age of improvement under colonialism.[89]

The emergence of a beggar problem amidst a situation of scarcity of labour appears contradictory, but it reveals the anomaly inherent in the penetration of capital in colonial social formations. The beggar problem was a symptom of the gradual dissolution of traditional means of labour control coupled with the harsh labour discipline of the plantation and mining systems which forced people to head for the urban areas rather than elsewhere. In England Henry VIII had responded to a similar situation by hanging '30,000 mendicants, who had no means of livelihood'. From 1531, 'any person found begging without a licence was shipped.' Later loiterers were branded with red-hot irons, and transported.[90] They could not in this case be returned to the rural areas because in England, with the enclosure system, land was being reserved as pasture.[91] With the rise of the industrial system vagabonds, children and others were forced into factories. In colonial Africa, however, this was not the case.

P. P. Rey singles out three stages in the articulation of capitalism with precolonial 'modes of production in which agriculture and petty craftsmanship are closely associated'. These are:

> The first one, in which the role of agriculture is to supply the nascent capitalist sector with manpower and raw materials to help realize primitive capitalist accumulation; the second, in which agriculture is left out of the rapid growth of productive forces in the industrial sector; and the third, when agriculture itself becomes not only the supplier of raw materials for industry but also the recipient of various industrial products which will serve as inputs for the transformation of the mode of production in agriculture itself.[92]

Capitalist penetration in the colonies was not so neat, because of the tendency of capital to concentrate in specific areas (the metropolitan countries) and because the backward economies emerged mainly during the monopoly stage of capital when cartels coupled with plunder acquired new proportions.[93]

Super-exploitation rather than revolutionization of the process of production has dominated development in the age of monopoly capital, especially in colonial and postcolonial social formations. The commencement of the age of monopoly capital was accompanied with doctrines like Social Darwinism, whose variant in the colonies, indirect rule, was intended to perpetuate super-exploitation. The colonial policy consciously adopted at that time was geared to maintaining rural life with a view to ensuring the reconstitution and reproduction of the colonial labour force.[94] This was the basis of the colonial doctrine of paternalism: reproducing African rural life with a view, allegedly, to saving the colonial people from the traumatic effects of the 'cultural shock' engendered by the 'cultural encounter'.[95]

There was nothing natural or peculiarly African about colonial social formations on the African continent being exclusively agrarian. Colonial policies were fashioned in such a way as to make this appear natural. Among the policies which were geared to achieving this were the educational ones. That the colonial system of education was elitist, and that there were possibilities of primary school drop-outs becoming the cynosure of anti-colonial activity, made it an urgent matter to formulate policies considered complementary to colonial economic policies. Agricultural education in schools, therefore, prepared those pupils who would not have the advantage of further education or white-collar employment for life in the countryside.

The guiding principles of this policy were enshrined in the Phelps-Stokes Commission Report. They were also reiterated from time to time by the Advisory Committee on African Education based in London, whose duty it was to advise the Colonial Secretary on how best to run African education in the colonies.[96] Other recommendations followed subsequently, but at all times agriculture in schools was emphasized. The Committee's report of 1944 noted that 'to educate school children in the ideas and techniques of the Western world would lead to disaster if it resulted in setting a gulf between them and the African society of which they are members. Education of the school child must be accompanied by education designed to help the whole community towards better living.[97] This was called 'education for adaptation'. Nowadays the same thing is called education for self-reliance. It is only right, it was argued, that in areas that are largely agricultural, education must be related to the countryside. Thus farming was considered an important part of the school timetable.[98] This was considered a logical outcome of the colonial environment, but it was not long before racism was smuggled in to justify the anomaly created by the fact that European schools in the colonies were not required to perform manual labour. 'The African,' it was said, 'is a peasant farmer at heart and should be trained rather than educated.'[99]

In this situation the school garden turned into an arena of struggle into which nationalist politics had to penetrate.[100] For many, this has been interpreted as a sign of the fact that Africans did not like rural life. Indeed there is no reason to like rural life just for its own sake. Moreover, with colonial penetration, rural life - especially in the labour reserves - began to deteriorate; famines became more severe, and in the cash-crop areas social differentiation and class formation worsened the conditions of poor peasants.[101] The struggle against the school gardens was in fact a struggle against colonial oppression. Even a small arena like that of the teacher in the classroom has thus been on occasion a place of intense class struggle.[102] When the nationalist struggle in Tanzania gained momentum, school gardens were among the areas attacked, and subsequently the colonial government abolished them.[103] When Tanzania became independent in 1961, therefore, agricultural education in schools was no longer an issue worth discussing.

Besides removing agriculture from the school curriculum, segregated education was abolished in Tanzania. Schooling, especially secondary schooling, was stepped up, and university education was introduced with the inauguration of the University College, Dar es Salaam. The establishment of the University College was regarded as an important adjunct of nationhood. In reality, the necessity to have so-called 'high-level manpower' following the departure of colonial personnel seems a more plausible explanation. The colonial regime had foreseen this when it supported the founding of Makerere University College after the Second World War. Similar trends were noticeable in West Africa with the establishment of, for example, Ibadan University College.[104] The expansion of higher education was complemented by the people's efforts to expand primary school education, especially of the middle school category, or what is nowadays called the upper primary school. This was in response to the government's efforts to expand higher education. Education, as has been observed with regard to West Africa, and specifically Nigeria, was becoming a scarce commodity, and the demand was growing apace.[105]

If there was a market in education to which people responded by competing against each other, though, Marx's warning to political economists of his time apropos of their somewhat descriptive and empiricist studies is salutary. In his criticism he observed that such 'sagacity consists in observing the clouds of dust on the surface and presumptuously declaring this dust to be something mysterious and important'.[106] Such apparent mystery is in fact the phenomenon whose essence has to be ascertained. Initially, force had been used to procure students for the few schools established by the colonial government which had needed a steady supply of clerks and other types of colonial factotum. Small wonder, then, that the colonial schools resorted to so much violence; it was necessary to knock the primitive instinct out of the heads of pupils who were prepared to undergo this kind of purgatory! The harsh discipline in school continued, but pupils who volunteered to endure it increased. Some commentators have used this to argue that the so-called age of colonial improvement was a reality. It would, however, be more appropriate to note that the real reason lay in the failure of peasant households in the countryside to reproduce themselves, because of the colonial destruction of the traditional means of doing so.

Impoverishment in the countryside increased with the entrenchment of the capitalist mode of production. This was particularly the case with the labour reserves which were established to serve the colonial growth areas. In the growth areas, too, of course there was impoverishment of the poor peasants. For such people education became one of the means that might lead them to some form of wage employment. As for the rich peasants, education was also a means through which they could reproduce themselves in an amplified manner. All classes joined in the competition for the scarce commodity, education.[107]

The attainment of independence in Tanzania, as has already been indicated, was accompanied by much enthusiasm. This was shown in the education reforms which were introduced. But it was not long before contradictions began appearing. Complaints about school leavers migrating to urban areas grew louder and louder. In October 1966 students at the University College of Dar es Salaam went on the rampage.[108] Meanwhile the price of sisal on the world market began to fall noticeably. Sisal was then Tanzania's chief export. Sisal farms had to be abandoned. Unemployment for migrant labourers grew.[109] The Tanzanian Government was pushed into a tight corner. Following the attainment of independence, the government had expected to industrialize rapidly with the aid of foreign capital. This hope was not realized. The realities of a backward capitalist economy were being revealed nakedly.

In view of this, the Tanzanian Government and the ruling party, TANU, which was also the only political party in the country,[110] were forced to come to grips with the Tanzanian situation more firmly. The confusion of imperialist mystagogy, however, still loomed large. Hence came the declaration that the predominance of agriculture in the Tanzanian economy was natural, a fact which was then defended by all kinds of government policies. Colonial education policy had argued that the '*jembe* should not be forsaken' for the urban environment. Now this was resurrected, but in radical garb. The 1966 student revolt also highlighted the need to control the emergent intellectual stratum. Agricultural education and the teaching of manual labour through the National Service scheme were considered the appropriate answer. But far from there being a once-and-for-all answer to the problems of unemployment (an illusion which political rhetoric has tended to perpetuate), the problems of school leavers, and unemployment in general, are on the increase.

Towards the end of 1974, the Musoma Resolution was introduced, stipulating that only employed people would be allowed to pursue university education. The idea then was that since, after graduating, students of this sort would return to their former jobs, the possibility of being faced with an unemployed graduate population was small. In this way, too, the country was sure to have a docile university population disciplined not only by employers, but also by the university and the government. But control of this kind also tends to produce a strong antithesis, real rebels. Such was the cause of the subsequent 1978 student revolt.

Conclusion

In the section above, the fundamental, as opposed to apparent, causes of the so-called school leavers' problem have been delineated. The idealism rampant in descriptions of education reform has been challenged. In emphasising agriculture as an important aspect of the school curriculum, it was hoped that any anomalies which arose in the course of implementing the policy would be explained in terms of the character of those who did not abide by the tenets of the steamroller under which they passed. If the nation, it has been asserted, spends so much on education, it is only legitimate that those who enjoy this privilege should reciprocate by working in the villages after graduating. If this does not happen, then it is not the policy which is wrong, but the aberrant behaviour of those who refuse to respond to the nationalist call. Perhaps so, but nationalist as contrasted with national policies have to be examined closely, and their class content located.[111] Moreover, the essence of men is not an assemblage of things innate in them, but the ensemble of their social relations.[112] In backward capitalist countries, the disintegration of rural life is a social fact. The failure of the peasantry, especially the poorest amongst them, to reproduce themselves in the countryside is becoming more pronounced, and migration to towns is consequently on the increase. Any policy which fails to come to grips with this reality will be but a palliative; the 'disease' will recur, albeit in a different form. Cosmetic surgery is not intended to arrest old age but to disguise its appearance.

This observation applies not only to this section but throughout this study. It is an observation which has also been emphasized constantly: that to come to grips with reality there is a need to go beyond the level of appearances. It is particularly relevant to Africanist studies, which in the course of emulating works produced in the metropolitan countries have caricatured the African reality and turned it into a 'negative mirror image'.[113] An 'historical sense', it has already been quoted, 'is, in the hands of the oppressed, a powerful tool for revolutionary mobilization.'[114] Little wonder, then, that Africanist historians have distorted this sense so much. Isn't Africa, if one were to be allowed to speculate, one of the weakest links in the imperialist chain? Is it any wonder then that the crude violence meted out to African producers should be coupled with equally violent intellectual assault?

References

1. A. Kuper, *Anthropologists and African Anthropology*, Harmondsworth 1973.
2. M. Perham, *Ten Africans*, London 1973.
3. S. Avineri (ed.), *Karl Marx on Colonialism and Modernization*, New York 1969. T. Hodgkin, 'Where the paths began', C. Fyfe (ed.), *African Studies Since 1945*, London 1976. R. H. Davies, 'Interpreting the

colonial period in African history', *African Affairs*, 72, 1973.
4. R. O. Collins (ed.), *Problems in the History of Colonial Africa 1860-1960*, Englewood Cliffs, NJ, 1970.
5. Quoted by Davies, 'Interpreting the colonial period in African history'.
6. S. H. Alatas, *The Myth of the Lazy Native*, London 1976.
7. M. Kidron, *Capitalism and Theory*, London 1974, pp. 16-19.
8. I. Wallerstein, 'The three stages of African involvement in the world economy', in P. C. W. Gutkind and I. Wallerstein (eds.), *The Political Economy of Contemporary Africa*, London 1976.
9. See M. Nicolaus's foreword in K. Marx, *Grundrisse*, Harmondsworth 1973, p. 18.
10. H. Bernstein, 'Concepts for the analysis of contemporary peasantries', Dar es Salaam 1978, mimeo.
11. Kidron, *Capitalism and Theory*.
12. K. Buttner (ed.), *Theories on Africa and Neo-Colonialism*, Leipzig 1971.
13. H. Odera-Oruka, 'Marxism and African history', *Kenya Historical Review*, II, 1973. See also his 'The development of black consciousness', Universities of East Africa Social Science Conference 1973.
14. Report of the Syllabus Committee of the Workshop of the Teaching of History in African Universities, University of Lagos 21-4 September 1977, p. 1. O. Ikime, 'History and the historian in developing countries of Africa', *ibid.*. W. M. Freund, 'Conflict and challenge in the historiography of South Africa', Zaria 1977, mimeo. N. Osolo-Nasubo, 'Benign neglect of Africa's contribution to world civilization', *The Pan-Africanist*, 7, 1977.
15. K. O. Dike and J. F. A. Ajayi, 'African historiography', in D. L. Shills (ed.), *International Encyclopedia of the Social Sciences*, New York 1967.
16. T. O. Ranger, 'How should we approach and assess African history?', African History Teachers' Seminar, Dar es Salaam 1965, mimeo.
17. L. Seve, *Marxism and the Theory of Human Personality*, London 1975. N. Abercrombie, B. Turner and J. Urry, 'Class, state and fascism: the work of Nicos Poulantazas', *Political Studies*, XXIV, 1976.
18. P. M. Kennedy, 'The decline of nationalistic history in the West 1900-1970', *Journal of Contemporary History*, 8, 1973.
19. V. I. Lenin, *Imperialism: The Highest Stage of Capitalism*, Moscow 1974. See also his 'The socialist revolution and the right of nations to self-determination', in Lenin, *Selected Works*, Moscow 1968.
20. J. Blaut, 'Are Puerto Ricans a national minority?', *Monthly Review*, 29, 1977. See also my 'The African intellectual and the colonial state', *Tanzania Zamani*, 22, 1979.
21. K. Marx, *Capital*, I, Moscow 1974, pp. 76-87, for a discussion of the notion of fetishism.
22. A. Kozharov, *Monism and Pluralism in Ideology and Politics*, Sofia n.d. Shih Chun, *On Studying some World History*, Peking 1973.
23. Blaut, 'Are Puerto Ricans a national minority?'.
24. W. R. Ochieng, 'Undercivilization in Black Africa', *Kenya Historical Review*, II, 1974.
25. B. Davidson, *Guide to African History*, London 1963. See also his *Can Africa Survive?*, London 1975.

26. J. Iliffe, *Agricultural Change in Modern Tanganyika*, Nairobi 1971.
27. Quoted by G. Connell-Smith and H. A. Lloyd, *The Relevance of History*, London 1972, pp. 48-9.
28. G. Kay, *Development and Underdevelopment*, London 1975, p. 3.
29. M. Elkin, *The Pattern of the Chinese Past*, London 1973.
30. W. Rodney, *How Europe Underdeveloped Africa*, London 1972. H. Kjekshus, *Ecology Control and Economic Development in East African History*, London 1977.
31. H. Rose and S. Rose (eds.), *Science and Society*, Harmondsworth 1969.
32. Ochieng, 'Undercivilization in Black Africa'.
33. C. Coquery-Vidrovitch, 'The political economy of the African peasantry and modes of production', in Gutkind and Wallerstein (eds.), *The Political Economy of Contemporary Africa*.
34. *Ibid.*
35. B. Moore, *Social Origins of Dictatorship and Democracy*, Harmondsworth 1969.
36. Coquery-Vidrovitch, *op. cit.*
37. Quoted in the introduction in Gutkind and Wallerstein (eds.), *The Political Economy of Contemporary Africa*.
38. F. Engels, *On Marx's Capital*, Moscow 1972, p. 105.
39. G. Williams, 'Taking the part of peasants: rural development in Nigeria and Tanzania', Gutkind and Wallerstein (eds.), *The Political Economy of Contemporary Africa*.
40. M. E. Wuyts, 'On the nature of underdevelopment: an analysis of two views on underdevelopment', Dar es Salaam 1976, mimeo.
41. J. Depelchin, 'The "beggar problem" in Dar es Salaam in the 1930s: a discussion on the reproduction of labour power', Dar es Salaam 1978, mimeo.
42. L. Cliffe, 'Rural political economy in Africa', in Gutkind and Wallerstein (eds.), *The Political Economy of Contemporary Africa*. O. Leburn and C. Gerry, 'Petty producers and capitalism', *Review of African Political Economy*, 3, 1975.
43. K. Marx, *Capital*, I, Moscow 1974, p. 716.
44. F. J. Kaijage, 'Proletarianization versus peasantization in Tanganyika: a colonial dilemma in rural transformation', Dar es Salaam 1978, mimeo, pp. 2-3.
45. Depelchin, 'The "beggar problem" in Dar es Salaam'.
46. J. D. Bernal, *Science in History*, IV, Harmondsworth 1969, p. 1017.
47. G. Novack, *Empiricism and its Evolution*, New York 1971.
48. S. Marks, 'South African studies since World War Two', in C. Fyfe (ed.), *African Studies Since 1945*, London 1976.
49. T. Valentine, *The Great Pyramid*, St Albans, Herts., 1977, p. 9.
50. D. A. Low, *Lion Rampant*, London 1974.
51. On an opposite view of the idea of local initiative in African history see J. S. Saul, 'Nationalism, socialism and Tanzanian history', in L. Cliffe and J. S. Saul (eds.), *Socialism in Tanzania*, I, Nairobi 1972.
52. R. P. Wolff, 'Beyond tolerance', in R. P. Wolff, B. Moore and H. Marcuse, *A Critique of Pure Tolerance*, Boston 1969, p. 3.
53. W. Boyd, *Plato's Republice for Today*, London 1964, pp. 60-1.
54. Wolff, 'Beyond tolerance'.

55. M. Garaudy, *Marxism in the Twentieth Century*, London 1970.
56. A. Bose, *Marxian and Post-Marxian Political Economy*, Harmondsworth 1975.
57. H. Bernstein and J. Depelchin, 'The object of African history: a materialist perspective', *History in Africa*, 5, 1978.
58. See above pp. 143-4.
59. 'Problems of African history and anti-colonial resistance', *Asia, Africa and Latin America*, 2, 1977. Bonaventure Swai, *Antinomies of Local Initiative in African History*, Dar es Salaam 1979; 'The contradictory past: historians and African history', Southern African Universities Social Science Conference, 1979; 'European merchant capital and state formation in Eastern Africa', Nairobi 1979, mimeo.
60. This section also appeared in *Taamuli*, 9, 1979.
61. J. K. Nyerere, *Freedom and Socialism*, Dar es Salaam 1969, pp. 269-90.
62. G. Novack, *Marxism and Pragmatism*, New York 1974.
63. J. S. Saul, 'The state in post-colonial societies: Tanzania', *The Socialist Register*, 1974.
64. S. R. Nkonoki, 'Ten years of national education for self-reliance in Tanzania 1965-77', Dar es Salaam 1977, mimeo.
65. K. F. Hirji, 'School education and underdevelopment in Tanzania', *Maji Maji*, 12, 1973.
66. For more information on the educational experiment in Tanzania see: J. K. Nyerere, *Ten Years after the Arusha Declaration*, Dar es Salaam 1977. I. N. Resnick (ed.), *Tanzania: Revolution by Education*, Dar es Salaam 1968; J. R. Sheffield (ed.), *Education, Employment and Rural Development*, Nairobi 1967; D. R. Morrison, 'Education and political development: the Tanzanian case', D.Phil. Thesis, University of Sussex, 1970; N. V. Zanolli, *Education Towards Development in Sukumaland, Tanzania*, London 1969. S. Toroka, 'Education for self-reliance: the Litowa experiment', in L. Cliffe and J. S. Saul (eds.), *Socialism in Tanzania*, II, Nairobi 1973. S. N. Eliufoo, 'Education: a new era begins', in K. E. Svendsen (ed.), *Self-Reliant Tanzania*, Dar es Salaam 1969. For other African countries see A. Callaway's work, especially his article, 'Unemployment and school leavers', *Journal of Modern African Studies*, I, 1963; D. B. Abernathy, 'Political and administrative factors affecting development strategies in independent African states', Universities of East Africa Social Science Conference, 1969.
67. L. M. Hacker, *The Triumph of American Capitalism*, New York 1959, p. 3.
68. K. Marx and F. Engels, *The German Ideology*, quoted by M. Levitas, *Marxist Perspectives in the Sociology of Education*, London 1974.
69. L. Seve, *Man and Marxist Theory*, Hassocks, Sussex, 1978.
70. S. Bowles and H. Gintis, *Schooling in Capitalist America*, New York 1976. M. Carnoy, *Education as Cultural Imperialism*, New York 1974.
71. J. Stein, 'Of Mr. Booker T. Washington and others: the political economy of racism in the United States', *Science and Society*, XXXVIII, 1974-5.
72. Bonaventure Swai, 'Class seven and after', BA dissertation, University of Dar es Salaam, 1970.
73. 'Do not hesistate: P.M. tells leaders', *Daily News*, Dar es Salaam,

6 January 1978. 'Directive to curb loitering', *ibid.*, 4 January 1978. 'Rounding up of loiterers: peasants, workers, are exploited', ibid., 12 January 1977. 'Beggers to be imprisoned', *ibid.*, 2 October 1978.
74. Detailed information is obtainable from the dissertation, Swai, 'Class seven and after'.
75. *Ibid.*, pp. 11-14.
76. *Ibid.*, pp. 15-20.
77. E. H. Moshi, 'Land shortage in Kilimanjaro and the consequences of population pressure', BA dissertation, University of Dar es Salaam, 1976.
78. Swai, 'Class seven and after', p. 30.
79. *Ibid.*, p. 25.
80. *Ibid.*
81. *Ibid.*, p. 30.
82. Nyerere, *Freedom and Socialism*, pp. 269-90.
83. For Marx's position on attitudinal surveys see M. Shaw, *Marxism and Social Science*, p. 42.
84. J. Cameron and W. A. Dodd, *Society, School and Progress in Tanzania*, Oxford 1970.
85. H. Bernstein, 'Concepts for the analysis of contemporary peasantries', Dar es Salaam 1978, mimeo.
86. R. Lubetsky, 'Sectoral development and stratification in Tanganyika 1890-1914', Universities of East Africa Social Science Conference, 1972. G. T. Mishambi, 'The creation of labour-force in Tanzania', Dar es Salaam 1977, mimeo. D. Bryceson, 'Peasant food production and food supply in relation to the historical development of commodity production in precolonial and colonial Tanganyika', Dar es Salaam 1978, mimeo. See also Bonaventure Swai, *Antinomies of Local Initiative in African History*, Historical Association of Tanzania 1978.
87. W. Rodney, 'Migrant labour reserves in the Tanganyika colonial economy', SOAS 1976, mimeo. M. Mamdani, *Politics and Class Formation in Uganda*, London 1976. J. Weeks, 'Imbalance between centre and periphery and the "unemployment crisis" in Kenya', in I. Oxaal, T. Barnett and D. Booth (eds.), *Beyond Sociology of Development*, London 1975.
88. Bonaventure Swai, ' "Native" labour in the age of capital', Dar es Salaam 1979, mimeo.
89. F. J. Kaijage, 'Proletarianization versus peasantization in Tanganyika: a colonial dilemma in rural transformation', Dar es Salaam 1978, mimeo. G. Williams, 'Law and socialist rural development', Dar es Salaam 1973, mimeo. C. B. Macpherson, *The Political Theory of Possessive Individualism*, London 1962. C. Hill, 'Pottage for freeborn Englishmen: attitudes to wage labour in the sixteenth and seventeenth centuries', in C. H. Feinstein (ed.), *Socialism, Capitalism and Economic Growth*, Cambridge 1968.
90. J. Iliffe, *Agricultural Change in Modern Tanganyika*, London 1971. J. Depelchin, 'The "beggar problem" in Dar es Salaam in the 1930s ...'. 'Beggars are back – why?', *Blitz* (Bombay), 1 May 1976.
91. B. Moore, *Origins of Dictatorship and Democracy*, New York 1969.
92. H. Mapolu and G. Phillipson, 'Agricultural cooperation and the

development of productive forces: some lessons from Tanzania', *Africa Development*, I, 1976.
93. V. I. Lenin, *Imperialism: The Highest Stage of Capitalism*.
94. A. B. Lyall, 'Land law and policy in Tanganyika 1919-1932', LIM 1973, Dar es Salaam.
95. S. Marks, *Reluctant Rebellion*, Oxford 1970.
96. K. J. King, 'The politics of agricultural education for Africans in Kenya', Nairobi 1969, mimeo.
97. C. Batey, *African Education*, London 1953, p. 4.
98. *Ibid.*, p. 21.
99. M. J. Mbilinyi, 'Education for rural life or education for socialist transformation', Universities of East Africa Social Science Conference 1973, mimeo. See also her 'Education in the British colonial period 1919-61', Dar es Salaam 1974, mimeo.
100. King, 'The politics of agricultural education for Africans in Kenya'. P. Saul, 'Agricultural education in Tanganyika: the policy programmes and practices 1925-55', in S. M. Mbilinyi (ed.), *Agricultural Research for Rural Development*, Nairobi 1973.
101. L. E. Y. Mbogoni, 'Labour migration and famine in Dodoma district', Dar es Salaam 1969, mimeo. J. Sender, 'Some preliminary notes on the political economy of rural development in Tanzania based on a case study in the Western Usambaras', Dar es Salaam 1974, mimeo. L. Cliffe, W. L. Luttrell and J. E. Moore, 'Socialist transformation in rural Tanzania: a strategy for the Western Usambara', Universities of East Africa Social Science Conference, 1969, mimeo.
102. 'Put Mao Tse-tung through in command of cultural courses', *Peking Review*, 39, 25 September 1971. See also Antonio Gramsci's ideas on education in Q. Hoare and G. N.Smith (eds.), *Selections from the Prison Notebooks of Antonio Gramsci*, London 1971.
103. Mbilinyi, 'Education for rural life?'.
104. O. Ikime, 'History and the historian in the developing countries of Africa', Workshop on the Teaching of African History in African Universities, Lagos 1977.
105. O. Nnoli, 'Education and ethnic politics in Nigeria', *Africa Development*, I, 1976.
106. K. Marx, *Capital*, III, Moscow 1974, p. 357. Quoted by J. Depelchin and S. Lemelle, 'Some aspects of capital accumulation in Tanganyika 1920-1940', Dar es Salaam 1979, mimeo.
107. J. Wayne and L. Howard, 'Colonialism and the geography of opportunity: the Kigoma case', *Taamuli*, 5, 1975.
108. I. Shivji, *Class Struggles in Tanzania*, Dar es Salaam 1975.
109. S. Ndawula Kajumba, 'The collapse of the Tanzanian sisal plantation system', Dar es Salaam 1972, mimeo.
110. TANU has recently been merged with Zanzibar's Afro-Shiraz Party to form Chama Cha Mapinduzi (CCM).
111. G. F. Rudenko, *et al.*, *Revolutionary Movements of Our Time and Nationalism*, Moscow 1975.
112. J. Lewis, *The Uniqueness of Man*, London 1974.
113. N. N. Luanda, 'The negative mirror images of African initiative: colonial resistance and collaboration', Dar es Salaam 1979, mimeo.

114. Quoted by O. Onoge, 'The counter-revolutionary tradition in African studies: the case of applied anthropology', *Nigerian Journal of Economic and Social Studies*, 15, 1973.

Select Bibliography

Ajayi, J. F. Ade, *Christian Missions in Nigeria 1841-1891*, London 1965.
Ajayi, J. F. Ade, 'The continuity of African institutions under colonialism', in T. O. Ranger (ed.), *Emerging Themes of African History*, Nairobi 1968.
Ajayi, J. F. Ade, 'West African States at the beginning of the nineteenth century', in J. F. Ade Ajayi and I. Espie (eds.), *A Thousand Years of West African History*, Ibadan 1965.
Alpers, E. A., 'Re-thinking African economic history: a contribution to the discussion of roots of underdevelopment', *Kenya Historical Review*, I, 1973.
Alpers, E. A., *Ivory and Slaves in East and Central Africa*, London 1975.
Amin, S., 'Accumulation and development: a theoretical model', *Review of African Political Economy*, I, 1974.
Anderson, P., *Lineages of the Absolutist State*, London 1974.
Armstrong, R.G., 'The development of Kingdoms in Negro Africa', *Journal of the Historical Association of Nigeria*, II, 1960.
Arrighi, G., 'Labour supplies in historical perspective: the Rhodesian case', Dar es Salaam 1967, mimeo.
Bernal, J. D., *Science in History*, Vol. IV, Harmondsworth 1969.
Bernstein, B. (ed.), *Towards a New Past*, New York 1969.
Bernstein, H., and Depelchin, J., 'The object of African History: a materialist perspective', *History in Africa*, 5, 1978.
Bernstein, H., 'Sociology of underdevelopment versus sociology of development', in H. Bernstein et al., *Development Theory: Three Critical Essays*, London 1978.
Bernstein, H., 'Capital and peasantry in the epoch of imperialism', Dar es Salaam 1976, mimeo.
Bernstein, H., 'Concepts for the analysis of contemporary peasantries', Dar es Salaam 1978, mimeo.
Blaut, J., 'Are Puerto Ricans a national minority?', *Monthly Review*, 29, 1977.
Blackburn, R. (ed.), *Ideology in Social Science*, London 1978.
Bose, A., *Marxian and Post-Marxian Political Economy*, Harmondsworth 1970.
Bukharin, N., *Imperialism and World Economy*, New York 1973.
Bullock, A., *Is History Becoming a Social Science?*, Cambridge 1976.

Select Bibliography

Buttner, K. (ed.), *Theories of Africa and Neo-colonialism*, Leipzig 1971.
Callinicos, A., *Althusser's Marxism*, London 1976.
Carr, E. H., *What is History?*, London 1962.
Chanock, M. L., 'Development and change in the history of Malawi', in B. Pachai (ed.), *The Early History of Malawi*, London 1972.
Cliffe, L., 'Rural political economy in Africa', in P. Gutkind and I. Wallerstein (eds.), *The Political Economy of Contemporary Africa*, London 1973.
Cohen, P. A., 'Ching China: confrontation with the West 1850-1900', in J. B. Crowley (ed.), *Modern East Asia*, New York 1970.
Collins, R.O. (ed.), *Problems in the History of Colonial Africa 1860-1960*, Englewood Cliffs, NJ, 1970.
Connell-Smith, G., and Lloyd, H.A., *The Relevance of History*, London 1972.
Coquery-Vidrovitch, C., 'The political economy of the African peasantry and modes of production', in P. Gutkind and I. Wallerstein (eds.), *The Political Economy of Contemporary Africa*.
Cornforth, M., *The Open Philosophy and the Open Society*, New York 1976.
Curtin, P. D., *The Dimensions of the Atlantic Slave Trade*, Madison 1969.
Dachs, A. J., 'Politics of collaboration: imperialism in practice', in B. Pachai (ed.), *The Early History of Malawi*.
Davidson, B., *Guide to African History*, London 1963.
Davidson, B., *Can Africa Survive?*, London 1975.
Davis, R. H., 'Interpreting the colonial period in African history', *African Affairs*, 72, 1973.
Denoon, D., and Kuper, A., 'Nationalist historians in search of a nation: the new historiography in Dar es Salaam', *African Affairs*, 69, 1970.
Denoon, D., and Kuper, A., 'The new historiography in Dar es Salaam: a rejoinder', *African Affairs*, 70, 1971.
Depelchin, J., 'African history and the ideological reproduction of exploitative relations of production', *Africa Development*, II, 1977.
Depelchin, J., 'Towards a problematic history of Africa', *Tanzania Zamani*, 18, 1976.
Depelchin, J., 'The coming of age of political economy in African studies', *International Journal of African Studies*, XI, 1978.
Depelchin, J., 'Notes towards the production of a materialist precolonial Central African history', Dar es Salaam 1977, mimeo.
Depelchin, J., and Lemelle, S. J., 'Some aspects of capital accumulation in Tanganyika 1920-1940', Dar es Salaam 1979, mimeo.
Dumett, R. E., 'John Sarbah the elder and African mercantile entrepreneurship in the Gold Coast in the late nineteenth century', *Journal of African History*, 14, 1973.
van den Dungen, P. H. M., 'Changes in status and occupation in nineteenth century Punjab', in D. A. Low (ed.), *Soundings in Modern South Asian History*, London 1968.
Dutt, R. P., *Problems of Contemporary History*, London 1963.
Ehrensaft, P., 'The political economy, of informal empire in precolonial Nigeria', *Canadian Journal of African Studies*, VI, 1972.

Ehrlich, C., 'Some social implications of paternalism in Uganda', *Journal of African History*, IV, 1963.
Elton, G. R., *The Practice of History*, London 1969.
Engels, F., *Ludwig Feuerbach and the end of classical German Philosophy*, Peking 1979.
Engels, F., *Marx's Capital*, Moscow 1974.
Eriksen, T. L., *Modern African History*, Uppsala 1979.
Fanon, F., *The Wretched of the Earth*, Harmondsworth 1965.
Fage, J. D., 'Slavery and the slave trade in the context of West African history', in J. G. Roland (ed.), *Africa: the Heritage and the Challenge*, Greenwich, Conn., 1974.
Fischer, D. H., *Historians' Fallacies*, London 1971.
Fox, R. G., *Kin, Clan, Raja, and Rule*, Berkeley 1971.
Fyfe, C. (ed.), *African Studies Since 1945*, London 1976.
Gann, L. P., and Duignan, P., *The Burden of Empire*, New York 1967.
Garaudy, R., *Marxism in the Twentieth Century*, London 1970.
Gellner, E., 'Class before state: the Soviet treatment of African feudalism', *Arch. Europ. Social*, XVIII, 1977.
Genovese, E. D., *The Political Economy of Slavery*, London 1966.
Genovese, E. D., *In Red and Black*, New York 1968.
Genovese, E. D., *The World the Slaveholders Made*, New York 1969.
Genovese, E. D., *Roll, Jordan, Roll*, New York 1974.
Gerschenkron, A., *Continuity in History and other Essays*, Cambridge, Mass., 1968.
Girvetz, H. K., *The Evaluation of Liberalism*, New York 1966.
Gray, R., 'E. P. Thompson, history and communist politics', *Marxism Today*, 23, 1979.
Gray, R., and Birmingham, D. (eds.), *Precolonial African Trade*, London 1970.
Guy, J. J., 'Production and exchange in the Zulu Kingdom', *Journal of Southern African Historical Studies*, II, 1978.
Habib, I., 'Potentialities of capitalist development in the economy of Mughul India', *Journal of Economic History*, XXIX, 1969.
Hacker, L. M., *The Triumph of American Capitalism*, New York 1959.
Heussler, R., *Yesterday's Rulers*, Syracuse 1963.
Hill, C., *The World Turned Upside Down*, Harmondsworth 1975.
Hobsbawm, E. J., *The Age of Revolution 1789-1848*, New York 1962.
Hodgkin, T., 'Where the paths began', in C. Fyfe (ed.), *African Studies Since 1945*.
Hodgkin, T., 'Some African and third world theories of imperialism', in R. Owen and B. Sutcliffe (eds.), *Studies in the Theory of Imperialism*, London 1972.
Hughes, H. S., *Consciousness and Society*, St Albans, Herts., 1974.
Iliffe, J., 'The organization of the Maji Maji rebellion', *Journal of African History*, VIII, 1967.
Iliffe, J., *Tanganyika under German Rule 1905-1912*, Nairobi 1969.

Select Bibliography

Iliffe, J., 'Era of modernization and differentiation', in I. N. Kimambo and A. J. Temu (eds.), *A History of Tanzania*, Nairobi 1969.
Iliffe, J., 'The recent historiography of 19th and 20th century Tanganyika, SOAS, 1972, mimeo.
Iliffe, J., *Agricultural change in Modern Tanganyika*, Nairobi 1971.
Iliffe, J., *A Modern History of Tanganyika*, Cambridge 1979.
Iliffe, J., with Gwassa, G. C. K. (eds.), *Records of the Maji Maji Rising*, Nairobi 1968.
Isichei, E., 'The development of underdevelopment: some relevant debates among historians', Universities of East Africa Social Science Conference, 1970, mimeo.
Jenkins, R., *Exploitation*, London 1971.
Jones, G. S., 'History: the poverty of empiricism', in R. Blackburn (ed.), *Ideology in Social Science*.
Kapteijns, L., *African Historiography written by Africans 1955-1973: the Nigerian case*, Leiden 1977.
Kay, G., *Development and Underdevelopment*, London 1975.
Kennedy, P. M., 'The decline of nationalist history in the West 1900-1970', *Journal of Contemporary History*, 8, 1973.
Kidron, M., *Capitalism and Theory*, London 1974.
Kimambo, I. N., 'Historical research in mainland Tanzania', Dar es Salaam 1968, mimeo.
Kitson Clark, G., *The Critical Historian*, London 1965.
Kjekshus, H., *Ecology Control and Economic Development in East Africa*, London 1977.
Kosambi, D. D., *An Introduction to the Study of Indian History*, Bombay 1975.
Kozharov, A., *Monism and Pluralism in Ideology and Politics*, Sofia n.d.
Lenin, V. I., *Imperialism: the Highest Stage of Capitalism*, Moscow 1974.
Lenin, V. I., *Collected Works*, Vol. 38, Moscow 1975.
Lenin, V. I., *Materialism and Empiriocriticism*, Moscow 1976.
Lonsdale, J. M., 'Some origins of nationalism in East Africa', *Journal of African History*, IX, 1968.
Low, D. A., *Lion Rampant*, London 1974.
Low, D. A., *Buganda in Modern History*, London 1970.
Lowith, K., *The Meaning of History*, Chicago 1960.
Luanda, N. N., 'The negative mirror images of African initiative: colonial resistance and collaboration', Dar es Salaam 1979, mimeo.
Lubetsky, R., 'Sectoral development and stratification in Tanganyika 1890-1914', Universities of East Africa Social Science Conference, 1972, mimeo.
Macpherson, C. B., *The Political Theory of Possessive Individualism*, London 1962.
Mafeje, A., 'The problem of Anthropology in historical perspective: an inquiry into the growth of the Social Sciences', *Canadian Journal of African Studies*, 10, 1976.
Mandel, E., *Marxist Economic Theory*, London 1971.

Mandel, E., *Late Capitalism*, London 1976.
Marcuse, H., *One Dimensional Man*, New York 1967.
Marks, S., 'South African studies since World War Two', in C. Fyfe (ed.), *African Studies Since 1945*.
Marks, S., *Reluctant Rebellion*, Oxford 1970.
Marwick, A., *The Nature of History*, London 1970.
Marx, K., *Grundrisse*, Harmondsworth 1973.
Marx, K., *Capital*, Vols. I and III, Moscow 1974.
Meszaros, I., *Marx's Theory of Alienation*, London 1975.
Milliband, R., *The State in Capitalist Society*, London 1973.
Mishambi, G. T., 'The mystification of African history: a critique of Rodney's *How Europe Underdeveloped Africa*', Dar es Salaam 1976, mimeo.
Mlahagwa, J. R., 'The Uluguru land usage scheme: a crisis in colonial production', Dar es Salaam 1977, mimeo.
Monteil, V., 'The decolonization of the writing of African history', in I. Wallerstein (ed.), *Social Change: the Colonial Situation*, New York 1966.
Moore, B., *Social Origins of Dictatorship and Democracy*, Harmondsworth 1969.
Mukherjee, R., *The Rise and Fall of the East India Company*, Berlin 1957.
Mutibwa, F., *The Malagasy and the Europeans*, London 1974.
Nairn, T., 'The English working class', in R. Blackburn (ed.), *Ideology in Social Science*, London 1978.
Nguyen Khac Vien, *The Long Resistance 1858-1975*, Hanoi 1975.
Novack, G., *Empiricism and its Evolution*, New York 1971.
Novack, G., *An Introduction to the Logic of Marxism*, New York 1975.
Novack, G., *Marxism versus Pragmatism*, New York 1975.
Nwala, T. U., 'Anthony William Amoo of Ghana on the mind-body problem', *Présence africaine*, 108, 1978.
Odera-Oruka, H., 'Marxism and African History', *Kenya Historical Review*, II, 1973.
Ollman, B., 'Marxism', *Monthly Review*, 30, 1978.
Onoge, O., 'The counter-revolutionary tradition in African studies: the case of Applied Anthropology', *The Nigerian Journal of Economic and Social Studies*, 15, 1973.
Onoge, O., 'Towards a Marxist Sociology of African Literature', Dar es Salaam 1977, mimeo.
van Onselen, C., 'The role of collaborators in the Rhodesian mining industry 1900-1935', *African Affairs*, 72, 1973.
Oxaal, I., *et al.* (eds.), *Beyond the Sociology of Development*, London 1975.
Palmer, R., 'Johnston and Jameson: a comparative study in the imposition of colonial rule', in B. Pachai (ed.), *The Early History of Malawi*.
Perham, M. (ed.), *Ten Africans*, London 1963.
Perham, M., Introduction to V. Harlow and E. M. Chilver (eds.), *History of East Africa*, Vol. II, Oxford 1965.
Petras, J., 'Popperism: the scarcity of reason', *Science and Society*, 30, 1966.

Plumb, J. H., 'The historian's dilemma', in J. H. Plumb (ed.), *Crisis in the Humanities*, Harmondsworth 1964.
Plumb, J. H., *Death of the Past*, Harmondsworth 1970.
Popper, K., *The Poverty of Historicism*, Vol. I, London 1972.
Primbs, E. R. J., 'The truth in science and labour', *Science and Society*, 26, 1962.
Ranger, T. O., 'African attempts to control education in East and Central Africa', *Past and Present*, 32, 1965.
Ranger, T. O., *Revolt in Southern Rhodesia*, London 1967.
Ranger, T. O., 'African politics in twentieth century Rhodesia', in T. O. Ranger (ed.), *Aspects of Central African History*, London 1968.
Ranger, T. O., 'Connections between primary resistance movements and modern mass nationalism in East and Central Africa', *Journal of African History*, IX-X, 1968.
Ranger, T. O., *The African Voice in Southern Rhodesia*, London 1970.
Ranger, T. O., 'The historiography of Southern Rhodesia', *Transafrican Journal of History*, I, 1971.
Ranger, T. O., 'Towards a usable past', in C. Fyfe (ed.), *African Studies Since 1945*.
Ranger, T. O., 'The people in African resistance', *Journal of Southern African Studies*, 4, 1977.
Ranger, T. O. (ed.), *Emerging Themes of African History*, Nairobi 1968.
Ranger, T. O. (ed.), *The Recovery of Local Initiative in Tanzanian History*, Dar es Salaam 1969.
Ranger, T. O. with Kimambo, I. N. (eds.), *The Historical Study of African Religion*, London 1972.
Robinson, R., and Gallagher, J., *Africa and the Victorians*, New York 1962.
Robinson, R., and Gallagher, J., 'Non-European foundations of European imperialism: sketch for a theory of collaboration', in R. Owen and B. Sutcliffe (eds.), *Studies in the Theory of Imperialism*.
Rodney, W., *The Groundings with my Brothers*, London 1969.
Rodney, W., *How Europe Underdeveloped Africa*, London 1972.
Rose, H., and Rose, S., *The Political Economy of Science*, London 1976.
Saul, J. S., 'Nationalism, socialism and Tanzanian history', in L. Cliffe and J. S. Saul (eds.), *Socialism in Tanzania*, Vol. I, Nairobi 1972.
Seve, L., *Man in Marxist Theory*, Hassocks, Sussex, 1978.
Shaw, M., *Marxism and Social Science*, London 1975.
Sheriff, A. M. H., 'The development of underdevelopment: the role of international trade in the economic history of the East African coast before the sixteenth century', Dar es Salaam 1973, mimeo.
Stern, F. (ed.), *The Varieties of History*, Cleveland, Ohio, 1956.
Stokes, E., 'Traditional resistance movements and Afro-Asian nationalism: the context of the 1857 mutiny rebellion', *Past and Present*, 48, 1970.
Swai, B., 'Notes on the colonial state', *Social Scientist*, 7, 1978.
Swai, B., 'Pragmatism, opportunism and professional African history', *Utafiti*, 5, 1979.

Swai, B., 'The new Cinderella in African history', *Tanzania Zamani*, 20, 1978.
Swai, B., 'Local initiative in African history: a critique', *Tanzania Zamani*, 19, 1977.
Swai, B., 'Crisis in Africanist history', *Tanzania Zamani*, Special Issue, 1980.
Swai, B., 'Contours of Tanzanian history', *Tanzania Zamani*, Special Issue, 1980.
Swai, B., 'The contradictory past: historians and African history', *Proceedings of the 1979 Southern African Universities Social Science Conference*.
Swai, B., 'Synthesizing the modern history of Tanganyika', *Utafiti*, forthcoming.
Szentes, T., *Underdevelopment and Socialism*, Dar es Salaam 1970.
Temu, A. J., 'The Giriama War 1914-1915', Dar es Salaam 1970, mimeo.
Temu, A. J., and Swai, B. (eds.), *Kenya under Colonial Rule*, London: Longman, forthcoming.
Temu, A. J., and Swai, B., 'Old and new themes in African history', *Proceedings of the Workshop on the Teaching of History in African Universities*, Lagos 1977; also to appear as 'Poverty of History: the Tanzanian case', in *Cahier d'etudes africaines*, forthcoming.
Thompson, E. P., *The Making of the English Working Class*, Harmondsworth 1965.
Thompson, E. P., *Poverty of Theory and other Essays*, London 1978.
Thorpe, E. E., *Negro Historians in the United States*, Baton Rouge 1958.
Tsomondo, M. S., 'Shona reaction and resistance to the European colonization of Zimbabwe (Rhodesia) 1890-1898', University of New York n.d., mimeo.
Unomah, A. C., 'Vbandevba and political change in a Nyamwezi Kingdom', Universities of East Africa Social Science Conference.
Usman, Y. B., 'History, tradition and reaction: the perception of Nigerian history in the 19th and 20th centuries', *Proceedings of the Workshop on the Teaching of History in African Universities*, Lagos 1977.
Uzoigwe, G. N., 'The Kyanyangire, 1907: passive revolt against British rule', University of East Africa Social Science Conference, 1969.
Wallerstein, I., *The Modern World-System*, New York 1974.
Weinstein, J., 'Can an historian be a socialist revoutionary?', *Socialist Revolution*, 3, 1970.
Wolfe, A., 'New directions in the Marxist theory of politics', *Politics and Society*, 4, 1974.
Wolff, R. P., *et al., A Critique of Pure Tolerance*, Boston 1969.
Wrigley, C. C., 'Historicism in Africa: slavery and state formation', *African Affairs*, 70, 1971.
van Zwanenberg, R. M. A., 'Anti-slavery: the ideology of 19th-century imperialism in East Africa', *Hadith*, 5, 1975.
van Zwanenberg, R. M. A., *Colonial Capitalism and Labour in Kenya 1919-1939*, Nairobi 1975.

Index

African Genius, 7, 73, 81, 87
Age of Improvement, 39, 42, 44, 48, 51, 89-90, 92, 165, 167
Agriculture/Rural Economy, 27, 36, 48, 132, 138-43, 160, 164-5, 166-9; *see also* Settler Production, Peasants, *and* Plantations
Ajayi, J.F.A., 67
Alatas, S.H., 43
Amoo, A.W., 19-20
Appropriation of Surplus Labour, 27, 35-6, 38, 40, 44-7, 49, 79, 94, 96, 122, 134

Brett, E.A., 68
Bureaucracy, 84, 125, 127, 157; *see also* Colonial Administration, Indirect Rule *and* State

Capitalism, 5, 10, 26-7, 33-40, 42, 44, 46, 49, 52, 71, 76-7, 90, 114, 120, 122, 130, 134, 140-2, 153, 155, 157-8, 160, 162, 166-9; *see also* Precapitalist Africa
Merchant Capitalism, 53, 79, 84-7, 93-8, 112; *see also* Trade
Monopoly Capitalism, 34, 62, 161, 166
Cesaire, A., 33-4, 83
Change, 9, 18-19, 22, 26, 61, 64, 71, 73-4, 76, 81-2, 132
Colonialism, 5, 9, 18-19, 21-5, 28-9, 33-9, 42-3, 45, 47-9, 52, 61, 67, 71-2, 75-6, 78, 83, 87, 89, 98, 119, 121, 131-2, 141-4, 154, 156, 158-61, 166-7; *see also* Precolonial Africa

Colonial Administration, 19, 23, 29-30, 36, 38-40, 43, 48-9, 65, 72, 86, 92, 95-7, 99, 141, 163, 164; *see also* Taxation
Colonial Historiography, 6, 20-1, 30, 61, 64, 81, 83, 98-9, 114
Continuity, 7, 9, 50, 51, 61, 64, 71, 73-4, 87, 116, 131
Coquery-Vidrovitch, C., 156-7
Critical Theory, 11, 51-2, 133, 135-8

Dar School of Historiography, 28, 61, 67; *see also* Radical Pessimism
Data Collection/Facts/Quantification, 1, 5, 8, 12, 18, 20-1, 25, 28-9, 31, 50, 61-2, 64, 66, 70, 73, 100, 120, 129, Ch. 4 *passim; see also* Empiricism *and* Oral History
Development/Underdevelopment, 9-11, 19, 26, 42, 48, 66, 68-9, 73-9, 82, 91, 112-13, 132, 134, 153; *see also* Modernization *and* Rodney, W.

Empiricism, 1, 3, 9, 11-13, 23, 61-2, 65, 70-3, 75, 84, 112-16, 118, 120-2, 128, 130-6, 140, 144, 158, 165, 167
Enlargement of Scale, 26, 68-9, 84, 87-8, 112-13

Fage, J.D., 67-9, 78
Fanon, F., 33, 83, 144
Fisher, H.A.L., 69

185

Historiographical Concepts; see
 African Genius, Continuity,
 Change, Enlargement of Scale,
 Internal/External Factors, Local
 Initiative, People's History,
 Progress, Pattern, Simple and
 Complex Societies, Tradition,
 Tribes; see also Colonial Histor-
 iography, Critical Theory, Dar
 School, Empiricism, Historicism,
 Imperial Historiography, *Journal
 of African History*, Nihilism, Oral
 History, Professional Historians
Historicism, 64, 66-70, 87, 112, 144
Hobsbawm, E., 4, 30, 32

Ideology, 13, 20-4, 32-4, 36, 40-2,
 53, 74-6, 81, 97-8, 112, 114,
 116, 119, 122-4, 126-8, 135,
 155, 158; see also Laziness,
 Paternalism, Racism
Imperialism, 6, 8, 18, 21, 27-8,
 32-9, 41, 48-9, 51-3, 64-5, 71-3,
 77-8, 83, 87-8, 93, 95, 99, 114,
 119-20, 134, 138, 141, 143-4,
 153-60
 Imperial Historiography, 19,
 21-2, 39, 49, 51, 61, 64, 72, 83
Internal/External Factors, 22, 52,
 82, 88, 153; see also Change
Indirect Rule, 72, 114, 141, 166

Journal of African History, 50, 63

Labour see Appropriation of
 Surplus Labour
Laziness, 37, 42-7, 52, 153
Liberalism, 9, 25, 29, 38, 82,
 120, 125
Local Initiative, 23, 25-32, Ch. 3
 passim, 75, 77-8, 84, 133, 140,
 143, 159
Low, D.A., 31, 39, 65

Manamba see Proletarization
Manufacturing, 36, 165
Metropole, 5-6, 27-8, 33, 36, 41,
 48, 50, 61-2, 64, 66, 73, 76-7,
 119, 127, 162, 164-5
Modernization, 22-3, 44, 53, 64,
 69, 76, 84, 92, 121-2; see also
 Development
Mishambi, G.T., 76
Myth/Religion, 24, 30-2, 40, 80,
 85, 123; see also Maji Maji *under*
 Resistance

Nationalism, 10, 24-5, 28, 41, 47-8,
 67, 75-6, 114, 121, 154-6, 158,
 167, 169
Nihilism, 8, 31, 64, 66-74, 77-8,
 80, 82, 112, 144

Oral History, 24, 99, 113, 126

Paternalism, 29, 35, 44, 47, 73, 83,
 142-3, 153, 166
Pattern, 8, 66, 71, 73, 81; see also
 Nihilism
Peasants, 7, 24, 29, 31, 36, 42,
 47-9, 52, 73, 86, 96-7, 122, 157,
 166-9
People's History/Social History, 2-7,
 13, 21, 61, 77
Petty Bourgeoisie, 21, 33, 41, 47,
 50-2, 66, 90, 98-9, 113, 144, 161
Petty Commodity Production, 27,
 30, 36, 49, 157-8; see also
 Agriculture *and* Peasants
Plantations, 29-30, 35-7, 42-3,
 46, 88, 93-4, 158; see also
 Settler Production
Popper, K., 4, 69-71, 136
Poverty, 42, 44, 52, 75-6, 144,
 167-8
Precolonial Africa, 18, 22-3, 38, 64,
 70, 73, 75, 83-7, 97, 132, 153,
 156, 162, 165
Precapitalist Africa, 27, 35-6, 38-9,
 47, 51, 56, 67-8, 82, 86-7, 97,
 114, 123, 132
Professional Historians/Academia,
 2-4, 6-12, 19-21, 25, 32, 39, 50,
 61, 63-4, 66-7, 69, 71, 74-7, 79,
 81-4, 98-9, 112-13, 116-17,
 119-29, 131, 133, 143-4, 154-5,
 158-9
Progress, 7-8, 19, 64, 66, 69, 120-1,
 134
Proletarianization, 30, 36, 42-8, 51-2

Protest, 67; *see also* Resistance

Racism, 19-20, 53, 83, 166
Radical Pessimism, 61, 74, 119, 133; *see also* Dar School *and* People's History
Ranger, T.O., 63, 67, 100
Ranke, O., 115, 117-19, 124-5
Religion *see* Myth
Resistance, 23-8, 30-1, 33, 36-7, 39-42, 48, 51, 62-5, 97-8, 126; Primary, 23-5, 36, 39-40; Secondary, 40 Abushiri, 27; Giriama, 36-8; Herero, 34; Maji Maji, 24, 26-32, 40-3; Ndonge-wa Kauti, 37
Robinson, R. and J. Gallagher, 64, 72, 82
Rodney, W., 9, 66, 75

Settler Production, 26-7, 36-7, 40, 42-4, 46, 94; *see also* Agriculture *and* Plantations
Simple and Complex Societies, 23, 69
Slavery, 20, 46-8, 53, 62, 67-8, 70, 78, 85, 88, 90, 95, 98, 112, 157
Social Darwinism, 18, 73, 118, 142, 156, 166
Social Sciences, 1, 4, 9, 20-1, 25, 62, 69, 70, 111, 120, 122-3, 133, 135, 141
Southall, E.A., 86
State, 25-6, 31, 33-6, 38, 41, 46-8, 53, 67, 69, 73, 79, 82-4, 86-8, 112, 126, 141, 153, 164

Taxation, 24, 36-9, 163
Technology, 132, 134, 156-8
Theory, 1-2, 12-13, 31, 70, 75, 123-4, 131, 136
Thompson, E.P., 13, 84, 136
Trade, 47, 66, 70, 72, 75, 78, 84, 88, 95-6, 120, 140, 157; *see also* Merchant Capitalism *and* Slavery
Tradition, 24, 35, 51, 70, 73, 76, 117, 157, 164
Tribes/Tribalism, 28-9, 31, 37, 43-4, 69, 75, 80, 98-9, 153-4

Unequal Exchange, 76
Usman, Yusufa Bala, 50-1, 100

Violence/Coercion, 27, 33-5, 38, 45-9, 51, 76, 79, 87, 97, 155, 164, 167, 169

Weber, M., 31, 87, 118
Wrigley, P., 42, 67-9, 71, 78